DECRYPTING GLOBALIZATION

First edition. July 8, 2024.

ISBN: 979-8227100450

Written by Waleed Mahmud.

Table of Contents

Decrypting Globalization:

Understanding the Economic, Cultural, And Political afflictions of Nationalism, Migration and the Environmental Crisis

By

Waleed Mahmud

Author of

*"**Probing Freewill:** A Story of Autonomy & Inevitability"*

and

*"**Power & Ethics:** A Brief History of Western Moral and Political Philosophy"*

In memory of my beloved brother,

Mashal,

And

For my Parents and Partner,

Who always nurtured the writer within me.

Preface

Globalization is an inescapable reality of the contemporary world, reshaping societies, economies, and cultures at an unprecedented pace. It is a process characterized by the increasing interconnectedness and interdependence of the global community through the continuous flow of goods, services, information, and people across borders. As such, globalization presents a complex array of challenges and opportunities that necessitates a profound and nuanced understanding from multiple disciplinary perspectives, most critically, from moral and political philosophy.

The relevance of moral and political philosophy to globalization lies in its capacity to provide deeper insights and normative frameworks that help navigate the ethical complexities and political dilemmas presented by this pervasive phenomenon. Globalization is not merely a political or economic process; it has profound ethical implications that affect individual lives and communities, influence cultural exchanges, and redefine the scope and impact of governance on a global scale. It matters because it compels us to ask not just what is happening or what the economic impacts are, but what *should* happen. It urges us to consider:

- **Justice:** *How can we ensure that the benefits and burdens of globalization are distributed fairly? What does justice demand from us in terms of obligations to those who are less advantaged or who suffer the negative impacts of global processes?*

- **Rights:** *What are the rights of individuals and communities in the face of global economic and cultural forces? How do we reconcile the right to cultural and political self-determination with the demands and benefits of a globalized world?*

- **Ethics:** *How do multinational corporations (MNCs) negotiate their responsibilities toward workers and communities in different parts of the world? What ethical guidelines should govern the transfer of technology and capital?*

The intersections of ethical, moral, and political dimensions in globalization are profound and far-reaching. For instance, consider the ethical concerns around labor practices in the global supply chain. Philosophically, this raises questions about the moral obligations of corporations and consumers in developed countries toward workers in less developed countries. Politically, it challenges us to think about the regulations and policies that can and should govern international labor rights.

Similarly, the environmental impact of globalization calls for a philosophical inquiry into our duties to future generations and the non-human world. It requires us to balance economic growth with sustainable practices, and to consider whether current international policies adequately protect the planet's ecological systems.

Culturally, globalization prompts an examination of how global media and communication technologies influence identity and social norms. Philosophically, this involves a critique of cultural imperialism and a defense of cultural diversity. It asks us to think about what it means to live in a world where cultural boundaries are both dissolving and being reinforced.

A philosophical examination of globalization is imperative because it provides the critical tools needed to assess, critique, and guide the transformations taking place. Without this critical lens, discussions about globalization risk being narrowly focused on economic benefits or losses, without considering the broader ethical, cultural, and political consequences.

In this book, we venture into these philosophical inquiries, aiming to provide a comprehensive analysis that not only describes the multifaceted impacts of globalization but also offers a normative critique that can guide future policies and individual actions. By integrating insights from moral and political philosophy, we endeavor to illuminate the paths toward a more just, ethical, and sustainable global order. This approach not only enriches our understanding but also empowers us as global citizens to act with both wisdom and compassion in the face of the world's shared challenges.

Globalization challenges traditional ethical norms by creating situations where diverse value systems often collide. For instance, what one culture considers ethical in business practices or human rights can vastly differ from another, leading to complex ethical dilemmas. Here, the philosophical contributions of Immanuel Kant's duty-based ethics provide a valuable framework. Kant's insistence on universalizability, that ethical principles must be applicable universally, raises significant questions in a globalized context. *How do MNCs reconcile profit motives with ethical obligations that transcend cultural and national boundaries?*

A pertinent example is the debate around fair trade practices. Philosophers like John Rawls, with his principles of *justice as fairness*, might argue that global trade should not only increase wealth but also distribute benefits in a manner that is fair and beneficial to all, particularly to the least advantaged. This perspective challenges current global trade policies and practices, advocating for a reevaluation that considers ethical implications alongside economic benefits.

Cultural integrity faces its tests as global interactions intensify. The spread of a dominant culture can often lead to a dilution or even erosion of local cultures, a phenomenon sometimes described as cultural imperialism. Here, the ideas of Edward Said on Orientalism can be instructive; they help us understand how cultural formations often involve power dynamics, where dominant cultures impose their values and practices, overshadowing local traditions and languages. However, globalization also offers opportunities for cultural exchange and enrichment. The philosophical notion of cosmopolitanism, championed by thinkers like Kwame Anthony Appiah, argues for embracing diversity while fostering a sense of global citizenship that respects local identities. This philosophy encourages a world where people can look beyond their immediate cultural boundaries to engage with and learn from others, creating a rich canvas of interconnected but distinct cultural identities.

On the political front, globalization necessitates a rethinking of governance and sovereignty. Traditional Westphalian sovereignty is increasingly challenged by non-state actors like MNCs and international organizations.

Here, the political theories of Thomas Hobbes and later, the transformational ideas of Michel Foucault on power and governance, offer deep insights into understanding the changing nature of power in global politics. Hobbes' notion of a social contract forming the basis of political authority becomes complex in a global context where allegiances and governance often transcend national borders. Examples of this shift are evident in the European Union's (EU) governance model, which presents a post-sovereignty political structure where member states share sovereignty in various domains. Similarly, global challenges like climate change and pandemics highlight the limitations of national governments and the necessity for global governance mechanisms, which philosophers like Martha Nussbaum argue should be guided by global justice and the capability approach, ensuring that all humans can live a life worthy of human dignity.

The philosophical approach to globalization is indispensable because it allows for a critical examination of these evolving dynamics. It encourages not just an understanding but also a questioning and reimagining of the principles and values that should guide global interactions. Philosophy offers the tools to critically assess the ethical, cultural, and political impacts of globalization, ensuring that progress in one area does not lead to regress in another. By leveraging the insights of influential philosophers and ethical theories, this book aims to provide a nuanced analysis of globalization's impacts. It seeks to explore ways in which a philosophical lens can help navigate the complexities of a world that is more connected than ever, ensuring that such connectivity fosters genuine progress that is ethical, respectful of cultural diversity, and conducive to effective and fair governance.

My engagement with globalization is deeply personal. Having observed diverse cultures and economic systems through travel and living in different parts of the world, I have experienced firsthand the interconnectedness of global communities as well as the disparities and tensions that arise from this interconnectedness. These experiences have driven home the urgent need for a deeper understanding of how global processes affect individuals and societies. Philosophically, my interests lie in the discourse of ethics, justice, and political theory. Seeing the inequalities bred by global trade, the erosion of cultural identities through cultural imperialism, and the challenges to governance posed by supranational entities has prompted me to question traditional ethical and moral frameworks. *How adequate are these frameworks in addressing the new realities of a globalized world?* This question lies at the heart of my philosophical inquiry.

Globalization challenges conventional ethical norms and moral frameworks in multiple ways. The global distribution of wealth, often dictated by the unseen hand of market forces and complex international trade agreements, raises questions about the fairness and justice of such distributions. *Are traditional theories of justice sufficient to address the global scale of inequality?* Similarly, the global environmental crisis challenges us to think about our ethical obligations not just to our own communities or nations but to the entire planet and future generations.

Significant global events have played a pivotal role in shaping my philosophical perspective. The 2008 global financial crisis, for instance, was a stark reminder of the vulnerabilities and interconnectedness of global financial systems. The crisis raised critical ethical questions about risk, responsibility, and the role of governmental and international institutions in regulating economies. More recently, the COVID-19 pandemic has underscored the necessity of global cooperation and the ethical implications of global health disparities. These events highlight the limitations of nation-centered approaches and the need for a global ethical perspective that considers the well-being of all humanity.

Reflecting on these events, it becomes clear that our philosophical approaches need to evolve to better address the complexities of globalization. The philosophical doctrines of the past, while foundational, must be expanded to incorporate the new realities of global interdependence. This is not merely an academic exercise but a practical imperative. Philosophical inquiry into globalization is essential for developing more equitable economic policies, more inclusive cultural policies, and more effective governance structures.

In this light, my exploration of globalization is both a response to personal experiences and a continuation of my philosophical interests. It is an attempt to bridge the gap between theoretical ethics and real-world issues, making philosophy not only relevant but essential in shaping global policies and practices. This book, therefore, is not just an academic endeavor but a call to action, a plea for deeper philosophical engagement with the issues that globalization presents to us today.

This book aims to serve multiple objectives, each designed to contribute meaningfully to the discourse on globalization from a philosophical standpoint. Firstly, it seeks to educate by providing a comprehensive analysis of how globalization impacts various spheres of human activity, economic, cultural, and political. Secondly, it challenges existing notions and widely held assumptions about these impacts, urging a reevaluation through a philosophical lens. Thirdly, the book aims to offer new insights that bridge the gap between theoretical discussions and practical applications, thereby enriching both academic discourse and real-world policy-making.

One of the primary goals of this book is to provide a nuanced exploration of how global economic practices, governance structures, and cultural exchanges operate and intersect in the context of globalization. By examining case studies and employing various philosophical perspectives, the book will illuminate the complex dynamics and interdependencies that characterize global interactions today. For instance, in discussing global economic practices, the book will dive into the ethical dimensions of trade and the distribution of wealth, providing readers with a deeper understanding of the principles that should govern fair and just economic interactions on a global scale.

Another key objective is to challenge the reader to question and critically evaluate the prevailing paradigms of thinking about globalization. By applying philosophical theories, ranging from Kantian ethics to Rawlsian justice and beyond, the book encourages a critical examination of how global policies are formulated and implemented. It questions the effectiveness and fairness of these policies, challenging readers to consider alternative approaches that might better address the underlying ethical and moral concerns. For instance, the book will critically analyze the concept of cultural imperialism through the lens of postcolonial theory, challenging readers to rethink how global cultural dynamics are shaped by historical and power structures.

The book also aims to bridge theoretical philosophy with practical policy-making. It seeks to demonstrate how philosophical insights can inform and improve decisions in international governance, business practices, and cultural conservation. For example, discussions on global governance will not only draw on philosophical concepts of sovereignty and democracy but also suggest how these ideas can be reconfigured to better address global challenges such as climate change and international conflicts. By doing so, the book provides policymakers, academics, and the general public with new tools for understanding and addressing the issues arising from globalization.

The application of philosophical theories and critical thinking to global phenomena is significant for several reasons. Philosophically informed approaches deepen our understanding of complex issues by highlighting ethical, moral, and existential dimensions that are often overlooked in conventional analyses. This enrichment of academic discourse is crucial for developing a holistic view of global issues, which in turn informs more nuanced and effective policy-making. Moreover, applying philosophy to practical global concerns empowers individuals, policymakers, business leaders, activists, and citizens, to make informed decisions that reflect ethical considerations and long-term sustainability rather than short-term gains. It helps build a foundation for global citizenship that is aware of and responsive to the interconnected nature of our modern world.

In essence, this book is an invitation to engage with globalization in a manner that is both reflective and forward-looking. It advocates for a global community that values philosophical inquiry as a fundamental component of navigating the challenges and opportunities presented by our interconnected world. Through this philosophical exploration, the book aspires not only to enhance academic discourse but also to influence practical actions and policies that shape our global future, striving for a world that is ethically sound, culturally respectful, and politically just.

"Ours is a world of nuclear giants and ethical infants."

Omar N. Bradley

Role of Philosophers in Shaping Global Ethics

Philosophers have long played a central role in shaping the ethical contours of society, challenging prevailing norms, and influencing policy and public opinion. Their ideas have historically provided frameworks for understanding justice, equality, and the responsibilities of individuals and states. In the context of globalization, the contributions of philosophers are indispensable for navigating the ethical conundrums of our interconnected world.

Historically, philosophers like Immanuel Kant, John Stuart Mill, and Karl Marx laid foundational ideas that still resonate in global ethics. Kant's notion of a cosmopolitan order, based on universal moral laws and perpetual peace, envisioned a world where states cooperate under shared principles of justice. His categorical imperative established a moral framework that emphasized treating individuals as ends in themselves, a principle echoed in modern human rights discourse. Mill's concept of utilitarianism, which sought to maximize happiness and minimize suffering, remains influential in policy decisions, particularly in public health and economic reforms. Meanwhile, Marx's critique of capitalism exposed the exploitative structures of economic globalization, inspiring movements for social justice and labor rights.

In the 20th century, the horrors of two world wars and the rise of international institutions brought philosophical ideas to the forefront of global governance. John Rawls' theory of justice, particularly his later work "The Law of Peoples," proposed a framework for international cooperation grounded in human rights and fairness among nations. Rawls argued for a global basic structure that would ensure fairness and justice, even as he balanced respect for national sovereignty. His work influenced the development of human rights norms and continues to shape debates on global justice. Similarly, Hannah Arendt's reflections on totalitarianism and the nature of evil illuminated the moral responsibilities of individuals and states in the aftermath of the Holocaust, providing philosophical grounding for the concept of "crimes against humanity."

Contemporary philosophers have continued to contribute to global ethical discourse. Thomas Pogge, building on Rawls' work, exposed the systemic injustices of global poverty, advocating for a more equitable distribution of wealth and resources. His global resource dividend concept challenges the status quo of international economic arrangements, proposing a framework where wealthier nations support global poverty alleviation. Martha Nussbaum's capabilities approach redefines human development by emphasizing the importance of individuals having the freedom to achieve their full potential. Her work has influenced international organizations like the United Nations in crafting development policies that prioritize human well-being over mere economic growth.

On the topic of environmental ethics, philosophers like Peter Singer and Arne Naess have provided frameworks that influence contemporary environmental policies. Singer's utilitarian argument for animal rights and environmental protection has shaped the ethical debate on sustainability, urging policymakers to consider the suffering of non-human beings. Naess, through his concept of deep ecology, argued for a fundamental shift in humanity's relationship with nature, advocating for intrinsic value in all living beings. Such ideas have gradually permeated global environmental movements, leading to more holistic approaches in international environmental agreements.

In addressing the ethical challenges of migration, Seyla Benhabib and Michael Walzer have offered contrasting yet complementary perspectives. Benhabib's cosmopolitan approach advocates for porous borders and inclusive citizenship, emphasizing the moral obligation to protect the rights of migrants and refugees. Walzer, on the other hand, supports a more communitarian view that recognizes the rights of states to control their borders while still upholding basic humanitarian principles. These perspectives have fueled debates on immigration policy, influencing both advocates and policymakers.

Philosophers also impact public opinion through their involvement in public discourse. Figures like Noam Chomsky, Cornel West, and Slavoj Žižek regularly challenge prevailing narratives, using their platforms to critique political and economic power structures. Chomsky's critique of American foreign policy, particularly in the Middle East, has shaped public understanding of global power dynamics. Cornel West's advocacy for racial and economic justice brings philosophical insights into grassroots movements, while Žižek's provocative critiques of capitalism and cultural politics stir debate in academic and public spheres alike.

Moreover, philosophical principles underpin key international documents and organizations. The Universal Declaration of Human Rights (UDHR), the foundation of global human rights norms, reflects philosophical ideals of universal dignity and equality. The International Criminal Court (ICC) and the Responsibility to Protect (R2P) doctrine, which seek to prevent atrocities and protect vulnerable populations, are rooted in moral principles that transcend national interests.

Essentially, philosophers have and continue to shape global ethics by providing the intellectual frameworks that guide policy decisions and public opinion. Their ideas challenge us to think beyond national borders, question economic and political structures, and envision a world where justice, human dignity, and sustainability are prioritized. As globalization presents new ethical conundrums, the role of philosophers becomes increasingly vital in offering clarity, critique, and direction for a just and equitable global future.

Philosophers can play a significant role in shaping debates on global issues like climate change, economic inequality, and human rights by providing conceptual clarity, ethical frameworks, and critical analysis. However, they face challenges in effectively communicating their ideas to policymakers and the broader public. Here's an analysis of their potential contributions, channels of communication, and the challenges they must navigate.

Philosophers contribute to climate change debates by elucidating ethical frameworks that inform policy decisions. For instance, philosophers like Derek Parfit and Henry Shue have examined the moral responsibilities toward future generations. This perspective emphasizes that current policies should not compromise the well-being of future generations. Similarly, Peter Singer and Simon Caney advocate for fair distribution of climate burdens between developed and developing nations, arguing that wealthy nations should shoulder more responsibility due to historical emissions and greater capacity to mitigate and adapt.

Philosopher Naomi Klein's work on climate change has reached a wide audience through her books and media appearances. Peter Singer has similarly contributed to public debates through op-eds and public lectures. At the same time, philosophers can join advisory bodies in international organizations like the United Nations Framework Convention on Climate Change (UNFCCC), providing ethical insights directly to policymakers. Additionally, publishing in journals like Environmental Ethics or Ethics, Policy & Environment is another way that allows philosophers to contribute to academic discourse that informs policy frameworks.

In terms of economic justice, philosophers provide valuable insights into the ethical dimensions of economic inequality, offering theories that guide policy reform. For example, consider distributive justice and capabilities approach. John Rawls' theory of justice, particularly the difference principle, has shaped contemporary discussions on welfare policies and income redistribution. Simultaneously, Amartya Sen and Martha Nussbaum advocate for policies that enhance individuals' 'capabilities', ensuring they have opportunities to pursue lives they value.

Public lectures and debates by Amartya Sen and Martha Nussbaum have brought the capabilities approach into mainstream discourse. Sen has served on the advisory board for the United Nations Development Programme's Human Development Report, ensuring that the capabilities approach informs international development policies. Similarly, collaboration with NGOs like Oxfam can bring philosophical insights into campaigns for economic justice.

On the subject of Human rights, philosophers clarify the moral basis and scope of human rights, providing theoretical guidance for global advocacy and legal frameworks. Charles Beitz and James Nickel explore how human rights can be grounded in global moral principles, informing international law. Seyla Benhabib and Joseph Carens analyze the ethical dimensions of migration, proposing frameworks for fair immigration policies.

Benhabib and Carens engage with the public through interviews, opinion pieces, and public talks, raising awareness on migration ethics. Additionally, serving as consultants to international bodies like the UN Human Rights Council can directly influence policy. Moreover, philosophers can contribute to human rights cases by submitting amicus curiae briefs that provide ethical perspectives to courts.

Challenges to Philosophical Impact on the World

PHILOSOPHICAL ARGUMENTS are often dense and abstract, making them less accessible to the general public and policymakers. Therefore, philosophers should present their ideas in clear, jargon-free language, as exemplified by Peter Singer's work.

Philosophers may struggle to translate their theoretical work into practical policy recommendations. Therefore, interdisciplinary approaches, such as working with economists, political scientists, and environmentalists can help philosophers craft more practical policy recommendations.

Policy frameworks often prioritize immediate economic and political considerations over ethical analysis, limiting the influence of philosophical ideas. Therefore, writing opinion pieces, giving public lectures, and appearing on media platforms can broaden the reach of philosophical ideas.

Philosophers should actively seek advisory roles in governmental and non-governmental organizations, ensuring their ethical insights influence policy discussions. Additionally, collaborating with educators and activists to integrate philosophical perspectives into curricula and advocacy campaigns can create a more ethically aware populace. In our society, philosophers have a vital role to play in shaping global debates on climate change, economic inequality, and human rights and by effectively communicating their ideas and engaging with policymakers, international organizations, and the public, they can provide the ethical guidance needed to address these pressing global challenges

Part 1: Understanding Globalization

———

Globalization is a multifaceted phenomenon that affects nearly every aspect of modern life. At its core, it refers to the process by which businesses, technologies, and philosophies spread across national borders, creating a network of global interdependencies. This process is not new, but its pace and impact have dramatically accelerated in the recent era due to advancements in technology, communication, and transportation.

Economically, globalization is characterized by the increased flow of goods, services, capital, and labor across borders. This integration of global markets has led to a surge in multinational corporations and international trade agreements that aim to reduce barriers to trade and investment. The economic dimension of globalization is often heralded for boosting economic growth, enhancing consumer choice, and reducing prices. However, it also raises significant challenges such as income inequality, job displacement in industrialized nations, and the disruption of traditional industries, particularly in less developed countries. These economic shifts require a balancing act between capitalizing on global opportunities and mitigating adverse effects on local economies.

Culturally, globalization involves the exchange and interaction of ideas, values, and artistic expressions among cultures. This dimension is evident in the global spread of information through the internet and social media, as well as the worldwide popularity of certain music genres, films, and fashion. While cultural globalization promotes understanding and the blending of cultures, it also poses risks to cultural integrity and identity. There is a tension between the homogenizing effects of a global culture, often dominated by Western values and consumerism, and the preservation of indigenous cultures and practices.

Politically, globalization has led to significant changes in the way governance is conducted and how political power is organized. The rise of international and supranational organizations, such as the United Nations, the World Trade Organization, and the EU, reflects an attempt to manage the complexities of global interdependence through cooperative political mechanisms. These bodies work to address issues that transcend national borders, such as climate change, international trade disputes, and global security challenges. However, the increasing influence of these organizations also prompts debates about national sovereignty, democratic accountability, and the distribution of power on the global stage.

The interdependence of these dimensions is crucial to understanding the full impact of globalization. Economic changes can lead to cultural shifts, as increased trade and communication expose individuals to new ideas and lifestyles. Similarly, political agreements often facilitate or constrain economic and cultural exchanges. The dynamic interplay between these dimensions suggests that globalization is not merely a series of isolated events but a complex process of transformation that influences and is influenced by multiple factors simultaneously. This comprehensive view of globalization highlights the necessity of approaching it through a multi-dimensional lens. Each aspect, economic, cultural, and political, does not operate in isolation but in a continuous interaction that shapes and reshapes the contours of global society.

The seeds of globalization were sown with the establishment of ancient trade routes, such as the Silk Road, which connected Asia, Africa, and Europe. These routes facilitated not only the exchange of goods like silk, spices, and precious metals but also the flow of ideas, technologies, and cultural practices across continents. Philosophical concepts, religious beliefs, and scientific knowledge traversed these routes, significantly influencing societies along their paths.

The Age of Discovery marked a significant escalation in the process of globalization, characterized by European colonial expansion. Nations such as Portugal, Spain, Britain, and France established colonies across the Americas, Africa, and Asia. This era was pivotal in shaping the modern world but also raised profound ethical and moral questions about conquest, domination, and the impact on indigenous populations. The colonial period saw the global spread of European legal, political, and economic systems, often at the expense of local cultures and governance structures.

The Industrial Revolution was another critical milestone, introducing new manufacturing processes and technologies that radically increased the volume and speed of production. Innovations such as the steam engine and later, the internal combustion engine, revolutionized transportation and communication, shrinking distances and knitting the world closer together. These technological advancements laid the groundwork for the modern phase of globalization, characterized by an unprecedented integration of global markets.

In the late 20th and early 21st centuries, digital technology has been the driving force of globalization. The advent of the internet and digital communication technologies has connected the globe in real-time, dissolving physical barriers and creating a new digital marketplace. Social media platforms, e-commerce, and mobile connectivity have transformed economic and social interactions, making it possible to live, work, and interact in a globally interconnected way.

The evolution of globalization raises significant philosophical questions, particularly regarding ethics, justice, and governance. Philosophers like Emmanuel Levinas and Martha Nussbaum have contributed to our understanding of the ethical responsibilities that arise in a deeply interconnected world. Levinas's emphasis on the ethical responsibility to the 'Other' and Nussbaum's capabilities approach suggest frameworks for considering how global interactions should be structured to respect human dignity and promote equitable development. From a political philosophy perspective, thinkers such as Thomas Paine and Immanuel Kant have laid down early ideas about cosmopolitanism, advocating for global governance mechanisms that respect individual rights while promoting collective responsibilities. These philosophical explorations are crucial in assessing the implications of globalization on global governance structures, questioning how power and resources are allocated and governed across borders.

Critically assessing the historical evolution of globalization involves acknowledging the benefits of increased global connectivity and economic growth while also confronting the disparities and disruptions it has caused. The challenge lies in balancing these scales in a way that promotes global equity and justice, aligning with philosophical theories that advocate for fairness and the ethical treatment of all individuals, regardless of geographic location.

Chapter 1: The Economic Dimension of Globalization

———

The economic dimension of globalization is perhaps the most visible and frequently discussed aspect, encompassing the expansion and integration of global markets and trade networks. This integration has been driven by a series of developments and policies that have progressively removed barriers to trade and investment across borders, shaping the economic landscapes of nations around the world.

The roots of modern global trade can be traced back to the mercantilist policies of the 16th and 17th centuries. Mercantilism was characterized by the belief that national power depended on the accumulation of wealth, particularly precious metals like gold and silver. European powers sought to maximize exports and minimize imports through high tariffs and other trade barriers. This period saw the rise of colonial empires, where the metropole (colonizing country) exploited the colony's resources to enrich itself. The mercantilist approach not only spurred the first wave of globalization but also laid the groundwork for subsequent economic theories and practices.

The Industrial Revolution marked a significant shift in global trade dynamics. The advent of industrial production methods allowed European countries, particularly Britain, to produce goods on an unprecedented scale, leading to the search for new markets and sources of raw materials. The steam engine, railways, and steamships reduced the cost and increased the speed of transporting goods across long distances, making global trade more feasible and profitable.

The post-World War II era ushered in a new phase of market integration. The establishment of institutions like the International Monetary Fund (IMF), the World Bank, and later the World Trade Organization (WTO), aimed to create a stable economic environment by promoting free trade, reducing tariffs, and regulating financial interactions. The General Agreement on

Tariffs and Trade (GATT), established in 1948, and its successor, the WTO, have been instrumental in this global economic integration by providing a forum for negotiating trade agreements and a mechanism for dispute resolution.

In recent decades, the proliferation of bilateral and multilateral free trade agreements (FTAs) has further diminished barriers to trade. These agreements, which often include provisions that go beyond traditional trade issues, such as intellectual property rights and labor standards, aim to enhance economic cooperation and integration between member countries. Notable examples include the North American Free Trade Agreement (NAFTA) and the Comprehensive and Progressive Agreement for Trans-Pacific Partnership (CPTPP). The growth of international trade and the integration of markets have had profound implications for global economies:

- **Economic Growth:** Countries that have embraced open markets tend to experience faster economic growth by capitalizing on their comparative advantages.

- **Job Creation and Loss:** While globalization has led to job creation in many sectors, it has also resulted in job losses, particularly in industries exposed to international competition.

- **Income Inequality:** Although trade can contribute to overall economic growth, its benefits are not always evenly distributed, leading to increased income inequality within and between countries.

- **Economic Dependence:** Smaller and developing economies often become economically dependent on larger, developed countries, creating imbalances in economic power and decision-making.

The economic dimension of globalization raises significant philosophical and ethical questions. Philosophers like Adam Smith and David Ricardo provided early justifications for free trade based on the principle of mutual benefit. Adam Smith's concept of the "invisible hand" is a cornerstone of classical economics, suggesting that individuals' pursuit of self-interest inadvertently benefits society as a whole. Originally, Smith introduced this idea in the context of domestic market behavior, positing that when producers and consumers operate in a free market, resources are allocated efficiently, and the economy grows without any central planning.

Smith's idea can be applied to explain how global trade increases efficiency. Countries engage in trade based on their comparative advantages, leading to a more efficient allocation of global resources. This has been a driving force behind the push for reducing trade barriers and liberalizing economies worldwide. However, the "invisible hand" theory in its purest form often overlooks the negative externalities associated with unregulated markets. For example, environmental degradation, labor exploitation, and economic inequality can arise from unchecked market forces. These outcomes challenge the notion that market forces always result in beneficial outcomes for all, highlighting the need for regulatory frameworks and ethical considerations in global trade practices.

On the other hand, David Ricardo's theory of comparative advantage explains why it's beneficial for countries to engage in trade even if one country is less efficient in the production of all goods. According to Ricardo, each nation should specialize in producing and exporting goods in which it has a relative efficiency advantage. His principle underpins the structuring of global supply chains, where production processes are fragmented across different countries. Each segment of production is located where it can be accomplished most efficiently, from manufacturing components to assembly. While this theory supports the idea of efficiency through specialization, it also contributes to economic dependency. For example, some developing countries have become overly reliant on exporting a narrow range of commodities, which can be volatile and limit their industrial development.

Both theories explain the economic logic behind free trade and market liberalization, which are foundational to contemporary globalization. They provide a rationale for why globalized trade can lead to wealth generation and efficiency improvements. However, these theories were developed in the context of relatively simple economies compared to today's complex global system. They do not fully account for modern issues such as digital economies, intellectual property, and multinational corporations that exert significant influence over global economics and politics.

Contemporary ethical discussions also focus on the responsibilities of global actors, be they states or corporations, to ensure that the benefits of globalization are shared equitably. The challenge is to craft policies and practices that not only promote economic efficiency but also adhere to principles of justice and fairness in the global context. As globalization has evolved, MNCs and global financial institutions have emerged as pivotal actors in shaping the global economic landscape. Their influence permeates various aspects of economic, cultural, and political life worldwide, dictating patterns of investment, production, and consumption across borders.

MNCs, with their vast resources and transnational reach, play a central role in the global economy. Companies like Apple, ExxonMobil, and Toyota, which operate production facilities in multiple countries and market their products globally, are prime examples. These entities leverage economies of scale and access to diverse markets to maximize profits, often influencing local economies significantly. MNCs contribute to job creation and technological advancement in the countries where they operate. However, they also face criticism for practices that can undermine labor standards and economic equity. For example, the practice of offshoring manufacturing jobs to low-wage countries raises significant ethical questions about workers' rights and working conditions. Instances where multinational corporations pay minimal wages in developing countries while generating substantial profits have sparked debates about economic justice and the ethical obligations of large corporations towards their workers.

Global financial institutions such as the IMF, the World Bank, and regional development banks play a crucial role in providing financial stability and development funding. They influence economic policies in developing countries through structural adjustment programs, loans, and aid initiatives aimed at fostering economic growth and stability. However, the conditions often attached to these financial supports, such as austerity measures and liberalization policies, can lead to significant social pushback. Critics argue that these conditions may prioritize financial markets and foreign investors over the welfare of the local population, exacerbating income inequality and undermining sovereign economic decision-making. The ethical implications of such influence highlight the need for policies that are not only economically effective but also socially just and respectful of national autonomy.

As MNCs and global financial institutions increasingly dominate the global economic landscape, their influence extends far beyond mere economic metrics, deeply impacting the ethical fabric and equity of societies worldwide. The complexity of these impacts necessitates a thorough exploration, informed by philosophical principles and economic realities.

For instance, the global operations of MNCs often bring them into regions where labor laws may be less stringent or less strictly enforced than in their home countries. This disparity can lead to practices that, while legally permissible, raise significant ethical concerns. For example, the textile industry in countries like Bangladesh and Vietnam has repeatedly been scrutinized for labor violations in factories producing goods for global brands. From a philosophical perspective, the Kantian imperative to treat individuals as ends in themselves and not merely as means to an end calls into question practices that exploit workers for profit. Furthermore, the capability approach advocated by philosopher Amartya Sen emphasizes enhancing individual freedoms and abilities, which includes fair labor practices that allow workers to live a life they have reason to value.

The activities of MNCs and global financial institutions also play a critical role in shaping the distribution of global wealth, often leading to significant economic disparities. While globalization has lifted millions out of poverty, it has also exacerbated income inequality both within and between countries. The wealth generated by global operations frequently accumulates to the benefit of corporate shareholders and top executives, often at the expense of the broader workforce. This concentration of wealth, especially in the context of globalization, presents a challenge to Rawlsian principles of justice, which advocate for social and economic inequalities to be arranged so that they are to the greatest benefit of the least advantaged members of society. The global scale of modern corporations and their impact on economic disparity demand a reevaluation of these principles to ensure that they encompass global contexts.

The sustainability of global economic policies is another area of significant ethical concern. The environmental degradation resulting from unchecked industrial growth poses not only ecological risks but also raises moral questions about the responsibilities of the current generation to future generations. This aspect touches on environmental ethics, a field that examines the moral relationship between humans and the natural world. Philosophers like Peter Singer and Julian Simon have debated the extent of our obligations to preserve the environment, with arguments ranging from the utilitarian perspective, which might justify environmental damage for greater good (an argument often used to defend economic development), to more radical ecological ethics that place intrinsic value on nature and demand its preservation.

Global financial institutions wield considerable influence over the economic policies of developing countries through loans and financial aid packages. While these institutions argue that their policies and recommendations are designed to nurture economic stability and growth, critics claim that they often prioritize repayment of debts over economic development and welfare improvements in these countries. These practices can be examined through the lens of distributive justice theories, questioning whether the conditions imposed by such institutions fairly distribute the benefits and burdens of economic activities. Ethical considerations include not only the immediate impacts of policy recommendations but also their long-term effects on national sovereignty and economic independence.

In institutions like the IMF and the World Bank, voting power is disproportionately held by wealthy countries based on their financial contributions. This structure inherently gives greater decision-making power to developed nations, which can shape policies and fund allocation in ways that prioritize their interests over those of poorer nations. Simultaneously, these institutions often impose conditions on loans and aid that require recipient countries to implement specific economic policies, such as austerity measures, privatization of state-owned enterprises, and liberalization of markets. Critics argue that these conditions can undermine economic sovereignty, forcing developing countries to adopt policies that may not be well-suited to their socio-economic contexts and can lead to long-term economic dependency. Moreover, the economic models promoted by these institutions tend to favor a one-size-fits-all approach, typically advocating for neoliberal economic principles. This can lead to the homogenization of global economic policies, which might not take into account the diverse economic realities and needs of different countries.

In light of these ethical and economic impacts, incorporating philosophical perspectives into global economic policy-making is crucial. This integration ensures that policies are not only economically sound but are also ethically justified, promoting a more equitable and just global economic system. Engaging with these philosophical issues encourages policymakers, corporate leaders, and stakeholders to consider the broader implications of their decisions and to strive for solutions that respect human dignity and promote genuine economic equity.

Authoritative sources such as the World Economic Forum (WEF), the United Nations Conference on Trade and Development (UNCTAD), and academic journals provide empirical data and analyses that support the discussion of these topics. Case studies from these sources illuminate the real-world implications of the theoretical debates on economic justice and ethics. Incorporating philosophical perspectives into the analysis of globalization challenges us to think critically about the ethical dimensions of economic activities. It encourages a dialogue not just about what is economically feasible but also about what is ethically desirable, aiming to create a global economic system that is just, equitable, and sustainable.

1.1 Wealth Distribution Disparity

Economic globalization has reshaped the distribution of wealth across and within countries, presenting a sophisticated web of economic outcomes that have fueled debates on equity and justice globally. This discussion explores how globalization has influenced wealth accumulation, highlighting the disparities it has either exacerbated or mitigated.

Globalization has often been touted as a vehicle for economic growth and prosperity, with the potential to uplift developing nations through increased trade, foreign direct investment (FDI), and technology transfer. However, the reality is more nuanced, with benefits unevenly distributed between and within countries. While some developing countries have experienced rapid economic growth and integration into the global economy, like China, India, and some Southeast Asian nations, others, particularly in sub-Saharan Africa and parts of Latin America, have not seen the same benefits.

Wealth accumulation in developed countries has generally been bolstered by globalization, thanks to their capacity to invest abroad, higher technology adaptation rates, and robust institutional frameworks that attract FDI. In contrast, many developing countries, despite some gains, often find themselves exporting raw materials and importing finished goods, a dynamic that perpetuates a colonial-style economic pattern. This model benefits developed nations and keeps developing countries in a dependent position, often referred to as the "***resource curse.***"

The economic theories of dependency articulated by scholars like Andre Gunder Frank in the 1960s and the more contemporary perspectives of Thomas Piketty highlight these issues. They argue that economic practices under globalization tend to favor capital-rich countries, leading to a concentration of wealth in nations with the capital necessary to invest and innovate, thus widening the gap between rich and poor countries.

Within individual nations, globalization has also significantly impacted wealth distribution. The opening of markets and the expansion of MNCs have created new wealth for some but have also often led to significant disruptions in local economies. In many cases, globalization has resulted in job losses in traditional sectors such as manufacturing in the developed world and agriculture in developing countries, due to competition from more efficient or cheaper foreign industries. MNCs sometimes exploit lower labor standards in developing countries to reduce costs, resulting in poor working conditions, unfair wages, and inadequate labor rights. This practice can exacerbate income disparities and contribute to the perpetuation of poverty in regions where they operate. Additionally, MNCs' pursuit of lower production costs can also lead to environmental degradation in developing countries, where environmental regulations may be less stringent or less rigorously enforced. This only impacts the global environment but also disproportionately affects the poor communities, least able to deal with environmental changes.

These changes have led to increased income inequality within countries. For instance, in the United States and other developed economies, there has been significant growth in income inequality since the late 20th century, coinciding with the acceleration of globalization. The top earners often benefit disproportionately from globalization, gaining from new markets and broader investment opportunities, while the middle and lower income brackets may face job displacement and stagnating wages.

Philosophically, these dynamics challenge the ethical frameworks proposed by both utilitarian and deontological theorists. From a utilitarian perspective, although globalization may increase overall wealth, the uneven distribution can lead to greater societal discontent and instability, which could negate the total gains. Deontological ethics, particularly those focusing on rights-based approaches as discussed by philosophers like John Rawls, would critique the fairness of a system that privileges a small segment of society at the expense of the majority.

The disparities in wealth distribution under globalization call for a reevaluation of policies from the standpoint of economic justice.

Philosophical perspectives such as Rawls's theory of justice advocate for structures that ensure not only equality of opportunity but also support for the least advantaged. Rawls's principle of the "*difference maxim*" suggests that economic inequalities are only justifiable if they benefit the least well-off members of society, a principle that could guide the restructuring of global economic policies to be more equitable.

While globalization has the potential to generate wealth and promote economic development, its current structure often leads to significant disparities in wealth distribution both between and within countries. A philosophical reevaluation of these outcomes is essential to develop more just economic policies that can address these disparities effectively, ensuring that the benefits of globalization are more broadly and equitably shared. These disparities in wealth distribution associated with economic globalization can be attributed to a variety of factors, including trade policies, investment flows, and corporate practices. These elements interact in multiple ways to shape the economy of countries and influence the socioeconomic stratification within societies.

Trade Policies: Trade policies play a crucial role in determining the distribution of wealth both between and within countries. Tariffs, quotas, and trade agreements have significant impacts on which industries thrive and which do not. For instance, developed countries often advocate for free trade policies in manufacturing and technology sectors where they have a competitive advantage but might protect their agricultural sectors which developing countries could competitively export. This selective approach to free trade can undermine the economic prospects of developing countries, perpetuating wealth inequalities. Furthermore, the structure of trade agreements can also influence wealth distribution. Agreements that favor the interests of economically powerful countries or that are negotiated without equal representation can exacerbate wealth disparities. For example, intellectual property rights provisions in some trade agreements have been criticized for favoring MNCs from developed countries, limiting the ability of firms in developing countries to access and develop new technologies and generics.

Investment Flows: Foreign Direct Investment (FDI) is another significant factor in globalization that affects wealth distribution. While FDI can contribute to economic growth in host countries by creating jobs and transferring technology, the benefits are often unevenly distributed. Investment tends to flow into sectors that promise the highest returns, which can lead to sectoral imbalances in the economy. For instance, if most FDI flows into extractive industries, it might not contribute significantly to broader economic development or might even lead to environmental degradation, which disproportionately affects poorer communities. Moreover, the conditions attached to investments and the stability of investment flows can also impact wealth distribution. Volatile investment flows can lead to economic instability in countries heavily reliant on FDI, affecting the poorest who are often least able to absorb economic shocks.

Corporate Practices: The practices of MNCs can significantly impact wealth distribution. Corporate decisions on where to locate factories, how much to pay workers, what prices to charge for goods, and how to manage supply chains have profound impacts on economies and societies. While corporations may bring jobs and technology to a region, their practices in wage setting, labor rights, and local engagement determine the extent to which the benefits are shared. Corporations may engage in practices such as transfer pricing and tax avoidance that can deprive local economies of significant sources of revenue. These practices, while often legal, raise ethical questions about the responsibility of corporations to contribute fairly to the economies from which they profit.

From a philosophical perspective, these factors challenge fundamental ethical and justice principles. The ethical theories of distributive justice, such as those proposed by John Rawls and Robert Nozick, offer frameworks for assessing these disparities. Rawls's principle of justice as fairness would critique policies and practices that lead to significant inequalities, suggesting that economic structures should benefit the most disadvantaged members of society. Nozick's entitlement theory would call for a reexamination of how rights over properties and goods are acquired and transferred in the global economy, emphasizing fair dealings and the rectification of past injustices.

Addressing these disparities requires a multi-faceted approach that involves rethinking trade policies to be more equitable, ensuring that investment flows contribute to sustainable development, and holding corporations accountable for their impacts on global wealth distribution. This approach not only seeks economic efficiency but also strives to fulfill ethical imperatives that advocate for equity and justice in the global economic order.

Let us consider both utilitarian and distributive justice frameworks to explore how these ethical theories can inform real-world solutions.

Utilitarianism, which advocates for actions that maximize overall happiness and well-being, provides a critical lens through which to examine the outcomes of economic globalization. From a utilitarian standpoint, the expansion of global trade and investment might be justified if it increases total global wealth. However, this justification often overlooks how this wealth is distributed and whether it contributes to the greatest good for the greatest number. The practical implications of a utilitarian approach can be seen in the push for economic policies that prioritize aggregate growth, often at the expense of increasing socio-economic inequalities. For instance, the rapid economic rise of countries like China has lifted millions out of poverty, which could be seen as a utilitarian success. However, this growth has also led to significant environmental degradation and a widening income gap, raising questions about the long-term sustainability of such growth from a utilitarian perspective.

Distributive justice, as discussed above, offers a different approach by focusing on how economic goods should be fairly distributed to achieve social justice. Rawls argues for a theory of justice based on two principles: that *each person should have equal access to basic liberties*, and that *social and economic inequalities should be arranged so that they are both reasonably expected to be to everyone's advantage and attached to positions open to all under conditions of fair equality of opportunity*. Applying Rawls's principles to global wealth distribution would necessitate a reevaluation of current economic structures. For example, the exploitation of labor in developing countries by MNCs might increase profits and contribute to economic growth, but it does not meet the criterion of benefiting the least advantaged in a way that compensates for the inequalities it creates.

Case studies from around the world illustrate the real impacts of these ethical considerations. For example, the extraction of minerals in the Democratic Republic of Congo for use in consumer electronics has generated significant profits but at the cost of human rights abuses and local impoverishment. Another case is the garment industry in Bangladesh, where factory conditions have sometimes been dire, illustrating a failure of both utilitarian and distributive justice frameworks. To address these inequalities, several philosophical insights and solutions can be proposed, like:

- **Global Minimum Wage:** Implementing a global minimum wage standard for multinational corporations could help ensure that workers everywhere receive fair compensation, aligning with both utilitarian (improving overall well-being) and distributive justice (fair distribution of economic goods) principles.

- **Strengthening Global Governance:** Enhancing the power and reach of international bodies like the International Labour Organization (ILO) could help enforce labor rights and fair trade practices globally.

- **Corporate Social Responsibility (CSR):** Encouraging or mandating CSR initiatives can align corporate practices with ethical standards that prioritize the welfare of all stakeholders, not just shareholders.

- **Fair Trade:** Supporting and expanding fair trade practices can help ensure that the benefits of globalization reach small producers in developing countries, fostering more equitable global trade relationships.

By applying these ethical frameworks and considering practical case studies, it becomes possible to formulate strategies that not only address the inequalities caused by globalization but also align with broader ethical imperatives. Supporting the above initiatives are crucial in this regard. *For instance, reforming the governance structures of global financial institutions to ensure more equitable representation and decision-making power for developing countries, like revising voting systems and considering greater input from a broader range of stakeholders. Or encouraging the development and adoption of alternative economic models that prioritize sustainability, equity, and local context can help counter the homogenization of global economic policies.* Such strategies would contribute to a more just global economic system, where the benefits and burdens of globalization are more equitably shared among all global citizens.

1.2 Ethical Conundrums of Labor and Production

———

The globalization of production has interconnected economies worldwide, leading to significant changes in labor practices and production processes. This integration, while economically beneficial, has brought forth significant ethical concerns that require a comprehensive analysis.

One of the most pressing ethical issues in global supply chains is labor exploitation. This often manifests as exceedingly long working hours, inadequate wages, unsafe working conditions, and the suppression of workers' rights to organize and bargain collectively. These practices are particularly prevalent in industries that are labor-intensive and operate in jurisdictions with weak labor laws or poor enforcement, such as the textile and electronics manufacturing sectors in parts of Asia and Latin America. From a philosophical standpoint, such exploitation can be analyzed through the lens of Immanuel Kant's categorical imperative, which posits that individuals should never be treated merely as a means to an end but always also as ends in themselves. Labor exploitation in global supply chains clearly violates this principle by treating workers primarily as tools for profit generation rather than as individuals with rights and dignity.

The disparity in working conditions between developed and developing countries is another ethical concern. Workers in developing countries often face hazardous conditions, such as exposure to toxic chemicals, extreme temperatures, and unsafe machinery. The collapse of the Rana Plaza building in Bangladesh in 2013, which housed several garment factories, is a stark example, resulting in over 1,000 deaths and highlighting the unsafe conditions that are all too common in global supply chains. This issue raises questions about the responsibility of MNCs in ensuring safe working conditions across their operations. According to the principle of distributive justice; social and economic inequalities are to be arranged so that they are to the greatest benefit of the least advantaged. Applying this principle, corporations would have a moral obligation to improve working conditions, even when local standards are lower.

Additionally, the environmental degradation resulting from production practices in global supply chains also poses significant ethical concerns. Industries such as mining, agriculture, and manufacturing often result in pollution, habitat destruction, and the depletion of natural resources. The global nature of these supply chains can lead to a scenario where the environmental costs of developed nations' consumption are outsourced to poorer countries. From an ethical perspective, this situation can be critiqued using utilitarian principles, which advocate for actions that maximize overall happiness and minimize suffering. The environmental damage caused by unsustainable production practices has long-term consequences for global populations, particularly impacting those who are least able to mitigate these effects and adapt to environmental changes. Addressing these ethical concerns could involve:

- **Enforcing ILOs:** International organizations, such as the ILO, need to be empowered to enforce labor standards globally. This could include stricter monitoring and penalties for non-compliance.

- **Corporate Accountability:** Corporations should be held accountable not only by regulatory bodies but also through mechanisms like public reporting, ethical certifications, and consumer advocacy. Transparency in supply chain operations and the implementation of Corporate Social Responsibility (CSR) initiatives can play a critical role.

- **Sustainable Production Practices:** Adoption of sustainable practices that reduce environmental impact should be incentivized. This might include adopting cleaner technologies, reducing waste, and ensuring that the environmental costs of production are factored into the pricing of goods.

MNCs operate complex supply chains that span multiple countries and often involve thousands of workers. The management of these supply chains and the responsibilities corporations hold towards their workers are crucial elements that dictate both operational success and ethical conduct. A comprehensive analysis of ethical concerns in global labor practices and production processes reveals significant challenges. Addressing these requires a multi-pronged approach that combines regulatory enforcement, corporate accountability, and a commitment to ethical principles. By integrating considerations of justice, rights, and utility, stakeholders can work towards a more equitable and sustainable model of global production.

Global corporations typically manage their supply chains through a centralized strategy that aims to optimize efficiency and reduce costs. This often involves sourcing materials from regions where inputs are cheapest and labor costs are lower, and distributing production across various countries to mitigate risks and exploit local advantages. For instance, a company like Apple sources components from over 40 countries, assembling products in places like China where labor costs have traditionally been lower than in Western countries.

The ethical responsibilities of global corporations towards their workers include ensuring fair wages, safe working conditions, and respect for labor rights. These responsibilities are guided by international labor laws and the principles of CSR. However, the enforcement and adherence to these standards can vary significantly between regions, influenced by local laws, economic conditions, and the corporation's commitment to ethical practices.

From the perspective of **Kantian ethics**, which emphasizes treating individuals as ends in themselves and not merely as means to an end, many supply chain practices can be seen as ethically problematic. For example, the exploitation of workers through low wages and poor working conditions in some factories in Southeast Asia used by Western corporations could be viewed as treating these workers as mere tools for profit. Kantian ethics would demand that these workers be treated with dignity and given rights commensurate with their inherent worth as human beings. Meanwhile, **Virtue ethics,** which focuses on the moral character of the individuals and organizations involved, would inherently demand that corporations value justice, benevolence, and prudence, translating these values into its supply chain management. This ethical framework would encourage companies to go beyond minimal compliance with legal standards to embody virtues in their corporate culture, impacting all aspects of their businesses.

As mentioned earlier, the Rana Plaza disaster in Bangladesh tragically highlighted the consequences of neglecting ethical practices in supply chains. Its collapse due to safety violations resulted in over 1,000 deaths, primarily of garment workers producing clothing for several global fashion brands. This event sparked an international outcry and led to calls for better regulatory oversight and corporate responsibility in global supply chains. Another example is the criticism faced by companies like Nike and Adidas over labor practices in their supply chains. These companies have since made significant efforts to improve transparency and labor conditions, showcasing how public pressure and ethical considerations can lead to positive changes. However, improving ethical practices in global supply chains is a continuous process and can involve other strategies, like:

- **Implementation of International Labor Standards:** Corporations should commit to implementing standards set by international bodies like the ILO. This includes adhering to conventions on wages, hours, and safety conditions.

- **Third-Party Audits and Certifications:** Regular audits by independent third parties can help ensure compliance with labor standards. Certifications like SA8000 are useful for companies to demonstrate their commitment to fair labor practices.

- **Strengthening Worker Voices:** Empowering workers through union representation or worker councils can ensure that labor concerns are heard and addressed directly, fostering a more ethical and inclusive workplace culture.

- **Corporate Policy Reforms:** Corporations can reform their policies to prioritize ethical considerations. This might include developing clear CSR policies, investing in worker welfare, and creating grievance mechanisms to address workers' concerns.

By critically assessing and addressing these issues through the lens of ethical theories like Kantian ethics and virtue ethics, global corporations can manage their supply chains more ethically, contributing to more just and sustainable business practices globally.

1.3 Utilitarian viewpoint

The ethical dilemmas posed by economic globalization, particularly wealth disparity and labor rights exploitation, demand a rigorous and pragmatic approach for resolution. The utilitarian viewpoint, with its emphasis on maximizing happiness and minimizing suffering, offers a compelling framework for navigating these complex issues. This perspective assesses actions based on their consequences, advocating for policies and practices that produce the greatest good for the greatest number.

The stark wealth disparities exacerbated by globalization represent a significant challenge from a utilitarian perspective. The concentration of wealth in the hands of a few, creates a situation where the well-being of the majority is compromised for the benefit of a minority. A utilitarian approach to this issue would advocate for economic policies that redistribute wealth more equitably, such as progressive taxation, social welfare programs, and investment in public goods like education and healthcare. These measures aim to enhance overall societal well-being by ensuring that economic gains from globalization benefit a broader segment of the population, thereby reducing poverty and improving quality of life for all.

Similarly, the exploitation of labor in the globalized economy presents a clear ethical dilemma from a utilitarian standpoint. Such practices not only cause significant suffering to workers but also undermine social stability and global justice. A utilitarian approach would advocate for the enforcement of international labor standards, corporate social responsibility initiatives, and fair trade practices. By prioritizing the well-being of workers and ensuring fair compensation and safe working conditions, the global community can work towards minimizing harm and maximizing the benefits of economic globalization for all stakeholders involved.

Addressing the ethical challenges of economic globalization requires robust global governance mechanisms and cooperation among nations, corporations, and civil society. Policies that promote economic justice, such as international agreements on tax evasion, labor standards, and environmental protection, are essential for ensuring that globalization leads to positive outcomes for the largest number of people. Furthermore, empowering international organizations to monitor and enforce compliance with these standards can help to mitigate the negative consequences of globalization.

The utilitarian perspective on economic globalization's ethical challenges emphasizes the importance of considering the broader implications of economic policies and practices. By focusing on the consequences of actions and striving to maximize overall happiness, it is possible to navigate the complexities of wealth disparity and labor exploitation in a globalized world. This approach calls for a commitment to justice, equity, and the well-being of all individuals, highlighting the need for moral and political philosophies that are attuned to the realities of the contemporary global economy.

1.4 Deontological ethics

The deontological critique of wealth disparity under economic globalization hinges on principles of fairness and justice. The accumulation of wealth in the hands of a few, at the expense of the many, violates the moral duty to treat all individuals with equal respect and consideration. Deontologists, drawing on Kantian ethics, would argue that economic systems and policies must be designed in a way that respects the moral worth of every person. Measures such as progressive taxation, equitable distribution of resources, and access to essential services like healthcare and education are not just strategies for social betterment; they are moral imperatives that recognize the equal worth of every individual.

The exploitation of workers in the global economy is particularly egregious from a deontological perspective. Practices that undermine basic human rights, subject workers to unsafe conditions, or fail to provide fair wages are fundamentally unjust. They treat individuals as means to an end, violating the Kantian principle that people should always be treated as ends in themselves. Deontologists would advocate for strict adherence to international labor standards, ethical business practices, and the protection of workers' rights as non-negotiable moral duties. These commitments are essential for honoring the intrinsic dignity of laborers and ensuring that economic activities are conducted within the bounds of moral and ethical principles.

In addressing the ethical implications of economic globalization, deontological ethics underscores the importance of principled action at both the individual and institutional levels. It calls for the establishment and enforcement of global standards that reflect moral duties towards fairness, human rights, and dignity. International organizations and agreements play a crucial role in this framework, setting out clear ethical guidelines for economic conduct and providing mechanisms for accountability.

A deontological approach to the ethical challenges of economic globalization emphasizes the primacy of moral duties and principles in guiding actions and policies. It calls for a reevaluation of global economic practices to ensure they align with imperatives of justice, respect for human rights, and the inherent worth of every individual. By adhering to deontological principles, societies can strive toward an economic system that not only fosters growth and development but does so in a manner that is ethically justifiable and morally sound. This perspective highlights the need for a foundational commitment to ethical norms that transcend economic considerations, advocating for a global order that upholds the dignity and rights of all individuals in the face of globalization's complex challenges.

1.5 Virtue ethics

Aristotle's virtue ethics approach, emphasizing character and the pursuit of a virtuous life, focuses on the development of moral character and the virtues necessary for a flourishing society. The stark wealth disparities accentuated by economic globalization call into question the moral character of both individuals and societies. Virtue ethicists would argue that a just and flourishing society is one where resources are distributed in a manner that enables all members to lead fulfilling lives. The accumulation of excessive wealth, particularly when it contributes to the deprivation of others, is seen as indicative of vices such as greed and injustice.

A virtuous approach to economic participation involves practicing generosity, fairness, and justice. These virtues guide individuals and corporations in making decisions that not only seek profit but also contribute to the common good. Policies that ensure fair wages, support social safety nets, and encourage philanthropy are aligned with the virtuous aim of promoting a more equitable and flourishing society for all.

The exploitation of workers in a globalized economy significantly contrasts with the principles of virtue ethics, which values dignity, respect, and the development of communal relationships. The virtue of justice demands fair treatment of all individuals, which includes just compensation, safe working conditions, and respect for workers' rights. Exploitative practices are not only unjust but also undermine the development of a moral community, eroding trust and solidarity. Virtue ethics emphasizes the role of moral exemplars; individuals and organizations that embody virtues in their practices. By championing ethical labor practices and corporate responsibility, these exemplars set standards for others, fostering a culture where virtues such as fairness, compassion, and respect are embedded in the core of global economic interactions.

Virtue ethics advocates for the cultivation of a global ethos centered on shared virtues that transcend cultural and national boundaries. This involves cultivating global citizenship and solidarity, where individuals and institutions are committed to the well-being of the global community. Education plays a crucial role in this process, cultivating virtues and ethical sensitivity that guide actions in an interconnected world. A virtue ethics perspective on economic globalization encourages a shift in focus from merely navigating ethical dilemmas to actively cultivating a virtuous society. It emphasizes that true flourishing, both individual and collective, depends on the development and practice of virtues that foster equity, justice, and respect for human dignity. Addressing wealth disparity and labor exploitation thus becomes not only a matter of rectifying injustices but also an opportunity to cultivate a global community grounded in virtue.

1.6 Marxist Philosophy

From a Marxist perspective, the economic wealth disparities and labor rights' exploitation are not mere byproducts of globalization but inherent features of the capitalist system it propagates. Marxism, with its critical analysis of capital and class struggle, provides a robust framework for understanding and challenging the ethical issues engendered by economic globalization.

Marxist analysis posits that wealth disparity is a direct outcome of the capitalist mode of production, where the value generated by the labor of workers is appropriated by the owners of capital (the bourgeoisie) in the form of profits. Globalization, in this context, is viewed as an extension of capitalism's inherent need to expand and exploit new markets and labor pools. The resulting concentration of wealth in the hands of a global elite is seen as an inevitable consequence of capitalism's exploitation and alienation of the working class. The ethical imperative from a Marxist standpoint is to challenge the structural inequalities of capitalism and work towards a more equitable economic system. This involves mobilizing the working class (the proletariat) to recognize their collective power and to strive for the overthrow of capitalist structures, replacing them with socialist ones where the means of production are owned and managed by the community, thus ensuring a more equitable distribution of wealth.

Marxist theory highlights labor exploitation as a fundamental characteristic of capitalism, where workers are paid less than the value they produce, a discrepancy that is the source of capitalist profit. In the context of globalization, this exploitation is magnified as corporations seek out the cheapest labor markets to maximize profits, often at the expense of labor rights and working conditions. From a Marxist perspective, the fight for labor rights is inseparable from the struggle against capitalism itself. It involves organizing workers globally to resist exploitation through unions, strikes, and other forms of collective action. Moreover, Marxism advocates for the ultimate abolition of the capitalist system and the establishment of a socialist society, where labor is not a commodity to be exploited but the means by which individuals contribute to and benefit from the collective well-being.

Marxism views the ethical challenges of globalization through the lens of class struggle and calls for solidarity among the working class across national boundaries. The goal is to create a global movement against capitalism, aiming for a radical transformation of society into a classless, stateless, and cooperative commonwealth. This vision includes not just an equitable distribution of wealth but the realization of human potential unimpeded by economic exploitation and inequality. A Marxist perspective on economic globalization emphasizes the systemic nature of wealth disparity and labor exploitation. It challenges us to question the ethical foundations of capitalism and to seek alternatives that prioritize human dignity, social justice, and economic equity. By advocating for a revolutionary restructuring of society, Marxism offers a radical but coherent critique of globalization and presents a vision for a more equitable and just world order.

1.7 Cosmopolitanism

Cosmopolitanism challenges us to consider how wealth disparities and labor exploitation might be addressed through principles of global justice, mutual respect, and shared responsibility. From a cosmopolitan standpoint, the vast wealth disparities exacerbated by economic globalization call into question our global ethical commitments. It argues for a sense of global solidarity and a duty to alleviate suffering and poverty wherever it exists, not just within our own national borders. This approach suggests that individuals and nations alike have a moral responsibility to contribute to the welfare of all humanity, advocating for policies and practices that aim to redress global inequalities.

Philosophers have articulated visions of cosmopolitanism that emphasize the importance of recognizing and addressing the interconnectedness of global communities. They argue that in a globalized world, the well-being of individuals is intrinsically linked across societies, necessitating a reevaluation of how wealth and resources are distributed on a global scale.

Cosmopolitanism also addresses the issue of labor rights and exploitation within the global economy by calling for universal standards of labor rights that ensure fair wages, safe working conditions, and the right to collective bargaining for all workers, regardless of their location. It challenges the ethical acceptability of a global economic system that allows for, and in some cases encourages, the exploitation of workers in less developed countries for the benefit of consumers and corporations in more affluent nations. The cosmopolitan approach demands a restructuring of global governance mechanisms to better protect the rights and dignity of workers worldwide. This includes advocating for stronger international labor laws and regulations, enforced by global institutions like the International Labour Organization (ILO), to ensure that globalization becomes a force for good, uplifting workers everywhere rather than exploiting them for profit.

Cosmopolitanism envisions a world where global governance, guided by principles of justice and equality, actively works to mitigate the negative impacts of economic globalization. It promotes the idea of a global community bound by shared values and a collective responsibility to ensure the well-being of all its members, advocating for international cooperation to address issues of poverty, inequality, and injustice. Through cosmopolitanism, the ethical challenges of economic globalization are not insurmountable but require a concerted effort from individuals, nations, and international bodies to create a more equitable and just global order. By emphasizing our common humanity and shared moral obligations, cosmopolitanism offers a hopeful perspective on addressing the profound disparities and exploitation that have accompanied globalization, urging us towards a more inclusive and compassionate world.

1.8 A Pragmatic View: Sweatshop Labor

The ethical conundrums of economic globalization are marred by the presence of sweatshop labor, a contentious issue that epitomizes the exploitation inherent in the global economy. Sweatshop labor, characterized by substandard working conditions, inadequate wages, and a blatant disregard for workers' rights, presents a complex challenge that demands a nuanced ethical response. This issue calls for an examination through a composite philosophical lens, blending insights from utilitarianism, deontology, virtue ethics, Marxism, and cosmopolitanism to forge a comprehensive understanding and propose morally informed solutions.

At the heart of the ethical dilemma posed by sweatshops is the sharp disparity between the economic benefits accrued by MNCs and the dire conditions faced by the laborers. Utilitarianism, with its principle of the greatest happiness for the greatest number, initially challenges us to evaluate the role of sweatshops in global economics. On the surface, sweatshops may seem to offer a pragmatic solution to poverty by providing jobs to those in dire need. However, this view quickly unravels when scrutinizing the dire consequences these jobs entail: subhuman working conditions, negligible wages, and the erosion of dignity. A refined utilitarian critique argues for a recalibration of global labor practices, where the happiness calculus is not skewed towards corporate profit but balanced to genuinely uplift workers' lives globally. It beckons a shift towards business models that ensure fair wages and humane working conditions, thereby harmonizing economic development with genuine welfare enhancement.

Deontology, anchored in the moral philosophy of Kant, unequivocally condemns sweatshops for violating the categorical imperative that demands we treat humanity, whether in our own person or that of another, always as an end and never merely as a means. The exploitation inherent in sweatshop labor, where individuals are instrumentalized for profit, sharply contravenes this moral law. Deontological ethics, therefore, calls for a reformation of global labor standards that respect the inherent dignity of all workers, advocating for stringent enforcement of labor rights that transcend profit motives

Viewing sweatshop labor through the lens of virtue ethics draws attention to the moral character of the societies and corporations that enable and sustain such practices. This perspective emphasizes the cultivation of virtues like justice, compassion, and prudence in economic decision-making. Virtue ethics criticizes the greed and shortsightedness that underpin sweatshop exploitation and posits that true economic progress is achieved when businesses and societies prioritize the common good, building environments that nurture the flourishing of all individuals.

Marxism offers a systemic critique of sweatshop labor, identifying it as a symptom of capitalism's inherent exploitation. Marxists view the global division of labor, which relegates the most exploitative and dangerous jobs to the world's poorest populations, as a manifestation of capitalist oppression. This perspective advocates for a revolutionary overhaul of the economic system, aiming to dismantle the capitalist structures that commodify human labor and to establish a more equitable socio-economic order where labor is valued not for its exploitative potential but for its contribution to the collective well-being.

The cosmopolitan view expands the ethical discourse on sweatshop labor to a global scale, arguing for a world where every individual's rights and dignity are respected regardless of national boundaries. It stresses the interconnectedness of humanity and the shared responsibility to combat injustices like sweatshop exploitation. Cosmopolitanism advocates for global governance mechanisms that enforce labor rights universally, promoting policies that ensure equitable treatment and fair wages for workers worldwide.

1.9 A Pragmatic Response: Fair Trade Initiatives

Fair trade initiatives emerge as a key response to the ethical quandaries posed by sweatshop labor, presenting a model that prioritizes the dignity, well-being, and empowerment of workers across the global supply chain. By focusing on equitable trade practices, fair trade aims to rectify the injustices inherent in conventional trade systems, which often exploit vulnerable populations for economic gain. Here we must explore the specifics of how fair trade initiatives effectively counteract the issues associated with sweatshop labor, illustrating their impact through a composite moral and political philosophical lens.

Fair trade initiatives challenge the status quo by ensuring that a greater portion of the profits generated from goods and services returns to the workers who produce them. This economic redistribution is achieved through fair wages that exceed local minimum wages, often accompanied by social premiums that communities can invest in development projects. From a utilitarian perspective, this redistribution contributes to a greater overall good by elevating the quality of life for workers and their communities, thus aligning economic incentives with the welfare of the global majority.

At the heart of fair trade is a commitment to respecting and safeguarding the rights and dignity of workers. This involves not only fair compensation but also safe working conditions, the right to organize, and freedom from discrimination and child labor. Deontological ethics applauds fair trade for treating workers as ends in themselves, honoring their inherent worth by ensuring their labor is justly rewarded and their rights are protected. Fair trade's adherence to international labor standards embodies the deontological imperative to act in ways that can be universally endorsed as just and ethical.

Fair trade initiatives can be seen as a practical application of virtue ethics in the economic realm. By prioritizing ethical considerations in trade practices, fair trade encourages businesses and consumers to act with justice, compassion, and integrity. This approach fosters a culture of ethical consumption where the virtues of producers and consumers alike contribute to a more equitable and sustainable global economy. The emphasis on long-term relationships and community development within fair trade further exemplifies virtues such as loyalty and commitment to the common good.

From a Marxist perspective, while fair trade may not dismantle the capitalist system, it represents a significant effort to mitigate some of its most exploitative aspects. By advocating for a fair distribution of economic gains, fair trade challenges the capitalist dynamics that commodify labor and exacerbate global inequalities. It offers a model for how economic activities might be restructured to prioritize human welfare over profit maximization, thus providing a blueprint for more radical systemic transformations toward economic justice.

Fair trade embodies the cosmopolitan ideal of global solidarity and shared responsibility. It acknowledges the interconnectedness of our global economy and asserts that ethical obligations extend beyond national borders. By choosing fair trade, consumers and businesses participate in a global effort to uphold the dignity and rights of workers, regardless of where they live. This cosmopolitan approach champions the notion that ethical trade practices are an essential component of global justice, advocating for policies and practices that recognize and respect the moral worth of every individual in the global supply chain.

The convergence of these philosophical views unveils a composite ethical framework for addressing the challenges posed by economic globalization. This framework calls for a holistic approach that integrates the consequentialist focus of utilitarianism, the principled stance of deontology, the character-based approach of virtue ethics, the systemic critique of Marxism, and the global ethos of cosmopolitanism. This framework crystallizes into five key principles that serve as foundational pillars for constructing a morally and politically enlightened approach to contemporary global issues: *global economic justice, dignity and rights, ethical consumption and production, systemic reform, and global solidarity.*

I. Global Economic Justice

IN A WORLD INCREASINGLY defined by globalization, the call for global economic justice rings louder, drawing attention to systemic disparities and deep-rooted inequalities that pervade our global economy. This principle is not merely a plea for humanitarian aid or a push for charity; it's a demand for a fundamental restructuring of the economic systems that dictate the distribution of wealth and resources across the globe. It confronts the harsh reality that while globalization has propelled unprecedented economic growth and technological advancement, it has also exacerbated wealth disparities, leaving billions without access to basic necessities like **food, shelter, healthcare, and education**.

The principle of economic justice challenges the neoliberal economic paradigms that have dominated the global stage for decades, where profit maximization and market efficiency have often been prioritized over the well-being of populations and the sustainability of the planet. It calls into question the fairness of an economic system where the wealth of the world is concentrated in the hands of a few, while a significant portion of the global population struggles to meet the most basic needs.

In advocating for economic justice, there's a push towards models that ensure equitable growth and wealth distribution. Fair trade practices emerge as a beacon of hope in this context, representing a tangible move towards economic systems that value people over profit. Fair trade initiatives aim to provide fair wages, safe working conditions, and a sustainable livelihood for producers and workers in developing countries by offering them a fair share of the profit their labor generates. This model stands in severe contrast to the exploitative practices that have become all too common in global supply chains, where workers in less developed regions are often subjected to poor working conditions and meager wages.

Reformations for achieving Global Economic Justice:

1. **Global Financial Regulations:** *To curb tax evasion and avoidance, implement global tax standards such as the Base Erosion and Profit Shifting (BEPS) actions by the OECD. This includes transparency requirements and the exchange of information between countries. Strengthen international cooperation to combat illicit financial flows that deprive developing countries of crucial resources. This can involve enhancing the capabilities of international institutions like the Financial Action Task Force (FATF).*

2. **Fair Trade Practices:** *Support and expand fair trade initiatives that ensure producers in developing countries are paid fair wages and work under ethical conditions. This can involve governmental and consumer support for fair trade certified products. Enforce regulations that require MNCs to adhere to the same labor and environmental standards abroad as in their home countries, preventing practices that exploit weaker regulatory systems.*

3. **Debt Relief Initiatives:** *Forgiving Debt for Developing Countries: Support international debt forgiveness initiatives, especially for the least developed countries, to enable them to invest in growth and development instead of debt repayment. Encourage sustainable lending practices that consider the economic stability and growth potential of debtor nations to prevent cycles of debt and dependency.*

4. **Equitable Resource Distribution:** *Invest in global initiatives to ensure equitable access to essential services such as healthcare, education, clean water, and sanitation. This includes supporting international development programs and partnerships with NGOs. Facilitate the transfer of technology and expertise to developing countries to help them move up the value chain and build sustainable economies.*

5. **Labor Rights and Protection:** *Promote and enforce international labor standards established by the International Labour Organization*

(ILO), including the right to collective bargaining, elimination of forced and child labor, and safe working conditions. Develop policies that support workers' rights globally, including mechanisms for workers to report abuses and seek redress without fear of retribution.

6. ***Inclusive Economic Policies:*** *Implement policies that support SMEs in developing countries, including access to finance, markets, and capacity-building programs. Promote gender equality by supporting initiatives that empower women economically, including equal pay, access to education, and opportunities for entrepreneurship.*

7. ***Environmental Sustainability and Economic Development:*** *Promote investment in green technologies and sustainable practices that also generate employment and foster economic growth in developing regions. Increase climate finance commitments to help vulnerable countries adapt to climate impacts and transition to low-carbon economies.*

Economic justice is about creating a world where prosperity is not only achievable but also sustainable and shared equitably among all inhabitants of the planet. It involves implementing policies that promote progressive taxation, protect workers' rights, ensure access to essential services, and support the development of economies in ways that do not deplete natural resources or degrade the environment.

At its core, the principle of economic justice demands a reimagining of global economic governance. It calls for international cooperation to address tax evasion, implement global minimum wage standards, and regulate multinational corporations to prevent them from exploiting cheap labor and lax environmental regulations. Moreover, it emphasizes the importance of local empowerment and self-sufficiency, encouraging economies to develop in ways that are responsive to their own needs and respectful of their cultural and environmental contexts.

Global economic justice is not an unattainable ideal but a necessary foundation for a future where all individuals can live with dignity, free from the shackles of poverty and inequality. It requires a collective effort and a commitment to principles of fairness, solidarity, and sustainability. As we move forward, the discourse on moral and political philosophy must continue to champion economic justice as a critical component of a just and equitable global order, ensuring that the benefits of globalization are shared by all, not just a privileged few.

II. Dignity and Rights

CENTRAL TO OUR DISCOURSE on moral and political philosophy is the unwavering respect for the inherent dignity and rights of every individual, irrespective of their economic or social status. This fundamental principle demands that all aspects of global economic activity, from labor practices to corporate governance, uphold and protect human rights. These rights include, but are not limited to, the right to fair wages, safe working conditions, freedom from discrimination, and protection from exploitation. It underscores the ethical imperative to treat individuals not merely as instruments of production but as ends in themselves, deserving of respect and full consideration in all economic activities.

Respecting Dignity and Upholding Rights:

1. ***Strengthening Labor Laws Globally:*** Advocate for and implement stringent labor laws that enforce minimum wage standards, work hours, and safety regulations across all countries to prevent exploitation and ensure fair treatment for all workers.
2. ***Corporate Accountability:*** Develop international frameworks that hold corporations accountable for human rights violations in their supply chains. This includes mandatory human rights due diligence for companies to identify, prevent, rectify, and report how they address their impact on human rights.
3. ***Empowering Workers:*** Support the formation and operation of independent labor unions globally, enabling workers to negotiate for better wages and conditions, and establish legal protections for union members and activists to operate without fear of intimidation or retaliation.

4. ***Addressing Workplace Discrimination***: Implement comprehensive policies that actively fight discrimination based on gender, ethnicity, age, sexual orientation, religion, or disability within workplaces to ensure inclusive and fair treatment of all employees.

5. ***Promoting Right to Education and Development***: Increase investment in education systems in developing countries to ensure universal access to basic education and opportunities for higher learning and vocational training. Encourage partnerships between governments, non-profits, and the private sector to create education programs tailored to the needs of local economies.

6. ***Legal Aid and Advocacy:*** Establish legal aid mechanisms to help workers in low-income countries combat exploitation and abuse, providing them with the means to seek justice and enforcement of their rights without fear of retaliation. Support the formation of local and international advocacy groups that can bring attention to and campaign against violations of workers' rights.

The respect for dignity and rights is not only about creating fair working conditions but also about fostering an environment where each individual has the opportunity to thrive and contribute positively to their community and the global economy. It involves a shift from seeing labor as a commodity to recognizing workers as valuable stakeholders in globalization whose rights and dignity are non-negotiable.

This principle requires a commitment from all sectors of the global economy; governments, businesses, and civil society, to collaborate in creating an economic system that fundamentally respects and enhances human dignity. By embedding these ethical considerations into the fabric of global economic policies and practices, we can ensure that the benefits of globalization are distributed more equitably and justly, contributing to a more stable and prosperous global community.

In championing dignity and rights within the context of economic globalization, we are advocating for a paradigm shift that places human well-being at the center of economic activities. This not only enhances the moral fabric of global trade and business but also serves as a cornerstone for sustainable development and peace. As we progress, it is imperative that our discussions and actions in the realm of moral and political philosophy continuously reflect a deep commitment to upholding these fundamental human values.

III. Ethical Consumption and Production

THE CALL FOR ETHICAL consumption and production addresses the responsibility of both producers and consumers in developing a more just and sustainable global economy. This principle encourages practices that are not only environmentally responsible but also socially equitable, promoting products and services that contribute positively to the welfare of communities and ecosystems. It invites consumers to exercise their purchasing power in support of ethical businesses, thereby incentivizing corporations to adopt practices that align with moral virtues such as fairness, compassion, and stewardship.

Principles and Practices of Ethical Consumption and Production:

1. ***Sustainable Sourcing:*** Companies are encouraged to prioritize renewable over finite resources to ensure long-term sustainability. This includes utilizing sustainably managed natural resources and integrating circular economy principles to minimize waste. Businesses should support sustainable agricultural and mining practices that conserve biodiversity, reduce environmental impact, and ensure the health of ecosystems. Collaborating with local communities to achieve these goals can also enhance social benefits.

1. ***Fair Trade Practices:*** Adopt fair trade certifications to ensure that workers and producers receive fair compensation. This not only improves the economic stability of communities in developing regions but also contributes to higher living standards. Ensure that all products bearing the fair trade mark are produced under conditions that uphold international labor standards, including

health, safety, and worker rights.

1. ***Transparent Supply Chains:*** Companies should adopt policies that ensure complete transparency in their supply chains. This includes regular reporting on sourcing locations, manufacturing conditions, and the steps taken to mitigate environmental and social risks. Provide consumers with accessible, clear, and reliable information about product origins, the sustainability of production processes, and the social conditions under which products are manufactured, enabling informed purchasing decisions.

1. ***Consumer Education:*** Develop comprehensive campaigns to educate consumers about the environmental and social impacts of their purchases. Highlight the benefits of choosing ethically produced goods, including the positive effects on global sustainability and human rights. Encourage consumers to opt for products that align with global ethical standards, creating a market that values sustainability and human dignity over mere cost-saving.

1. ***Regulations and Standards:*** Implement stringent regulations that require businesses to adhere to high environmental and social standards in their production processes. This may include setting benchmarks for emissions, waste management, and labor conditions. Introduce incentives such as tax breaks, subsidies, or public recognition programs for companies that demonstrate leadership in ethical production practices.

1. ***Innovation in Production Technologies:*** Support R&D in cleaner production technologies that reduce environmental impacts, such as reducing water usage, minimizing chemical pollutants, and lowering energy consumption. Facilitate the widespread adoption of these technologies across industries to ensure that production processes become progressively more sustainable.

1. ***Supporting Local and Small-Scale Producers:*** Bolster initiatives

that support local and small-scale producers to help maintain cultural traditions and reduce the environmental impact associated with long-distance transportation of goods. Assist these producers in gaining access to global markets under fair conditions, which can help preserve local industries and promote diverse cultural products.

Ethical consumption and production are about making conscious choices that prioritize sustainability and fairness over convenience and cost. It involves a collaborative effort between consumers, businesses, and policymakers to cultivate a global economy that respects environmental boundaries and promotes social equity.

By integrating ethical considerations into consumption and production, we not only address the immediate impacts of these activities but also contribute to a broader cultural shift towards sustainability and responsibility. This shift is vital in a globalized world where the environmental and social repercussions of production and consumption choices are no longer confined by geographical boundaries.

Promoting ethical consumption and production is an essential step towards mitigating the negative impacts of globalization. It aligns with the broader goals of economic justice, environmental sustainability, and global solidarity, ensuring that progress in one area does not come at the expense of others. As we advance in our moral and political discourse, it is imperative that the principles of ethical consumption and production are championed as foundational to a just and sustainable global order.

IV. Systemic Reforms

RECOGNIZING THE LIMITATIONS of piecemeal solutions, the principle of systemic reform advocates for comprehensive changes to the global economic and political structures that perpetuate inequality and injustice. This involves reimagining and reengineering institutions, policies, and legal frameworks to ensure they serve the common good, rather than the interests of a privileged few. Systemic reform calls for a collaborative, multi-stakeholder approach that engages governments, corporations, civil society, and individuals in the collective task of building a more equitable and just world.

1. *Redefining Global Governance:* Reform international institutions such as the United Nations, the World Bank, and the International Monetary Fund to make them more inclusive and representative of the global population. This involves ensuring that decisions are made not only by the most economically powerful countries but also take into account the voices and concerns of smaller nations and underrepresented populations.

1. *Strengthening International Law:* Develop and enforce international laws that bind countries and multinational corporations to high standards of human rights, labor rights, environmental protection, and corporate accountability. This includes creating mechanisms for individuals and communities to hold these entities legally accountable for actions that lead to social, economic, or environmental harm.

1. *Innovative Economic Models:* Promote economic models that prioritize sustainable development over short-term profits. This includes supporting the circular economy, which emphasizes reuse, recycling, and sustainability, and exploring alternative models such as cooperative business structures and social enterprises that aim to balance profit with social good.

1. *Tax Justice:* Implement global tax reforms to prevent tax evasion and avoidance by multinational corporations and wealthy individuals. Establishing a universal tax regime that closes loopholes and ensures that wealth generated globally contributes fairly to the communities from which it is derived.

1. *Political Reforms:* Encourage political reforms that enhance

democratic governance and ensure greater public participation in decision-making. This can involve electoral reforms, the strengthening of public institutions, and the protection of media freedom and civil liberties, which are essential for a vibrant democracy.

1. ***Technological and Digital Governance:*** Address the ethical and social implications of rapid technological advancements, particularly in the realms of artificial intelligence and biotechnology. Develop global standards and regulations that ensure these technologies are used responsibly and that their benefits are widely distributed.

1. ***Empowering Civil Society:*** Strengthen the role of NGOs, community groups, and other civil society actors in the global governance framework. These organizations often play a crucial role in highlighting issues of injustice and advocating for change, and their active participation ensures that a wide range of perspectives are included in global decision-making processes.

Systemic reform is not merely an adjustment to the existing order but a profound transformation aimed at creating a global system that genuinely reflects the principles of justice, equity, and sustainability. It involves a holistic reevaluation of how power and resources are distributed and governed on a global scale.

By advocating for systemic reforms, we acknowledge that the challenges of globalization cannot be effectively addressed through isolated measures or incremental changes. Instead, they require a bold reimagining of the global order. This vision for systemic reform is driven by the understanding that our shared future depends on our ability to craft institutions and policies that reflect our deepest values and aspirations for a fair and sustainable world. This comprehensive approach is crucial for ensuring that the benefits of globalization are shared more equitably and that all individuals, regardless of nationality or status, can participate fully and fairly in the global community.

V. Global Solidarity

FINALLY, THE PRINCIPLE of global solidarity embodies the cosmopolitan spirit of mutual respect and shared responsibility among all members of the global community. It recognizes the interconnectedness of our challenges and destinies, advocating for a unified approach to addressing global issues such as poverty, climate change, and social injustice. Global solidarity emphasizes the need for empathy, understanding, and cooperation across cultural, national, and ideological divides, fostering a sense of belonging to a single human family committed to safeguarding the welfare and dignity of all its members.

A Framework for Global Solidarity:

1. ***Enhanced International Cooperation:*** Global solidarity is predicated on the belief that international cooperation is essential for solving complex global issues. This involves collaborative efforts between nations through diplomatic channels, international organizations, and treaties that focus on collective action and resource sharing to tackle common problems.

1. ***Empathy and Cultural Exchange:*** Cultivating empathy through cultural exchange and education is crucial for global solidarity. Understanding different cultural contexts and histories can foster a deeper appreciation of global diversity and the unique challenges faced by various communities. Educational programs and media that promote global citizenship can play pivotal roles in building bridges and reducing prejudices.

1. ***Unified Response to Global Crises:*** Global solidarity calls for a unified response to crises that affect multiple nations or the planet as a whole, such as pandemics, climate change, and refugee crises. This involves pooling resources, sharing knowledge, and coordinated action plans to ensure that responses are swift, effective, and equitable.

1. ***Support for Multilateralism:*** Strengthening multilateral institutions that promote global governance and cooperation is a practical step towards actualizing global solidarity. Organizations like the United Nations, the World Health Organization, and the International Criminal Court are pivotal in facilitating discussions and actions that reflect a commitment to collective problem-solving and adherence to international law.

1. ***Equitable Resource Distribution:*** True global solidarity must address the economic disparities that separate rich from poor nations. This involves fair trade practices, aid that respects the sovereignty and development goals of recipient nations, and policies that ensure that globalization benefits are more evenly distributed.

1. ***Advocacy and Activism:*** Civil society organizations, non-governmental organizations, and individual activists play critical roles in fostering global solidarity. They bring attention to injustices, advocate for change, and hold governments and corporations accountable. Supporting and protecting these voices is essential for a vibrant and effective global civil society.

1. ***Technological and Information Sharing:*** In our digital age, global solidarity can be significantly bolstered by open and equitable access to technology and information. Initiatives that expand internet access, promote open-source technologies, and facilitate educational exchanges can empower communities worldwide and foster a more connected and informed global populace.

Global solidarity is not merely a philosophical ideal but a pragmatic necessity in the face of our interconnected challenges. It recognizes that no nation can thrive in isolation or at the expense of others. Instead, it emphasizes a shared commitment to the well-being and dignity of all people, advocating for policies and actions that reflect our common humanity and our collective responsibility to future generations. By embracing global solidarity, we commit to building a world where the values of empathy, justice, and cooperation are not just upheld but are woven into the fabric of our global interactions. It is a call to action for all members of the international community to work together in spirit and deed to create a more just, sustainable, and peaceful world.

Philosophical reflections on these issues push the discourse beyond legal and economic dimensions, highlighting the moral imperatives that should guide our approach to globalization. This discourse invites a broader philosophical reflection on the kind of world we aspire to create; *one where economic globalization serves not just the interests of a privileged few but the wellbeing of all humanity.*

Economic globalization presents a paradox of progress and disparity, of wealth creation and persistent poverty. As we dive into the ethical implications of this phenomenon, the philosophical challenge lies in reconciling the benefits of a globalized economy with the moral imperative to address its inherent inequities. This chapter seeks to illuminate paths toward a more just and equitable global economic order; *one that harmonizes the principles of freedom, justice, and human dignity with the realities of a globalized world.*

1.10 Future Developments in Global Economics

I. The Role of Digital Currencies in Global Finance:

Digital currencies, especially cryptocurrencies like Bitcoin and Ethereum, offer a form of financial inclusion that could potentially bypass traditional banking systems, offering direct access to capital and financial services for underserved populations. This decentralization could challenge the traditional monetary control mechanisms and regulatory frameworks, raising questions about sovereignty, privacy, and financial security. The proliferation of digital currencies could lead to greater financial autonomy but also poses risks such as increased volatility, potential for misuse in money laundering, and the ethical implications of unregulated financial flows. Philosophically, this raises questions about the balance between freedom and regulation, and the role of governments in safeguarding economic stability while promoting innovation.

II. Impact of Artificial Intelligence on Labor Markets:

AI AND AUTOMATION ARE poised to transform labor markets, potentially displacing large numbers of jobs in sectors like manufacturing, retail, and transportation. However, they also promise the creation of new jobs in tech, data analysis, and AI ethics management. This shift requires a rethinking of labor rights and employment laws to accommodate the new types of employment and work arrangements. The displacement of traditional jobs by AI raises ethical questions about the responsibilities of corporations and governments to the workers affected. How should the benefits of increased productivity and economic efficiency be distributed? This discussion taps into philosophical debates about justice, equity, and the right to work, challenging us to define what a fair and just economic system should look like in the AI era.

III. Evolving Nature of Global Trade Post-Pandemic:

THE COVID-19 PANDEMIC exposed vulnerabilities in global supply chains and highlighted the need for greater resilience and diversification of sources. Post-pandemic, there is likely to be a shift towards more localized production and the strengthening of regional trade blocs, which could alter the traditional models of globalization. These shifts require a reevaluation of global interdependence and the ethics of economic nationalism versus global solidarity. The philosophical underpinnings of trade policies will need to address fairness, the distribution of economic risks and benefits, and the duty to cooperate internationally in managing global crises.

Integrating the Future into Our Philosophical Framework:

These future developments call for an adaptive and responsive moral and political philosophy that can address the rapid changes in global economics. Philosophers and policymakers alike must engage with these emerging issues not just reactively but proactively, by anticipating changes and their impacts on different populations globally, crafting policies that are flexible and robust enough to handle the uncertainties of technological and economic transformations, and promoting ethical standards that ensure innovations such as AI and digital currencies contribute positively to societal welfare.

This tells us that our philosophical discourse must evolve to incorporate not only the current ethical issues but also those that are on the horizon. This proactive approach will ensure that our moral and political responses are well-suited to the dynamic and interconnected world of the future, nourishing a global economic system that is not only efficient but also just and equitable.

Throughout this chapter, we have navigated through the historical evolution of global trade, the pivotal roles of MNCs and global financial institutions, and the pressing ethical considerations arising from global economic practices. We've seen how theories from classical economists like Adam Smith and David Ricardo continue to inform modern economic policies, albeit with necessary adaptations to address today's complex global landscape. The critique of global institutions highlighted systemic biases and structural inequalities that often favor developed nations and multinational corporations at the expense of developing countries and vulnerable populations. This critique calls into question the fairness and sustainability of current global economic practices and points to the urgent need for reform.

Looking ahead, the path toward a more ethical and equitable form of globalization involves several strategic shifts like global economic policies that must be crafted with a more inclusive and representative approach. This includes reforming the governance structures of international financial institutions to ensure that all countries, especially developing ones, have a voice in shaping the policies that affect them. There is also a crucial need to strengthen international regulatory frameworks to ensure that MNCs operate in a manner that is socially responsible and environmentally sustainable. This includes enforcing labor rights, ensuring fair wages, and implementing strict environmental protections. Finally, promoting ethical leadership and enhancing corporate accountability are imperative. Corporations must be held to higher ethical standards, where they not only pursue profitability but also contribute positively to the societies in which they operate.

Globalization, as a dynamic phenomenon which presents both opportunities and challenges. By embracing a critical and philosophical approach to its economic dimension, we can begin to address the inequalities and ethical concerns it engenders. This requires a collective effort among governments, businesses, and civil societies to reimagine and reform the global economic architecture. Such efforts will ensure that globalization becomes a force for good, promoting not only economic efficiency but also equity, justice, and sustainability for all. As we continue to explore other dimensions of globalization in subsequent chapters, the insights gained from this economic analysis will provide a solid foundation for understanding the broader impacts of globalization on culture, politics, and society.

Chapter 2: The Cultural Dimension of Globalization

Cultural globalization refers to the intensified flow of cultural goods, ideas, and practices across national and continental boundaries, facilitated by advancements in communication and transport technologies. This phenomenon is characterized by the increased interconnectivity between diverse cultures, leading to greater exposure and exchange of cultural elements ranging from food and clothing to languages, arts, and religious practices. It manifests in the global spread of movies, music, consumer products, and even lifestyles, often mediated through digital media platforms that connect distant parts of the world instantaneously.

It is not a new phenomenon, as it has roots in ancient processes of cultural exchange; but its scale and speed have dramatically increased in recent times. The historical backdrop to modern cultural globalization is shaped by three major processes: **colonization, trade**, and **technological advancements**.

Colonization: From the 15th century onward, European powers expanded their territories across Asia, Africa, and the Americas, imposing their cultures, languages, and religions on indigenous populations. This form of cultural imposition often led to the suppression of local traditions and languages, but also resulted in the syncretic blending of cultures, as seen in the cuisines, languages, and religious practices in many colonized countries. The colonial legacy still influences contemporary cultural dynamics and can be seen in the global dominance of European languages like English and Spanish.

Trade: Long before the advent of modern globalization, trade routes like the Silk Road served as conduits for cultural exchange, spreading goods, ideas, and cultural practices across continents. Traders and travelers carried not just silk and spices but also technological innovations, artistic styles, and philosophical and religious ideas, creating a foundation of cultural interconnectivity that laid the groundwork for today's global cultural exchanges.

Technological Advancements: The technological revolutions of the 19th and 20th centuries, particularly in transport and communications, have been pivotal in accelerating cultural globalization. The invention of the steam engine, the telegraph, and later, the internet, has transformed the ability of cultural products and ideas to cross borders at unprecedented speeds. Today, social media platforms like Facebook, Instagram, and Twitter allow for the sharing of cultural content across global audiences instantly, creating a new form of cultural dialogue where every user can be both consumer and producer. Similarly, streaming services like Netflix and Spotify democratize access to a global catalog of music and film, allowing for a two-way flow of cultural influence. This has enabled shows from South Korea, movies from India, and music from Africa to find audiences in the most remote parts of the world.

These historical processes have collectively contributed to the web of modern cultural globalization, which is marked by both the widespread dissemination of certain cultural forms and the resurgence of local cultures that adapt and reassert themselves in global contexts. This interrelationship of global and local dynamics is crucial to understanding the current and future trajectory of cultural globalization.

This cultural globalization is often driven by economic forces. MNCs play a significant role in spreading cultural products and practices as they expand into new markets around the world. For instance, fast food chains like McDonald's and Starbucks not only sell food and drinks but also convey a lifestyle and set of cultural values associated with the Western way of life. This commercial spread of culture has led to the concept of the **'global consumer culture'** in which products, branding, and marketing strategies are tailored to transcend local markets, creating a globally recognized and consumed image.

Simultaneously, the globalization of media and entertainment industries highlights how cultural products such as films and music contribute to and are influenced by global economic trends. Hollywood movies and Korean pop music are examples of cultural exports that generate significant economic value and facilitate cultural exchanges on a global scale. These industries not only bring substantial revenue to their countries of origin but also shape global cultural tastes and preferences. For instance, Hollywood films and American television shows have long been global staples, showcasing American values and lifestyles that often set trends in other cultures. The portrayal of themes such as freedom, conflict, romance, and success has universal appeal but also carries the risk of overshadowing local narratives. Similarly, consider how international news outlets like CNN, BBC, and Al Jazeera shape perceptions of global events and cultures, often framing narratives in ways that reflect their own cultural biases or geo-political agendas.

Studying and understanding cultural globalization in relation to its economic and political dimensions is crucial for several reasons within our broader discourse on moral and political philosophy as it raises significant ethical questions about cultural homogenization, the preservation of cultural diversity, and the right of communities to maintain their cultural identities. These ethical considerations are central to debates on how we should govern a culturally diverse global society. Further, The economic aspects of cultural globalization touch on issues of global inequality and justice. For instance, who benefits from the global export of culture, and how are the profits distributed? Similarly, the political aspects raise questions about power disparities and the capacity of smaller or less powerful communities to participate equally in global cultural exchanges.

From a philosophical standpoint, cultural globalization challenges us to rethink concepts of identity, community, and belonging in a globalized world. It prompts us to consider how cultural practices can both bridge and create divisions among people and how these practices influence global ethical and political norms. Understanding the cultural dimension of globalization in conjunction with its economic and political facets will allow us to critically engage with the realities of our globalized world. This approach is vital for constructing informed and nuanced responses to the challenges and opportunities that arise from our increasingly interconnected global community. This discourse aims to not only analyze these interconnections but also propose ways in which globalization can be managed ethically and justly to enhance cultural diversity and global solidarity.

2.1 Cultural Homogenization

Cultural homogenization refers to the process through which diverse local cultures are increasingly overshadowed or absorbed by a dominant culture. This phenomenon is often driven by globalization, which facilitates the widespread dissemination of cultural symbols, practices, and artifacts across national borders. The result is a growing uniformity in cultural expressions and lifestyles, which can diminish the richness of cultural diversity that characterizes different societies and regions.

The mechanisms through which cultural homogenization occurs are multifaceted, involving economic, media, technological, and political dimensions. Economically, the global market's dynamics favor large multinational corporations that standardize their products and services to appeal to the broadest possible audience, often at the expense of local variants. Technologically, advances in communication technologies, such as the internet and mobile platforms, have allowed for an unprecedented flow of cultural products across geographical boundaries, making it easier for dominant cultural forms to penetrate and influence local cultures.

One of the most visible examples of cultural homogenization is the global proliferation of American fast food chains, such as McDonald's, KFC, and Starbucks. These brands have become symbols of Western lifestyle and consumption patterns, establishing a presence in virtually every corner of the world. Their global reach has not only changed eating habits and dietary preferences in different cultures but also introduced a standardized form of food consumption that mirrors Western fast-paced, convenience-oriented lifestyles.

Hollywood films and American television series also illustrate cultural homogenization as these media products dominate global entertainment markets, shaping perceptions and setting trends that often overshadow local film industries and cultural narratives. The global appeal of Hollywood's storytelling techniques, themes, and production values has led to a certain uniformity in cinematic experience, influencing how stories are told and received worldwide.

Additionally, the international fashion industry, led by brands like Nike, Adidas, and H&M, promotes a homogeneous global fashion sense, often inspired by Western aesthetics. This not only limits the visibility of local and traditional attire but also impacts local economies and cultural practices related to clothing and textiles.

While cultural homogenization can facilitate cross-cultural understanding and access to global markets, it often comes at a significant cost to cultural diversity. Local traditions, languages, and practices may become marginalized or perceived as less modern or valuable compared to dominant cultural norms. This can lead to a loss of cultural identity and heritage, especially among younger generations who are the most exposed to and influenced by global media and consumer culture.

In essence, while cultural homogenization offers certain economic and social benefits, such as increased connectivity and a shared cultural vocabulary, it poses serious challenges to cultural diversity and the preservation of unique cultural identities. Understanding this dynamic is crucial as we explore further the philosophical perspectives on cultural globalization and its practical implications for maintaining a diverse and vibrant global cultural landscape. So let's start by understanding the key drivers of this phenomenon. Each of these driving factors contributes to the reshaping of local cultures into a more uniform global culture. Here, we examine the primary drivers behind this trend: **economic globalization**, **media proliferation**, and the **role of MNCs**.

- **Economic Globalization:** Economic globalization is a significant catalyst for cultural homogenization. As markets become more integrated, there is a growing trend towards global consumer culture, which is often dictated by the economic principles of efficiency, profitability, and consumer appeal. These economic forces encourage the standardization of products and services to meet the broad, cross-cultural appeal, thus reducing the diversity of local alternatives. This is evident in various sectors including food, clothing, and entertainment, where global brands dominate local markets and influence local consumption patterns and lifestyles. For instance, global trade agreements and open market policies facilitate the entry of multinational companies into new markets, often at the expense of local businesses and practices. This economic integration allows for a more streamlined, homogeneous market environment that prioritizes large-scale efficiency and global branding over localized, diverse market conditions.

• **Media Proliferation:** The explosion of global media has been another powerful driver of cultural homogenization. With the advent of satellite television, internet streaming platforms, and social media, there has been an unprecedented increase in the availability and consumption of media content on a global scale. Media companies, especially those based in the West like Netflix, Disney, and HBO, distribute content that tends to reflect Western values, narratives, and aesthetics, which can dominate and marginalize local cultures and perspectives. This proliferation not only spreads certain cultural norms and values but also creates a form of cultural imperialism where the dominating media narratives shape public perceptions, ideals, and aspirations around the world. The global influence of popular culture, facilitated by these platforms, often leads to a dilution of local traditions and languages in favor of international or Western norms.

• **Role of MNCs:** MNCs play a pivotal role in cultural homogenization beyond just economic influence. Through their marketing strategies and global branding, MNCs promote a uniform image and lifestyle that are often rooted in Western consumerism. Whether it is through the global distribution of Coca-Cola or the worldwide retail presence of Apple, these corporations propagate a set of values centered on materialism, efficiency, and a Western style of modernity. MNCs also contribute to cultural homogenization through corporate policies and practices that standardize the work environment, employee behavior, and company culture, often modeled after their home country norms. This not only affects how business is conducted but also impacts cultural expressions, workplace norms, and even language use within these multinational environments.

The combined effects of economic globalization, media proliferation, and the influence of MNCs have accelerated the pace of cultural homogenization. This process challenges the preservation of cultural diversity, raising critical questions about the balance between global integration and cultural identity. As we delve deeper into the philosophical perspectives and practical implications of cultural globalization, it's essential to consider strategies that can mitigate the risks of homogenization while enhancing the benefits of cultural diversity and exchange. These strategies might involve promoting local content in media, enforcing cultural heritage protections, and encouraging MNCs to engage more deeply with local cultures.

2.2 Cultural Diversity

Cultural diversity represents the rich orchestra of human expression, encompassing a variety of languages, traditions, beliefs, and ways of life within a shared geographic or social space. This diversity is a fundamental aspect of human society, contributing to the vibrancy and resilience of communities by fostering a broad spectrum of ideas, practices, and innovations. It is the quality of diverse or different cultures, as opposed to monoculture, the global monoculture, or a homogenization of cultures, akin to cultural decay. The term cultural diversity can also refer to having different cultures respect each other's differences. The phrase "cultural diversity" is also sometimes used to mean the variety of human societies or cultures in a specific region, or in the world as a whole. It is often embodied in the concept of a "cultural mosaic," a metaphor that emphasizes a mixture of interactions and exchanges that retain distinct cultural identities within a shared space.

Think of Sushi! Originally a street food in Tokyo, which has become a global phenomenon, adapting to various local tastes and ingredients. Restaurants around the world serve sushi, reflecting both traditional and localized versions of the dish. Or perhaps, the Day of the Dead, a Mexican festival that honors deceased loved ones, which has been recognized by UNESCO as an Intangible Cultural Heritage of Humanity Its symbols, especially the "calaveras" (skulls) and "ofrendas" (altars), have been adopted and adapted in various cultural festivities worldwide, spreading its message of honoring ancestors and embracing mortality.

Similarly, South Korean pop music, or K-Pop, has transcended its national borders to become a global entertainment powerhouse. Bands like BTS and Blackpink are household names in many countries, influencing music styles, fashion, and fan culture across continents. "Capoeira," an Afro-Brazilian martial art which combines elements of dance, acrobatics, and music. It has gained international fame not only as a sport but also as a cultural expression of resistance and beauty, taught and practiced in many countries around the world. African Wax Prints which were once inspired by Indonesian batik have become symbols of African identity and heritage. They are celebrated on global fashion runways and are incorporated into mainstream fashion, showcasing their patterns and colors. Native American Pottery and Navajo Weaving is an art form celebrated for its beauty and craftsmanship. Museums and collectors worldwide seek these pieces, and they have influenced various art and design fields by highlighting traditional techniques and indigenous narratives.

Championing cultural diversity involves recognizing and promoting the inherent value found in the varied cultural expressions of communities worldwide. It is essential for fostering mutual understanding and respect among different cultures, which is increasingly important in our interconnected global society. By encouraging the recognition and international embrace of local cultural practices, we can enrich global culture and support the survival and thriving of these traditions in the modern world. This approach not only counters the forces of cultural homogenization but also contributes to a more colorful, inclusive, and dynamic global culture. Some of the benefits of preserving this cultural diversity, including innovation, ecological diversity, and societal resilience are discussed below. However, promoting and maintaining cultural diversity in the face of globalization poses significant challenges. Economic pressures, political conflicts, and social dynamics often threaten the preservation of unique cultural identities. Therefore, understanding these advantages and challenges is crucial for developing effective strategies to safeguard these diverse cultural expressions of the global heritage.

Innovation vs. Market Pressures: Cultural globalization has spurred innovation by incorporating diverse cultural perspectives into MNCs, driving creativity that leads to new products and market expansions. Research has shown that teams from varied cultural backgrounds often bring unique viewpoints and problem-solving strategies, enhancing creativity across sectors. For example, the global art scene demonstrates how cultural diversity fuels creativity, with artists blending influences to appeal to global audiences. However, this innovation faces a countervailing force from global economic systems that often favor homogeneity for market efficiency and profit maximization. MNCs can overshadow local businesses, replacing rich local traditions with uniform global products, such as American fast food chains. This economic pressure risks diluting local cultures and stifling local innovation by favoring mass-produced goods over artisanal, culturally specific products.

Environmental and Ecological Considerations: On the environmental front, cultural diversity promotes ecological sustainability through traditional practices that have evolved in harmony with local environments. Indigenous agricultural techniques like polyculture and agroforestry enhance biodiversity and build resilience to climate change, contrasting sharply with the ecologically disruptive practices of intensive, monoculture farming often promoted by global agricultural businesses. However, the globalization-induced demand for natural resources and agricultural products can lead to environmental degradation, as seen in deforestation and over-mining, which undermines these traditional, sustainable practices. Thus, while cultural diversity can offer ecological benefits, the global market's demands pose significant threats to these same systems.

Societal Resilience vs. Social Challenges: Culturally diverse societies gain resilience through a vast repository of knowledge and cultural strategies that enhance their capacity to address contemporary challenges. This diversity builds social cohesion and innovation, as communities draw upon varied experiences and historical resilience in times of crisis. Nevertheless, globalization's push for a singular global culture can erode this diversity, leading to social fragmentation. Pressures for cultural assimilation and integration into a global economic framework can marginalize minority cultures and erode traditional lifestyles, threatening the very foundation of societal resilience. Political movements that enforce a dominant cultural narrative can suppress the cultural practices of minorities, undermining societal cohesion and resilience.

Nationalism vs. Global Cooperation: Politically, cultural globalization can facilitate international cooperation through a cosmopolitan ethos that develops mutual respect and shared solutions to global issues. This global solidarity can enhance diplomatic relations and foster a cooperative approach to worldwide challenges. However, this potential is often challenged by nationalistic reactions that resist foreign cultural influences, viewing them as threats to national or cultural purity. Such ethnocentrism can lead to restrictive policies against perceived foreign elements, stifling cultural exchange and cooperation, and promoting a xenophobic backlash that opposes the integrative promise of globalization.

The preservation of cultural diversity is not merely a moral obligation; it is a strategic imperative that underpins innovation, ecological sustainability, and societal resilience. Each culture holds unique insights and knowledge that can contribute significantly to addressing global challenges. By actively promoting and protecting cultural diversity, societies not only enrich their own cultural environments but also contribute to the global good, founding a world that is vibrant, diverse, and resilient. As we move forward in our discourse on globalization, the dialectical nature of cultural globalization emphasizes a nuanced approach that recognizes and leverages the benefits of cultural diversity while actively countering the forces of homogenization. This discussion highlights the need for policies that protect cultural diversity and promote an equitable sharing of cultural and economic benefits, ensuring that globalization becomes a force for cultural enrichment and mutual respect rather than a cause of cultural erosion and conflict.

I. Stuart Hall and Cultural Identity

STUART HALL'S INSIGHTS into *cultural identity* are profoundly relevant in examining the transformative effects of globalization on individual and collective identities. He argued that cultural identity should be seen not as a static, inherent characteristic fixed at birth, but as an ongoing process of development and negotiation that occurs within a framework of representation. This perspective is essential for understanding how identities are shaped by the complex interaction between global influences and local traditions. Hall envisioned cultural identity as inherently hybrid, formed through the continuous interactions between the global and the local. This hybridity, according to Hall, can be deeply enriching; it promotes the emergence of new cultural forms and practices that are adaptive and inclusive, integrating diverse influences in creative ways. These emergent identities can enhance understanding and cooperation among different cultural groups by showcasing the potential for cultures to evolve and assimilate beneficial aspects of each other.

However, Hall was also acutely aware of the potential downsides of this process. He pointed out that the global flow of cultural influences often tends toward homogenization, where dominant cultures, particularly those of the West, may overshadow or even erase local cultures. This can lead to a dilution of distinct cultural practices and languages, resulting in what he termed *cultural hegemony*, situations where dominant cultural groups impose their values and norms on others, often marginalizing local traditions and languages in the process. Hall's theory highlights a critical tension in globalization: *the balance between enriching cultural exchange and the risk of cultural dominance*. This dynamic poses significant ethical and practical challenges as societies strive to preserve their unique cultural heritage while engaging with the inevitable influences of a globalizing world. His work encourages a critical examination of how cultural identities are articulated, challenging us to consider who has the power to define cultural norms and whose voices are amplified or silenced in the global cultural arena. By understanding and addressing these dynamics, we can work towards a more equitable global cultural landscape that respects and celebrates diversity rather than subsuming it under homogeneity.

II. Homi Bhabha and the Third Space

HOMI BHABHA'S CONCEPT of the "*Third Space*" provides a critical framework for understanding the complex dynamics of cultural interaction in the age of globalization. This notion introduces an innovative way of thinking about cultural intersections as spaces of hybridity where cultural meanings are continuously contested and redefined. The Third Space is not a physical location but rather a metaphorical domain where different cultures meet, clash, and grapple with each other. This interaction often leads to the emergence of new cultural forms that are neither the sum nor the simple synthesis of their parts but something altogether new and unanticipated.

In the Third Space, cultural identities and meanings do not remain fixed but are constantly being negotiated and renegotiated. This space is characterized by its inherent dynamism and fluidity, making it a powerful area of cultural innovation and creativity. Bhabha views this space as fundamentally empowering because it challenges the historical and authoritative claims to cultural purity and authenticity. By doing so, it disrupts the traditional hierarchies and binaries that have historically dominated discussions of culture and identity, such as center/margin or colonizer/colonized.

From an ethical standpoint, Bhabha's theory is particularly significant in its emphasis on resistance to cultural domination. This aspect of his work underscores the importance of the Third Space as a site where marginalized and subaltern groups can assert their agency and articulate their own voices. In a global discourse often dominated by Western narratives and perspectives, the Third Space provides a venue for these groups to challenge dominant cultural narratives and propose alternative visions. This process is not merely reactive but is a proactive reclamation of cultural agency, allowing marginalized communities to redefine their identities on their own terms rather than through the lens imposed by dominant cultures.

Bhabha's concept thus serves as a critical tool for analyzing how globalization impacts cultural identities, offering both a space of resistance and a creative crucible for the generation of new forms of cultural expression. It encourages a more nuanced understanding of global cultural exchanges, where the interaction is not merely additive but transformative, leading to the creation of new identities and possibilities that reflect the complex realities of a globalized world. This transformative potential highlights the ethical imperative to foster and maintain these spaces of cultural negotiation as they are crucial for the continued vitality and diversity of global cultures.

III. Convergence: Fluidity and Hybridity of Cultural Identities

BOTH HALL AND BHABHA argue against the notion of fixed or essentialist cultural identities. Hall conceptualizes identity as an ongoing production, a never-completed process that is subject to the continuous play of history, culture, and power. Bhabha, similarly, posits that cultural identity exists in a "Third Space" where it undergoes constant negotiation. For both, identity is inherently hybrid, formed and transformed under the pressure of encountering the Other. This hybridity allows for the creation of new cultural forms that are adaptive and inclusive of diverse influences, thus enriching cultural exchanges.

While Hall's framework emphasizes the descriptive process of how identities are shaped by and through cultural representation and the media, Bhabha's work is more prescriptive in highlighting the possibilities of cultural resistance and the reclamation of agency by marginalized groups. Hall is concerned with how identities are narrated through different, often competing, discourses and practices, highlighting the role of power in these narratives. His approach often portrays a passive reception of identity imposed by external conditions. In contrast, Bhabha's Third Space is an active site of resistance and construction. It is not just a middle ground of exchange but a battleground of appropriation and reappropriation, where marginalized groups can challenge and redefine cultural dominance. This notion places greater emphasis on the agency of cultural subjects to manipulate and reshape cultural meanings, thus offering a more empowering view of the potential for subaltern groups to exert influence over their identity narratives.

Bhabha's focus on the Third Space inherently carries a strong ethical dimension, advocating for the rights of marginalized groups to participate in the articulation of their cultural identities. This space provides a theoretical justification for resisting the cultural hegemony of dominant groups and promotes a more equitable participation in global cultural exchanges. Hall's analysis, while equally concerned with power dynamics, often lacks this direct call to action, focusing more on understanding the mechanisms through which cultural hegemony is maintained and contested. Both theorists critically assess the impact of globalization on cultural identities but from slightly different focal points. Hall sees globalization as a force that exacerbates the tension between the global and the local, leading to both the homogenization of culture and the simultaneous intensification of cultural differences. Bhabha, meanwhile, views globalization as offering unique opportunities for creating new hybrid forms through the interactions in the Third Space, which can potentially subvert traditional power structures and hierarchies.

Stuart Hall and Homi Bhabha offer frameworks that are instrumental in understanding the complex realities of cultural identity in a globalized world. Both scholars provide tools for analyzing how cultures adapt and resist in the face of global forces. However, where Hall provides a more grounded analysis of the processes and mechanisms through which identities are negotiated, Bhabha offers a normative approach that emphasizes the transformative potential of cultural interaction. Together, their theories enhance our understanding of the global cultural canvas, highlighting both the challenges and the transformative possibilities inherent in cultural globalization.

In the forthcoming section on Cultural Globalization and Identity, we will utilize a blend of existentialism, postmodernism, feminism, and philosophical responses to technological change as our primary analytical frameworks. Each of these perspectives offers unique insights into the complex dynamics of cultural globalization. Existentialism and Humanism will guide our understanding of personal and collective identity formation in a globalized world, emphasizing the choices individuals and communities make in response to global cultural forces. Postmodernism will help us deconstruct the narratives of cultural globalization, enabling a critical examination of how cultural values are disseminated, transformed, or resisted within global networks. Feminism and Gender Theory will provide a lens through which to view how global cultural flows impact gender norms and identities, highlighting issues of power and inequality. Technological Change responses will allow us to explore the significant role of digital media and technology in shaping and transmitting cultural content across borders, influencing both homogenization and cultural diversity.

These frameworks will deepen our analysis and ensure that it remains nuanced and sensitive to the complexities of global cultural interactions. This will, in turn, help us to critically assess the effects of cultural globalization, balancing the exploration of both its opportunities and challenges.

2.3 Existentialism and Humanism

———

Existentialism and Humanism provide a crucial philosophical framework to examine the cultural dimensions of globalization. This perspective emphasizes the centrality of individual freedom, choice, and the inherent responsibility that comes with shaping one's own essence in the world. In the context of cultural globalization, this framework invites us to consider how global cultural flows influence individual identity and personal autonomy across diverse cultural landscapes.

Existentialism posits that *essence follows existence*, implying that individuals define themselves through their actions and choices rather than adhering to predefined cultural scripts. In a globalized world, individuals are increasingly exposed to a vast array of cultural influences, from music and food to fashion and media. This exposure offers unprecedented opportunities for self-definition but also presents challenges as traditional cultural boundaries become blurred. For instance, young people around the globe may adopt and adapt cultural elements from foreign lands into their own identities, choosing to embrace global music styles like K-pop or hip-hop as expressions of their personal tastes and experiences. These choices reflect existential freedom but also raise questions about the authenticity and depth of cultural engagement. *Are these global influences merely superficial, or do they represent a deeper integration and redefinition of individual identities?*

From a humanistic viewpoint, cultural globalization can be seen as enriching the human experience, providing a broader palette from which individuals can paint their unique life stories. However, this freedom to choose can sometimes be overwhelming or illusory. The saturation of global culture might lead to a paradox of choice where individuals struggle to find genuine connections to any specific cultural tradition. Moreover, the humanistic aspect of existentialism would argue for the importance of creating meaning within one's cultural context. As cultures blend and interact, individuals must navigate complex cultural narratives to construct a sense of meaning that resonates with their personal and communal identities. This process can be empowering, as it allows for the creation of new cultural syntheses that reflect the nuanced realities of global interconnectivity.

Existentialism also carries an ethical imperative: ***the responsibility that comes with freedom.*** In the dimension of cultural globalization, this translates into the responsibility of individuals and societies to engage with foreign cultures in ways that are respectful and enriching rather than exploitative. It challenges the often one-sided narrative of cultural dominance, such as the imposition of Western values and lifestyles on other cultures, advocating instead for a more dialogic and reciprocal cultural exchange. For example, the global spread of English as a lingua franca opens numerous doors for communication and business, but it also poses significant challenges to linguistic diversity and can lead to the erosion of local languages and dialects. From an existential-humanistic view, the ethical response would be to promote policies and practices that respect linguistic diversity and encourage multilingualism, thereby supporting both global connectivity and local identity.

In essence, existentialism and humanism add to our understanding of cultural globalization by highlighting the individual's role in shaping and reshaping cultural identities in a global context. They remind us that while global cultural flows offer new opportunities for identity formation, they also require careful consideration of the choices we make and the responsibilities those choices entail. This philosophical lens advocates for a culturally aware globalization process, one that fosters genuine respect for diversity and promotes an ethical engagement with the world's myriad cultures. This approach not only respects individual agency but also promotes a collective ethos that values cultural plurality and mutual understanding in the global village.

2.4 Postmodernism in Cultural Globalization

Postmodernism offers a unique lens to examine cultural globalization, particularly through its emphasis on skepticism towards grand narratives and its focus on the fragmentation and multiplicity of truth. This philosophical perspective challenges the idea of a single, universal culture, promoting instead a view that recognizes the complex mosaic of global cultures, each with its own validity and significance.

Postmodernism argues against the concept of absolute truths, which is crucial when discussing cultural globalization. It critiques the idea that certain cultural norms or values are universally applicable, emphasizing instead the relative and constructed nature of these truths. For example, the global spread of Western ideals of democracy and capitalism is often critiqued by postmodernists who argue that these are not the ultimate solutions to political and economic issues worldwide but are rather narratives shaped by specific historical and cultural contexts. This perspective encourages a more nuanced understanding of cultural exchanges, highlighting how global interactions can lead to the hybridization of cultures rather than the dominance of one over the other. It suggests that the blending of Eastern and Western aesthetics in contemporary art and architecture, for instance, reflects a form of cultural negotiation rather than assimilation or domination.

In cultural globalization, postmodernism particularly emphasizes the role of media and technology. It explores how these tools both construct and disseminate fragmented cultural identities. Media platforms like social media allow for the creation and perpetuation of multiple realities and identities, enabling individuals to present themselves in diverse ways depending on different cultural contexts. This can lead to a more pluralistic understanding of identity that transcends traditional geographic and cultural boundaries. However, postmodernism also warns of the superficiality and commodification that can come with these technologies. The global marketing strategies of major brands often adopt a pastiche of cultural elements to appeal to a global audience, potentially leading to the dilution and commodification of distinct cultural identities.

Postmodernist critiques extend to cultural imperialism, where certain cultures, particularly those of the West, are seen as overpowering others. This perspective scrutinizes how global cultural flows might suppress local traditions and languages under the guise of modernization or globalization. Postmodernism calls for a recognition of the local, the specific, and the different, countering the trend towards a homogeneous global culture. It advocates for preserving local narratives and voices, particularly those of marginalized communities. The postmodern approach supports local art, music, and literature that reflect the unique experiences and histories of different cultures, providing a counter-narrative to mainstream global culture.

Finally, postmodernism's influence on cultural globalization carries significant ethical implications. It promotes activism that is attuned to the nuances of local contexts and respects the diversity of cultural expressions. Postmodern activism often takes the form of grassroots movements that use decentralized networks to challenge large-scale political or corporate entities. This activism can also be seen in movements that resist cultural homogenization, championing instead local traditions and practices.

Through its critical examination of universality, truth, and identity, postmodernism significantly enriches the discourse on cultural globalization. It offers tools for understanding the complex dynamics of global cultural interactions, emphasizing respect for diversity and the importance of local contexts. By challenging the dominance of any single cultural perspective, postmodernism helps pave the way for a more inclusive and pluralistic global community, encouraging a deeper appreciation for the myriad ways in which cultures interact and influence each other in the contemporary world.

2.5 Feminism and Gender Theory

Feminism and Gender Theory offer critical insights into how cultural globalization affects gender norms and identities. These frameworks explore the dynamics of power, representation, and identity through a gendered lens, highlighting how global cultural flows can both challenge and reinforce traditional gender roles.

Feminism has long critiqued the patriarchal structures that define and often limit the roles and identities of women and other marginalized genders within societies. Cultural globalization brings with it a proliferation of media and ideas that can challenge these traditional roles. For example, global movements such as #MeToo have used digital platforms to unite voices across the world against sexual harassment and assault, showcasing the potential of global networks to empower and enact change. Moreover, the global circulation of feminist literature, films, and art provides diverse perspectives on gender and power, inspiring local movements and discussions. For instance, films that depict strong, independent women can serve as powerful counter-narratives to local cultural norms that emphasize traditional, subservient roles for women.

Globalization has also facilitated the spread of ideas and support networks for LGBTQ+ communities, which are often suppressed in conservative societies. The global discourse on gender fluidity and rights has enabled more open discussions and acceptance in some regions, leading to legislative changes and greater social acceptance. The celebration of Pride events, supported by global solidarity, exemplifies how cultural globalization can foster inclusiveness and recognition of diverse gender identities. However, the influence of globalized media can also perpetuate stereotypes and commercialize aspects of gender identity. The international fashion and beauty industries, for example, often promote unrealistic standards of beauty that can reinforce harmful gender norms. Feminist and gender theorists critique these industries for shaping consumer culture in ways that commodify women's bodies and perpetuate gender inequalities.

Feminist economic analysis adds another dimension to our understanding of cultural globalization. It critiques how global economic policies often disadvantage women, particularly in the Global South. Women are disproportionately represented in low-wage sectors such as textiles, where labor abuses are common. Feminism calls for a reevaluation of economic policies to ensure they are equitable and support gender equality in the workforce. Furthermore, the global spread of MNCs can both provide opportunities and pose challenges for women. While they may offer employment, these jobs often lack security or equitable pay. Feminist theory pushes for global labor standards that include fair wages and safe working conditions for all, emphasizing the need for policies that consider the differential impacts on various genders.

Educational initiatives and advocacy are crucial in leveraging the benefits of cultural globalization for gender equality. Feminism and gender theory advocate for education that not only raises awareness of gender issues but also empowers individuals to challenge and redefine gender norms. Educational programs that focus on gender equality can help foster a new generation that values diversity and equality, equipped to address gender issues in a globalized context.

Feminism and Gender Theory provide essential perspectives on the intersections of culture, gender, and globalization. By examining how global flows of culture influence gender norms and identities, these frameworks highlight the complex ways in which globalization can both empower and marginalize. They advocate for a conscientious approach to cultural exchange, one that promotes gender equality and challenges patriarchal structures. This approach aims to ensure that cultural globalization contributes to a more equitable and just world, where gender diversity is not only recognized but celebrated.

2.6 Technological Change in Cultural Globalization

Technological Change plays a pivotal role in shaping the contours of cultural globalization. This section explores how advancements in technology not only transform how cultures interact but also redefine the very fabric of cultural identity and exchange. The intersection of technology and culture is a dynamic space where new forms of communication, expression, and connection emerge, profoundly influencing global cultural landscapes.

Technological advancements, particularly in communication technologies, have drastically accelerated the pace of cultural exchange. The internet, social media platforms, and mobile technology enable instant communication and the sharing of cultural content across the globe. This accessibility allows for an unprecedented flow of cultural symbols, languages, and practices that can be shared and adapted across different societies. For instance, platforms like YouTube and TikTok have become global stages where musical genres, dance forms, and digital art transcend their local origins to gain worldwide audiences. These technologies democratize cultural production and dissemination, allowing individuals and communities to contribute to global cultural dialogues without the need for traditional gatekeepers like media companies or cultural institutions. This has led to a more participatory cultural landscape where a diverse array of voices can be heard and where cultural innovation can arise from any corner of the globe.

Technology has also transformed the ways in which cultural goods are consumed. Streaming services, digital libraries, and online galleries provide global access to films, books, music, and art that were once limited to specific geographic regions. This ease of access contributes to a more integrated global culture but also raises questions about the sustainability of traditional cultural industries and local cultural forms. The shift to digital consumption changes the economics of cultural goods, affecting how they are valued and monetized. While it opens up new opportunities for creators to reach global audiences, it also introduces challenges related to copyright, compensation, and the preservation of cultural heritage. For example, while streaming platforms can offer independent filmmakers a global audience, they also challenge traditional film industries in countries where cinema is a significant cultural expression.

Technology influences the construction and perception of cultural identities. Social media, in particular, allows individuals to curate and express their identities in ways that blend multiple cultural influences. This can lead to the emergence of hybrid identities that reflect the complex realities of a globalized world. However, the same platforms can also reinforce stereotypes and enable the spread of misinformation, complicating the understanding of different cultures. Moreover, technology's role in surveillance and data collection raises ethical questions about privacy and autonomy. The datafication of cultural practices can lead to intrusive marketing practices and the commodification of cultural identities, where personal and cultural data are used to target consumers more effectively.

The benefits of technological advancements in cultural globalization are not uniformly distributed. The digital divide, the gap between those who have access to modern information and communication technology and those who do not, can exacerbate existing inequalities. This divide can prevent certain communities from participating fully in the global cultural exchange, leading to a form of cultural marginalization. Addressing the ethical implications of technological change involves ensuring that technology serves as a tool for inclusion and diversity rather than exclusion. It requires policies and initiatives that promote equitable access to technology and that protect against the exploitation of cultural communities for their data.

Technological change is a double-edged sword that facilitates a more connected, cultural world but also presents significant challenges that need to be managed carefully with ethical, social, and cultural consideration. As we navigate this rapidly changing landscape, it is crucial to build a global dialogue on the role of technology in cultural preservation and innovation, ensuring that technology enhances rather than diminishes the diversity of the world's cultural heritage. Thus, the philosophical framework for evaluating the consequences of technological change guides the development of responsible tech policies that honor and preserve cultural diversity.

2.7 A Pragmatic View: Netflix's Influence on Culture

Netflix serves as a potent case study to explore the multifaceted impact of cultural globalization, viewed through the philosophical lenses of the above frameworks, driving cultural globalization. Each perspective offers a distinct way of understanding how Netflix, as a global media giant, shapes and is shaped by the cultural dynamics of the modern world.

Netflix epitomizes the existentialist values of individual choice and freedom by providing a diverse array of content that allows viewers to shape their cultural consumption according to personal preferences and identities. This capacity for choice reflects the existentialist assertion that "existence precedes essence," with individuals defining their identities through actions, in this case, their selection of media consumption. Subscribers from various cultural backgrounds can find content that resonates with their specific tastes, whether it's American sitcoms, Korean dramas, or Bollywood films, thereby exercising personal autonomy in defining their cultural experiences. From a humanistic perspective, Netflix carries the responsibility to curate a content library that not only entertains but also respects and represents global cultural diversity. This responsibility is crucial in fostering an environment where all cultural identities are acknowledged and valued, thus enhancing the human condition through cultural respect and representation. However, the challenge lies in balancing this responsibility with commercial interests, often leading to tensions between maximizing subscriber engagement and promoting cultural diversity.

Postmodernism's critique of grand narratives provides a useful lens for analyzing how Netflix both challenges and perpetuates certain cultural dominances. The platform disrupts traditional media hierarchies by providing access to a multitude of voices, thereby facilitating a fragmentation of cultural authority that is characteristic of postmodern thought. Netflix's diverse catalog enables viewers to explore a vast range of cultural narratives, potentially democratizing media consumption by diluting the hegemony of dominant cultural producers like Hollywood. However, postmodernism also draws attention to how Netflix might still perpetuate Western cultural norms through its algorithm-driven recommendations that prioritize content with broad, global appeal. This algorithmic curation can inadvertently lead to a homogenization of viewer preferences, subtly shaping global cultural tastes towards a more uniform standard. Thus, while Netflix contributes to cultural hybridization, it also raises concerns about the subtle reinforcement of certain cultural norms at the expense of truly diverse representations.

Through the lens of feminism and gender theory, Netflix's role in shaping gender narratives becomes particularly salient. The platform has been instrumental in promoting shows that offer progressive portrayals of women and gender minorities, challenging traditional gender roles and contributing to a global discourse on gender equality. Series like "Jessica Jones" and "Sex Education" provide narratives that empower underrepresented voices and tackle complex issues surrounding consent, sexual identity, and gender equality. Yet, the global reach of Netflix also means it has the power to reinforce stereotypes, particularly when it streams content that adheres to conventional gender roles popular in certain cultures. The feminist critique thus extends to how effectively Netflix navigates the tension between depicting cultural authenticity and resisting the perpetuation of regressive gender norms. Furthermore, the global influence of such content has implications for how gender roles are perceived and enacted worldwide, potentially influencing societal norms and individual behaviors across diverse cultural contexts.

Technological advancements are central to Netflix's influence on cultural globalization. The company's sophisticated use of streaming technology and data analytics enables it to reach a global audience and tailor content to diverse viewer preferences. Netflix's recommendation algorithms, which suggest content based on previous viewing habits, exemplify how technology can both broaden and narrow cultural exposure. While these algorithms help users discover content from different cultures, they also risk creating filter bubbles that reinforce viewers' existing preferences, potentially limiting exposure to new cultural experiences. The digital architecture of Netflix not only facilitates the rapid dissemination of cultural content but also raises ethical concerns about digital colonialism and the commodification of cultural expressions. As Netflix shapes global cultural consumption, it must navigate the ethical implications of its technological influence, ensuring that it supports a diverse and inclusive cultural landscape rather than monopolizing cultural narratives.

Studying Netflix illustrates the multifaceted impact of cultural globalization mediated by a global streaming giant. Through the lenses of existentialism, postmodernism, feminism, and technological analysis, it becomes clear that Netflix plays a complex role in both promoting cultural diversity and influencing global cultural norms. The platform's ability to shape cultural identities and narratives across the world underscores the importance of critically engaging with the ways media giants like Netflix manage the profound responsibility that comes with their extensive reach and influence in shaping global culture.

2.8 A Pragmatic Response: Culturally Diverse Content

In response to the ethical and cultural challenges posed by Netflix's influence in global cultural globalization, enhancing cultural representation and inclusion emerges as a crucial strategy. This approach aims to rectify the potential cultural homogenization and ensure that Netflix promotes a diverse and authentically representative media landscape. Here, we explore how initiatives focused on increasing cultural representation effectively address the issues associated with global media platforms, examining their impact through a composite moral and philosophical lens.

Netflix is currently trying to amplify its positive impact by investing significantly in local content production across diverse cultural contexts. This not only provides a platform for local voices and stories but also enriches the global audience's viewing experience with a broad spectrum of cultural perspectives. From a utilitarian perspective, this approach enhances the overall cultural richness available to viewers, thus aligning business practices with the welfare of a global audience. Additionally, actively curating a diverse content library that goes beyond mainstream narratives to include marginalized and underrepresented groups can help counteract cultural homogenization. This commitment to diversity respects the inherent dignity and variety of global cultures, reflecting deontological ethics by treating each cultural expression as an end in itself. Moreover, collaborating with local filmmakers, artists, and cultural experts can help ensure that the content is not only culturally rich but also authentic and respectful of the source material. Such partnerships can nurture long-term relationships rooted in mutual respect and shared goals, embodying the virtue ethics principle of fostering community and mutual respect.

Additionally, embracing a postmodern approach, Netflix can deconstruct dominant cultural narratives by promoting a plurality of voices. This strategy challenges the traditional power dynamics within global media production and consumption, offering a platform for narratives that reflect the fragmented and diverse nature of global cultures. Further, integrating feminist and gender theories into content development and platform policies enhances the representation of gender diversity and promotes narratives that challenge traditional gender roles and stereotypes. This approach not only supports gender equality but also broadens the spectrum of stories and perspectives presented to a global audience. Leveraging technology to enhance accessibility and personalized content recommendations based on diverse cultural interests can help mitigate the risks of algorithmic biases that favor dominant cultures. Technologies that promote inclusion can transform how cultural content is recommended and consumed, ensuring a more equitable representation of global cultures.

Addressing some of the concerns that Netflix's audience has been voicing in recent times in response to the aforementioned. It should be noted that it is a common misconception that diversity and quality are mutually exclusive. It's important to clarify that promoting diversity in content does not inherently mean compromising on quality. Diversity in storytelling brings a plethora of perspectives, enriching the narrative complexity and depth of content. High-quality, diverse storytelling can enhance viewer engagement by offering new, often underrepresented perspectives that can resonate with a broader audience. Netflix's model is based on offering a wide array of content to cater to diverse global tastes. This strategy inherently includes shows and movies of various genres and qualities to meet different preferences and interests. While not every piece of content will meet the same quality standards or appeal to every viewer, the platform's strength lies in its vast selection, allowing users to choose content that best fits their taste. Criticisms about quality might often stem from viewers encountering content that does not align with their personal preferences but might be highly valued by other segments of Netflix's diverse audience.

The term "*agenda*" often gets used to criticize efforts aimed at increasing representation, suggesting a forced or unnatural inclusion. However, it's essential to differentiate between inclusivity as an agenda and inclusivity as a reflection of the world's diversity. Representation in media is crucial for promoting understanding and empathy across different cultures and communities. Netflix's initiative to enhance diversity is not just about ticking boxes but about reflecting the real, multicultural world we live in, which should naturally include a spectrum of stories and perspectives. It's also vital to consider that Netflix operates in a competitive market environment, where content decisions are driven by both creative ambitions and market dynamics. The diversity in content also responds to market demands from global audiences seeking representation and stories that resonate with their own experiences or curiosity about other cultures.

Netflix, like any content provider, benefits from engaging constructively with its audience's feedback. Understanding criticisms in context can help refine strategies to balance diversity and quality more effectively. This might involve investing in emerging writers and directors with diverse backgrounds to bring authenticity and high-quality storytelling that aligns with inclusive goals. It is crucial for Netflix to continually evaluate how they measure success and impact. Beyond viewership numbers, understanding deeper engagement metrics and audience satisfaction can provide insights into how well diversity and quality are being balanced.

Communicating the rationale behind content choices and diversity initiatives transparently can help audiences understand Netflix's objectives. This might include sharing insights into the creative process, the selection criteria, and how these strategies benefit a broad spectrum of viewers. Finally, it's about continuous improvement. Netflix can take criticisms as opportunities to refine their content acquisition and production processes to ensure both diversity and quality are upheld. This could mean providing more resources and support to projects that might require further development to meet high-quality standards while fulfilling the company's diversity and inclusivity goals.

I. Cultural Justice

CULTURAL JUSTICE IS a crucial principle in addressing the inequalities and disparities that arise within an increasingly globalized world. It involves ensuring fair representation and equitable treatment of all cultures, recognizing that globalization can often lead to the marginalization and silencing of certain communities or cultural expressions. The essence of cultural justice lies in creating systems and policies that not only prevent the dominance of any single culture but also foster environments where all cultures have the opportunity to thrive and be respected on a global scale.

The philosophical underpinnings of cultural justice draw from theories of fairness and recognition, integrating concepts from thinkers like John Rawls and Charles Taylor. Rawls' theory, which emphasizes equity and justice as foundational to societal well-being, suggests that just as social and economic inequalities demand systemic redress, so too do cultural disparities require careful attention and rectification. Taylor's ***politics of recognition*** further argues that justice is not only about treating individuals with equal respect but also involves acknowledging and affirming the unique identities and contributions of different cultural groups. This dual focus on fairness and recognition provides a robust framework for understanding and implementing cultural justice.

Central to the notion of cultural justice are several key focus areas: *the protection of cultural rights, representation in global media and institutions, and support for cultural preservation and promotion.* Legal frameworks must be established and enforced to protect cultural rights and prevent cultural domination by more powerful entities. This includes laws that safeguard intellectual property specific to cultural artifacts and traditional knowledge. Additionally, cultural sovereignty must be supported, allowing every culture the autonomy to manage how its knowledge is shared or commercialized globally.

Equitable representation in global media and cultural institutions is also paramount. Media outlets should strive to provide a balanced portrayal of diverse cultures, avoiding stereotypes and enabling marginalized voices to share their narratives. Similarly, global cultural institutions like UNESCO need to reflect the diversity of their memberships, not only in their staff but also in their decision-making processes and the projects they support.

Support for cultural preservation is another critical element of cultural justice. Initiatives need to be funded and supported that aim to preserve endangered languages, crafts, rituals, and traditions. Additionally, the promotion of cultural exchanges can enhance mutual understanding and respect among different cultures, fostering a global community that values and learns from its diverse constituents.

Implementing cultural justice requires a multifaceted approach, where policymakers must collaborate with international bodies to develop policies that promote cultural diversity and protection. Engaging with local communities is essential to ensure that cultural preservation efforts are aligned with the needs and desires of the people they aim to support. Technology can also play a pivotal role, helping to document and archive cultural expressions in digital formats, thereby preserving them for educational purposes and future generations.

However, cultural justice also faces significant challenges, such as balancing the benefits of globalization with the need to protect local cultures from being overshadowed or assimilated. Furthermore, there is a need to address the commercial exploitation of cultural expressions, ensuring they are not reduced to mere commodities in global trade.

In short, cultural justice is not just about preserving cultural diversity but actively engaging in creating a dynamic global society where all cultures can interact equitably. It involves building a world where diversity is seen as a strength and where each cultural identity is both acknowledged and valued. By striving towards cultural justice, the global community can work towards a more harmonious and respectful international landscape, where the rights and dignity of all cultural expressions are upheld.

II. Recognition and Respect for Cultural Diversity

RECOGNITION AND RESPECT for cultural diversity are essential for creating a globally inclusive society where different cultural practices and beliefs are not only acknowledged but valued. This principle involves understanding the intrinsic worth of diverse cultural expressions and the rights of individuals and communities to maintain and develop their cultural identities. In a globalized world, where interactions between cultures are frequent and varied, embracing cultural diversity is crucial for promoting mutual respect and reducing conflicts that stem from misunderstandings or cultural insensitivity.

Philosophically, the respect for cultural diversity is anchored in the concept of pluralism, which asserts that *diversity within a society is valuable and that different cultural perspectives can coexist harmoniously.* This approach aligns with the ideas of philosophers like Isaiah Berlin, who argued for the positive ramifications of acknowledging and celebrating pluralistic values in a society. Such recognition is not merely a passive acknowledgment but an active engagement with the differences that define various cultural groups, fostering a deeper understanding that each culture offers unique insights and ways of being that can contribute to the collective human experience.

Key areas that highlight the importance of recognizing and respecting cultural diversity include education, policy-making, and media representation. In education, curricula should be developed to reflect a broad spectrum of cultural histories and values, providing students with a global perspective that appreciates cultural differences and similarities. Such educational initiatives encourage open-mindedness and respect among young people, preparing them for constructive interactions in a diverse world.

In terms of policy-making, governments and organizations should implement policies that promote cultural inclusivity and prevent discrimination based on cultural, ethnic, or religious backgrounds. These policies must ensure that all cultural groups have equal access to opportunities and are protected under the law from hate crimes and other forms of cultural bias. Furthermore, the media plays a critical role in shaping perceptions of different cultures. Media outlets should strive to present diverse cultural perspectives fairly and accurately, avoiding stereotypes and providing a platform for underrepresented groups to share their stories and perspectives.

To effectively promote and respect cultural diversity, several strategies can be employed:

- **Cultural Competence Training:** Organizations and institutions can offer training programs that enhance understanding and respect for cultural differences among their members. Such programs prepare individuals to interact respectfully and effectively with people from different cultural backgrounds, which is increasingly important in our interconnected world.

- **Support for Cultural Festivals and Events:** Governments and community organizations can support cultural festivals and events that celebrate diverse cultural expressions. These events serve as platforms for cultural exchange and learning, nurturing community engagement and appreciation for cultural diversity.

- **Inclusive Policy Frameworks:** Developing inclusive policy frameworks involves revising existing policies and creating new ones that recognize and protect the rights of all cultural groups. This includes anti-discrimination laws, policies promoting multicultural education, and support for minority and indigenous cultural practices.

- **Empowerment of Minority Voices:** Ensuring that minority groups have the opportunity to be heard in public discourses and decision-making processes is vital. This can be achieved through representation in political offices, advisory boards, and media outlets, which helps to ensure that diverse perspectives are considered in societal developments.

- **International Collaboration:** Encouraging international collaboration on cultural projects can enhance mutual respect and understanding. These collaborations can include cultural exchanges, joint artistic productions, and international research projects that explore and celebrate cultural diversity.

In essence, recognizing and respecting cultural diversity involves a commitment to understanding and valuing the differences that define various cultural groups. It requires concerted efforts in education, policy-making, and media representation to ensure that diversity is celebrated and that all cultural groups are treated with respect and dignity. By embracing this principle, societies can work towards a more peaceful and cohesive global community, where cultural diversity is seen as a resource for learning and growth rather than a barrier to it.

III. Ethical Global Engagement

ETHICAL GLOBAL ENGAGEMENT is the principle that governs interactions between cultures to ensure they are conducted respectfully, justly, and in a manner that promotes mutual benefit. This concept is crucial in a globalized world where cultural exchanges are pervasive and impactful, influencing everything from business practices to educational content, media representations, and interpersonal communications. Ethical engagement seeks to foster interactions that are not only economically advantageous but also culturally enriching and socially responsible.

The philosophical roots of ethical global engagement can be traced to cosmopolitanism, which advocates for recognizing and acting upon our responsibilities to others irrespective of national, geographic, or cultural boundaries. Immanuel Kant's idea of cosmopolitanism, for instance, emphasizes the ethical duty of individuals and institutions to engage in cooperative and mutually beneficial relationships across borders. This duty is grounded in the belief that all human beings belong to a single moral community. Ethical global engagement, therefore, involves prioritizing the dignity and rights of all individuals in interactions, ensuring that global initiatives consider the welfare of the global community.

Key components of ethical global engagement include cultural sensitivity, fairness in economic transactions, and the promotion of sustainable and inclusive practices. Cultural sensitivity involves understanding the cultural contexts and nuances that shape interactions and ensuring that these differences are respected rather than overridden. Fairness in economic transactions ensures that global trade and cooperation lead to equitable outcomes for all parties involved, preventing exploitative practices that could arise from power imbalances.

To effectively implement ethical global engagement, several strategic approaches can be pursued:

- **Promoting Fair Trade Practices:** Fair trade is a model that emphasizes transparency, respect, and fairness in the global marketplace. It seeks to offer producers in developing countries fair payment for their goods and services, thereby contributing to sustainable community development. By adopting and promoting fair trade practices, businesses and consumers can partake in a more ethically engaged global economy that supports economic justice.

- **Enforcing CSR:** Corporations have a significant role in ethical global engagement. CSR initiatives can drive corporations to act beyond mere compliance with laws, to proactively improve social, economic, and environmental outcomes across their operations and supply chains. This includes ensuring fair labor practices, environmental conservation, and contributing positively to the communities in which they operate.

- **Cultural Exchange Programs:** Supporting and participating in cultural exchange programs can enhance mutual understanding and respect among different cultures. These programs often involve educational, artistic, and professional exchanges that provide participants with firsthand experiences of other cultures, fostering a global outlook and reducing cultural prejudices.

- **Global Educational Initiatives:** Integrating global education into school curricula around the world can prepare young people to engage ethically with the global community. This education should focus on teaching the values of empathy, respect for diversity, and the importance of sustainable development.

- **International Cooperation on Global Issues:** Ethical global engagement requires cooperative efforts to address international issues such as climate change, poverty, and human rights abuses. By working together through international agreements and concerted actions, countries and organizations can address these challenges more effectively and ethically.

Ethical global engagement is about creating a framework within which global interactions occur in a manner that is respectful to all parties involved, recognizing their dignity and rights. It involves a commitment from individuals, businesses, governments, and international bodies to engage in practices that are not only beneficial but also just and respectful of cultural diversity. By adhering to this principle, the global community can ensure that the interconnections and interdependencies that characterize our world lead to positive outcomes for all, fostering a spirit of global solidarity and cooperation.

IV. Protection of Indigenous and Marginalized Cultures

THE PROTECTION OF INDIGENOUS and marginalized cultures is a critical aspect of building a globally inclusive and ethical society. As globalization accelerates, these cultures often face significant threats from economic development, cultural assimilation, and environmental degradation, risking the erosion of their cultural identities and traditional ways of life. The principle of protecting these cultures is grounded in respecting their unique contributions to global diversity and recognizing their rights to maintain and develop their cultural practices and lands.

Philosophically, the protection of indigenous and marginalized cultures aligns with principles of justice and equity, particularly as articulated in theories of multiculturalism by philosophers like Will Kymlicka, who argue for the rights of minority cultures to self-determination and preservation.

These rights are not only essential for the well-being of the communities themselves but are also crucial for maintaining global cultural diversity, which enriches the human experience for all.

Key Aspects of Protecting Indigenous and Marginalized Cultures:

- **Legal and Political Recognition:** Ensuring that indigenous and marginalized groups receive formal recognition and legal protections at both national and international levels is fundamental. This includes recognizing their land rights, cultural rights, and political autonomy, protecting them from exploitation and ensuring they have a voice in decisions that affect their communities.

- **Cultural Preservation Initiatives:** Supporting initiatives aimed at preserving the languages, arts, rituals, and practices of indigenous and marginalized cultures is crucial. This can involve funding cultural heritage projects, supporting local schools that teach traditional knowledge and skills, and facilitating cultural revival programs that help restore and invigorate cultural practices that may be at risk.

- **Economic Support without Cultural Erosion:** Providing economic support that respects the cultural integrity of communities is essential. Development projects and aid should be designed in consultation with the communities they aim to assist, ensuring that these initiatives support sustainable development without imposing external cultural values or causing environmental damage that could undermine the communities' traditional ways of life.

Strategies for Implementation:

- **Community-Based Management:** Implementing community-based management of natural resources and cultural sites ensures that development or conservation efforts are aligned with the needs and wishes of the indigenous populations. This approach respects their traditional knowledge and practices, which are often sustainable and ecologically beneficial.

• **Representation in Governance:** Indigenous and marginalized groups should have direct representation in governmental and international bodies that make decisions affecting their rights and resources. This participation ensures that policies are informed by those who are directly impacted and that these policies support the communities' long-term cultural and environmental goals.

• **Education and Awareness Programs:** Broad public education and awareness campaigns can help increase understanding and respect for the cultures of indigenous and marginalized groups. These programs can also be aimed at tourists and businesses to promote respectful engagement and avoid the commodification of cultural practices.

• **Support for Legal Battles:** Many indigenous communities face legal challenges in securing land rights and protection against exploitation. Providing legal assistance and international advocacy can support these communities in their efforts to defend their rights against more powerful corporate or governmental interests.

• **Safeguarding Intangible Cultural Heritage:** Support initiatives that document and safeguard intangible cultural heritage, such as folklore, music, dance, and traditional crafts, ensuring that these cultural expressions are preserved and appreciated both within the community and globally.

Challenges and Considerations:

• **Balancing Development and Cultural Preservation:** One of the major challenges is finding the right balance between necessary economic development and the preservation of cultural identities. Development projects need to be designed in a way that they do not undermine the cultural fabric of the communities they are intended to help.

- **Navigating External Interests:** Indigenous and marginalized cultures often find themselves at odds with national and international corporations, especially in industries such as mining, logging, and agriculture. Ensuring that these cultures are protected from exploitative practices requires robust legal frameworks and vigilant enforcement.

- **Respecting Cultural Autonomy:** It is vital to approach the protection of indigenous and marginalized cultures with a mindset that respects their autonomy and avoids paternalistic attitudes. Communities must be regarded as active partners rather than passive recipients of protection and aid.

The protection of indigenous and marginalized cultures is not merely an ethical obligation but a necessity for maintaining the world's cultural diversity, which is a source of richness and resilience. By implementing the above strategies, societies can work towards a more just and equitable global community where the rights and dignities of all cultures are respected and upheld. The philosophical commitment to these principles involves recognizing the intrinsic value of diverse cultural expressions and ensuring that globalization becomes a force for cultural enrichment rather than cultural erosion. This commitment must be operationalized through thoughtful policies, respectful engagement, and a continuous dialogue with the communities at the heart of this discourse.

V. Promotion of Intercultural Competence

PROMOTION OF INTERCULTURAL competence is pivotal in amplifying effective and respectful interactions across diverse cultural boundaries, especially in a world increasingly interconnected by globalization. Intercultural competence involves the ability to communicate and function effectively across different cultural contexts, recognizing and respecting diversity while avoiding miscommunications and conflicts that may arise from cultural misunderstandings.

The philosophical foundation of promoting intercultural competence is embedded in the ethical principles of respect and empathy. It is informed by the concept of ethical relativism, which suggests that different cultural practices have their own internal logics and values that must be understood and respected on their own terms. This approach emphasizes the importance of seeing the world through others' perspectives, which is essential for cultivating a global society that values diversity and cohesion.

Key Aspects of Promoting Intercultural Competence:

- **Educational Programs:** Integrating intercultural education into school curricula at all levels is crucial. This should include teaching students about global cultures, religions, customs, and communication styles, as well as providing opportunities for direct interaction with diverse cultural groups through exchange programs and multicultural events.

- **Professional Development:** Offering intercultural training in workplaces, particularly in multinational corporations, healthcare, and government services, where interactions with people from diverse backgrounds are frequent. This training helps professionals develop the skills necessary to navigate cultural differences effectively, fostering a workplace environment that is both inclusive and productive.

- **Media Representation:** Encouraging media outlets to portray diverse cultures accurately and sensitively, helping to break down stereotypes and promote understanding. Media plays a powerful role in shaping perceptions and can be a potent tool for enhancing intercultural competence by providing audiences with nuanced portrayals of different cultures.

Strategies for Implementation:

- **Interactive Platforms:** Develop interactive platforms that facilitate cultural exchange and learning. These can be digital platforms that offer language learning opportunities, cultural exchange, and forums for dialogue about cultural issues, making it accessible for people from all over the world to engage and learn from each other.

- **Community Engagement Projects:** Implement community engagement projects that encourage diverse cultural expressions and collaborations. These projects could involve collaborative art installations, cultural festivals, and community service programs that bring people from different backgrounds together to work on shared goals.

- **Policies Promoting Cultural Exchange:** Governments can enact policies that encourage cultural exchange by simplifying visa processes for students and professionals, providing scholarships for international studies, and funding cultural festivals that showcase diverse cultural traditions.

- **Corporate Intercultural Initiatives:** Encourage corporations to develop intercultural initiatives that not only train employees in cultural competence but also promote diverse hiring practices and inclusive work environments. These initiatives can help harness the benefits of a culturally diverse workforce, which includes enhanced creativity, broader perspectives on problem-solving, and better market insights.

Challenges and Considerations:

- **Depth vs. Breadth in Cultural Education:** Balancing the depth and breadth of cultural education can be challenging. While it is important to cover a broad range of cultures to foster general cultural awareness, depth is necessary for the development of true competence and understanding.

- **Overcoming Cultural Bias:** Overcoming ingrained cultural biases and stereotypes remains a significant challenge. Intercultural competence requires ongoing self-reflection and openness to change, which can be difficult for individuals and institutions entrenched in their ways of thinking and operating.

- **Resource Allocation:** Allocating resources effectively to promote intercultural competence can be challenging, especially in areas with limited educational and financial resources. Ensuring that these initiatives are accessible and beneficial to all segments of society is crucial.

Promoting intercultural competence is essential for creating a world where individuals not only coexist but also cooperate and thrive together, despite cultural differences. By cultivating an environment that values and utilizes diverse cultural perspectives, societies can enhance their collective problem-solving capabilities and foster a deeper sense of global unity. The promotion of intercultural competence is a dynamic, ongoing process that requires commitment from educational systems, workplaces, and media, alongside continuous engagement from individuals seeking to broaden their cultural understanding and empathy.

2.9 Future Developments in Cultural Globalization

I. The Impact of Virtual Reality and Augmented Reality on Cultural Experience

Virtual Reality (VR) and Augmented Reality (AR) technologies are poised to redefine the way we experience and interact with culture. These technologies enable immersive experiences that can transport users to different cultural settings without leaving their homes. This has profound implications for education, allowing for interactive and experiential learning about diverse cultures through virtual tours of historical sites, museums, and cultural events. Philosophically, this raises questions about the authenticity of virtual experiences and the impact on traditional cultural tourism. *Will virtual experiences enhance cultural appreciation or diminish the value of physical presence in cultural immersion?* Additionally, there are ethical considerations regarding the representation of cultures in virtual platforms, ensuring that these representations are respectful and accurate, and do not perpetuate stereotypes or cultural appropriation.

II. Increased Global Connectivity and the Rise of a Global Culture

AS INTERNET PENETRATION increases and digital platforms become more accessible, we see the potential rise of a singular global culture. This culture is mediated by the internet, where cultural trends, memes, and media quickly spread worldwide, transcending geographical and cultural boundaries. This hyper-connectivity raises philosophical debates about cultural homogenization versus cultural diversity. While global connectivity can nurture understanding and unity, it also poses risks of diluting distinct cultural identities. Ethically, there's a need to balance the promotion of a global culture that celebrates shared human values with the preservation of unique cultural identities and practices. *How do we maintain cultural diversity in an increasingly interconnected world?*

III. Artificial Intelligence in Cultural Creation and Curation

AI'S ROLE IN CULTURAL sectors such as art, music, and literature is expanding, with algorithms now capable of creating artworks and composing music, or curating personalized cultural content for individuals. This technological intervention in cultural creation challenges traditional notions of creativity and artistic authenticity. Philosophically, it prompts us to reconsider the nature of art and the role of human agency in cultural production. Ethically, there are concerns about the transparency of AI processes and the potential for AI to reinforce biases in cultural representation. *Should AI have a role in cultural creation, and if so, how do we ensure that it enhances rather than diminishes human creativity?*

IV. Cultural Datafication and its Implications

THE GROWING TREND OF quantifying and analyzing cultural data has significant implications for how cultures are understood and managed. Big data can help in understanding complex cultural dynamics and predicting cultural trends, which can be useful for everything from policy-making to marketing. However, the datafication of culture also raises privacy concerns and questions about the ownership of cultural information. Philosophically, this trend touches on issues of surveillance and control, as well as the potential for commodifying cultural aspects that are deeply personal or sacred to communities. Ethically, it's crucial to develop frameworks that respect individual and community rights over cultural data and ensure that such data is used responsibly.

V. Promotion of Intercultural Competence in a Digitally Connected World

AS DIGITAL COMMUNICATION becomes a dominant medium for social interaction, there is an increased need for intercultural competence to navigate the complexities of global digital platforms. This involves understanding and managing cultural differences in online interactions, which can often be misinterpreted due to the lack of non-verbal cues and the immediate nature of digital communication. The development of digital literacy programs that include intercultural communication skills is essential. Philosophically, this situation challenges us to think about the nature of communication and relationship-building in a digital age. Ethically, there's a pressing need to develop online environments that are inclusive and respectful of diversity.

VI. Integrating the Future into Our Philosophical Framework

THESE CULTURAL DEVELOPMENTS require a dynamic and responsive philosophical approach that can adapt to the rapidly changing landscape of global culture. Philosophers, cultural theorists, and policymakers must proactively engage with these emerging issues, anticipating their impact on cultural identity, expression, and ethics. Crafting policies and educational programs that promote respect for diversity, ensure ethical use of technology in cultural contexts, and foster genuine intercultural engagement are essential for managing the future of cultural globalization effectively. This ongoing dialogue will help ensure that advancements in technology and connectivity contribute positively to a diverse and vibrant global cultural mosaic.

As we conclude our exploration of the cultural dimension of globalization, it becomes evident that our philosophical discourse must adapt to embrace not only the current cultural phenomena but also anticipate future shifts in global cultural dynamics. This forward-looking approach ensures that our moral and philosophical responses are aptly suited for an increasingly complex and interconnected world, nourishing a global cultural system that is not only diverse but also ethically sound and respectful.

Throughout this chapter, we have traversed the meadows of cultural exchange, the impactful roles of digital media and technology, and the critical ethical questions they raise about cultural preservation and identity.

We've examined how contemporary cultural theories, such as those proposed by thinkers like Stuart Hall and Homi Bhabha, inform our understanding of cultural identity in a globalized context, challenging us to consider the fluid and hybrid nature of modern identities. The analysis of virtual reality, AI, and digital platforms illustrated how these technologies are reshaping cultural experiences, offering both opportunities for enriched cultural interaction and challenges to cultural authenticity.

The critique of cultural datafication and the rise of a global culture emphasized the need to safeguard diverse cultural expressions against the risks of homogenization and cultural erosion. These discussions highlight the delicate balance required to maintain cultural diversity and integrity in the face of pervasive global influences. They call into question the sustainability of current global cultural practices and underscore the urgent need for ethical guidelines that respect and protect the richness of global cultural heritage.

Looking forward, the path toward a more respectful and inclusive global culture involves several strategic considerations:

- **Enhanced Intercultural Education:** Cultivating intercultural competence through education that spans schools to corporate training programs, ensuring that individuals are prepared to navigate and appreciate an increasingly diverse world.

- **Robust Policies on Cultural Exchange and Preservation:** Implementing policies that encourage cultural exchange while protecting and preserving the autonomy of indigenous and marginalized cultures, ensuring they are not overshadowed by dominant global forces.

- **Ethical Use of Technology in Cultural Production:** Developing guidelines that ensure technologies such as AI and VR contribute positively to cultural development without compromising cultural integrity or promoting inequality.

- **Promotion of Global Cultural Dialogue:** Facilitating a global dialogue on culture that includes diverse voices and perspectives, ensuring that all cultural narratives are valued and that global policies reflect this diversity.

- **Sustainable and Ethical Media Practices:** Encouraging media practices that responsibly portray and promote cultural diversity, avoiding stereotypes, and ensuring that media becomes a tool for cultural education and not misinformation.

Globalization presents a dynamic relationship between global integration and cultural distinction. By adopting a critical and reflective approach to its cultural dimension, we can strive to mitigate the risks associated with cultural convergence while enhancing the benefits of cultural diversity and exchange. This requires concerted efforts among governments, cultural institutions, businesses, and communities to reimagine and restructure global cultural interactions. Such efforts will ensure that globalization serves as a force for cultural enrichment and mutual understanding, promoting not only intercultural dialogue but also respect and appreciation for the world's myriad cultures. As we move forward to explore the political dimension of globalization in subsequent chapters, the insights from this cultural analysis will provide a robust framework for understanding the broader impacts of globalization on society, politics, and the global ethical landscape.

Chapter 3: The Political Dimension of Globalization

———

I n this chapter, we explore the web of political structures that define and regulate globalization, specifically focusing on the pivotal roles played by international organizations and global treaties. This analysis seeks to understand how such entities influence national sovereignty, frame global governance, and enforce international law, forming a bridge between the economic and cultural dimensions discussed in previous chapters.

The emergence and evolution of supranational entities represent pivotal moments in the history of international governance. These organizations, transcending individual national policies, aim to build cooperation and ensure peace and stability on a global scale. Their creation marks significant shifts in how states interact, share sovereignty, and address global issues together.

The United Nations, established in the aftermath of World War II, embodies the collective aspiration for peace and cooperation among nations. It was founded with the primary goals of preventing future conflicts, promoting human rights, and nurturing social and economic development. The UN operates through a complex system of councils and programs, each dedicated to different aspects of international relations, from peacekeeping and conflict resolution to health and environmental sustainability. This global body has been crucial in setting international norms and facilitating diplomacy in a world where unilateral actions by powerful states could otherwise dominate. The Universal Declaration of Human Rights, adopted in 1948, exemplifies the UN's role in promoting global norms that uphold human dignity and justice.

The UN, through its peacekeeping missions, endeavors to maintain peace and security worldwide. However, the effectiveness of these missions often varies due to political complexities, limited resources, and varying commitments from member states. For instance, missions have been successful in some contexts like Liberia or Sierra Leone, where they have helped to stabilize regions post-conflict. Conversely, in places like Rwanda or the former Yugoslavia, the UN's inability to prevent genocide and atrocities has been a significant failure, raising ethical questions about the responsibility and capability of international bodies in preventing humanitarian crises.

The enforcement of human rights norms by entities like the UN is hampered by geopolitical interests, sovereignty concerns, and the selective will of member states to intervene. The principle of non-interference in internal affairs often clashes with the need to protect human rights, leading to paralysis or ineffective responses to crises. Furthermore, the reliance on voluntary compliance without substantial enforcement mechanisms continues to be a significant challenge.

Similarly, the World Trade Organization, succeeding the General Agreement on Tariffs and Trade (GATT) in 1995, focuses on streamlining and regulating international trade. The WTO aims to create a level playing field for all nations by ensuring that trade flows as smoothly, predictably, and freely as possible. This is achieved through a comprehensive set of rules agreed upon by its members, who must abide by these rules to avoid unilateral trade policies that could lead to trade wars. The WTO also serves as a forum for negotiating trade agreements and a platform for resolving trade disputes among countries. This role is critical in managing the complexities of global trade, where conflicting national interests can often lead to disputes that impact the global economy.

The WTO has been integral in providing a regulated framework for resolving international trade disputes. This role is critical in preventing trade conflicts from escalating into more significant political conflicts. However, the organization faces criticisms regarding the dominance of wealthier nations in the decision-making processes, potentially compromising the fairness of rulings and reflecting a power imbalance that undermines its foundation of equitable trade.

In Europe, the European Union represents one of the most advanced forms of regional economic and political integration. It began as a series of economic agreements after World War II, aimed at fostering economic cooperation to prevent further conflicts in Europe. Over time, these agreements evolved into a comprehensive political and economic union involving 27 European countries. The EU operates through supranational institutions like the European Commission, the European Parliament, and the European Court of Justice, alongside intergovernmental decisions made in the European Council and the Council of the European Union. One of its hallmark achievements, the introduction of a single currency, the euro, has facilitated unparalleled economic integration among its member states. However, the EU also illustrates the challenges of supranational governance, balancing national sovereignty with broader regional policies, as seen in areas such as immigration, regulation, and fiscal policy.

These supranational entities are more than functional bureaucracies; they symbolize the shifting paradigms of global politics, where cooperation and collective action are increasingly seen as necessary for addressing complex global challenges. From fostering economic stability and development to addressing climate change and human rights abuses, their roles underline the interconnectedness of nations in the modern world. However, the evolution of these bodies also highlights the tensions inherent in global governance, between national sovereignty and international cooperation, between local interests and global imperatives. In an interconnected global stage, the sovereignty of nation-states is often perceived as being diluted, as international organizations and treaties demand a level of compliance that can influence domestic policies and priorities. The UN, WTO, and EU challenge and redefine the notion of sovereignty in the modern world. As such, they are central to understanding the political dimensions of globalization, influencing how laws are made, borders are defined, and how states and peoples interact on the global stage.

The concept of sovereignty, historically understood as the absolute authority of a state over its territory and domestic affairs, faces new pressures under global governance frameworks. Membership in international organizations often requires states to adhere to international agreements and conventions that can supersede national laws and regulations. This integration into global governance structures is seen as a trade-off between retaining traditional sovereign powers and gaining the benefits of global cooperation, which can include economic aid, security guarantees, and access to international markets. For example, UN member states are bound by the Charter of the United Nations to promote human rights and to respect the legal standards set forth in treaties such as the Geneva Conventions. Similarly, WTO agreements have direct implications for national economic policies and legislation. States must align their trade policies with WTO rules, potentially limiting their ability to impose tariffs or subsidies that they would otherwise use to protect domestic industries.

The European Union exemplifies the complexities of shared sovereignty in a supranational context. By agreeing to the treaties of the EU, member states accept that certain decisions, especially those concerning economic policies, competition law, and environmental standards, will be made at the European level. This arrangement is intended to ensure uniformity and fairness across the single market, promoting economic integration and reducing barriers to trade and mobility within the bloc. However, this sharing of sovereignty has sparked debates and controversies, particularly around issues like immigration, fiscal policy, and national identity. The principle of subsidiarity in the EU seeks to balance power by ensuring that decisions are taken as closely as possible to the citizen and that action at the European level is taken only when it is more effective than action taken at the national or local level. Despite this, the tension between national sovereignty and European governance remains a hotly debated topic within member states.

The influence of international organizations on national sovereignty is also evident in how they can shape domestic agendas through compliance mechanisms. For instance, to participate in the global trade system under the WTO, countries may need to reform their trade laws and regulations, which can lead to significant changes in their economic landscapes. The UN's agendas, particularly in sustainability and development, often require states to adjust their policies to meet international goals, such as those outlined in the Sustainable Development Goals (SDGs).

These adjustments, while beneficial in developing global cooperation and ensuring compliance with international norms, can also lead to a perception of loss of control over national issues. This perception can fuel nationalist and protectionist sentiments, as seen in the rise of populist movements advocating for a return to full national sovereignty and the rejection of international agreements perceived as unfavorable.

The challenge for modern states lies in navigating the balance between maintaining sovereignty and engaging in the global system that increasingly governs economic, political, and social realms. The ongoing debates and policies reflect a dynamic negotiation of power, where sovereignty is not merely relinquished but redefined in the context of global interdependence. The influence of supranational entities on national sovereignty thus shows a fundamental shift in international relations, highlighting the need for states to strategically engage with and shape international norms and policies. This dynamic forms a crucial part of the political dimension of globalization, reflecting the continuous evolution of sovereignty in response to global challenges and opportunities.

From a political philosophical perspective, these organizations are grounded in the theory of cosmopolitanism, which advocates for global justice and universal moral obligations across borders. Yet, the realpolitik of international relations often contradicts cosmopolitan ideals. Sovereign states prioritize national interests, sometimes at the expense of global ethical considerations, such as in cases of refugee treatment or climate change mitigation. Overall, the moral responsibilities of these organizations are complex. Ethically, they are expected to uphold the highest standards of justice, equity, and human dignity. Philosophically, they must balance these ideals with the pragmatic realities of international politics, where power dynamics and national interests often prevail. This tension raises profound ethical dilemmas about the nature of sovereignty, the limits of international law, and the extent of moral duty states have to individuals beyond their borders.

Managing these ethical and operational challenges requires robust governance frameworks that can adapt to the dynamic nature of global politics. Reforming voting systems in organizations like the WTO and the UN Security Council could help address inequalities in representation and power imbalances. Enhancing the transparency and accountability of international institutions can also increase their legitimacy and ethical standing. Moreover, fostering greater collaboration between supranational entities and non-state actors, such as NGOs and civil society, can help bridge gaps in enforcement and implementation of global norms. These partnerships could enhance the responsiveness and effectiveness of international organizations in managing complex global issues.

The governance of global issues by supranational entities involves navigating a labyrinth of ethical dilemmas, political challenges, and philosophical questions about justice, responsibility, and equity. While these organizations have made significant strides in addressing some of the world's most pressing problems, their effectiveness is often limited by structural flaws, resource constraints, and conflicting state interests. A critical reevaluation of their roles and responsibilities, informed by both ethical considerations and practical realities, is essential for enhancing their capability to manage the complexities of globalization effectively. This philosophical inquiry not only sheds light on their current operations but also guides future reforms necessary for a just global governance system.

3.1 Global Justice: Cosmopolitanism vs. Realism

In the discourse on global justice, two prominent theoretical frameworks offer contrasting perspectives on how to address issues like global inequality, human rights, and international responsibilities. These are cosmopolitanism, which advocates for a global approach to justice, and realism, which prioritizes national interests and state sovereignty. An in-depth analysis of these theories helps elucidate their implications for global governance and ethical norms.

Cosmopolitanism is rooted in the idea that all human beings, irrespective of nationality or geographic location, belong to a single global community with shared moral obligations. This theory posits that global justice should transcend state borders and that individuals have rights and responsibilities toward others globally, not just within their own country. Cosmopolitan theorists argue that disparities in wealth and resources between countries should be addressed through global redistribution mechanisms. Philosophers like Thomas Pogge have argued that wealthy nations have a moral duty to aid in alleviating global poverty because they often benefit from global economic systems that disadvantage poorer countries. This view supports initiatives like international aid, debt relief for developing nations, and fair trade as ethical imperatives.

From a cosmopolitan viewpoint, human rights are universal and non-negotiable. This theory supports international human rights law and advocates for supranational legal frameworks to enforce these rights. It challenges states' rights to non-interference when they are violating basic human rights, supporting humanitarian interventions in cases of gross human rights abuses. It also calls for enhanced cooperation among nations to address global challenges such as climate change, pandemics, and migration. It encourages the formation of global governance structures that can make and enforce rules binding all members of the international community, promoting a sense of shared responsibility for the planet and its people.

In contrast to cosmopolitanism, realism emphasizes the role of the state as the primary actor in international relations. Realists argue that the international system is anarchic and that states must primarily act in their own interest to ensure their survival and security. Realists view global inequality as an inevitable consequence of international politics where states pursue their own interests. They are skeptical about international redistribution, arguing that such policies are often not in the national interest. Realists focus on state sovereignty and non-interference, holding that states have no moral obligations to others beyond their borders unless directly serving their own strategic interests.

Realism tends to prioritize national security and interests over universal human rights. Realists may support human rights when it aligns with national interests, but they are generally skeptical about international human rights enforcement, viewing it as a potential infringement on sovereignty. They are cautious about international obligations that might constrain national sovereignty. They argue that states should only engage in international agreements when they serve their own interests, and they are skeptical of global governance structures that limit state power.

The contrast between cosmopolitanism and realism lies in their ethical orientation and practical implications. Cosmopolitanism champions a moral perspective that prioritizes global solidarity and collective action, advocating for a world where justice does not stop at borders. Realism, on the other hand, focuses on the pragmatic aspects of state behavior in an anarchic international system, where security and power are paramount.

The debate between these theories affects how global issues are approached. For cosmopolitans, global justice requires reforming international institutions to be more inclusive and accountable, ensuring they serve humanity as a whole rather than the interests of powerful states alone. For realists, such reforms may undermine the autonomy and security of individual states, suggesting a more cautious approach to international cooperation. Therefore, understanding these two theories provides a comprehensive view of the philosophical and practical tensions in addressing global justice. It highlights the complexities of formulating policies that balance ethical imperatives with political realities, a central challenge in the ongoing discourse on globalization and international relations.

These approaches propose fundamentally different frameworks for addressing international policies and humanitarian interventions. These perspectives not only guide the theoretical discourse but also have practical implications for international relations and global policy-making. Influential philosophers like Thomas Pogge, John Rawls, and Michael Walzer offer insights that enhance our understanding of these approaches.

Cosmopolitanism is deeply rooted in the philosophy of global egalitarianism, which argues for extending justice beyond national borders. Thomas Pogge, a prominent advocate for this approach, argues that wealthy countries have moral obligations that stem from a global order that disproportionately benefits them at the expense of poorer nations. Pogge's perspective challenges international and domestic policies to be more responsive to global suffering and injustice. Whereas Realism, influenced by thinkers like Michael Walzer, emphasizes the primacy of the state and the anarchic nature of international relations. Walzer argues that states have rights to political independence and territorial integrity, and thus, international actions must respect state sovereignty. Realists are skeptical of moral arguments that require significant sacrifices of national interest in the name of global justice.

Hence, adopting a cosmopolitan approach encourages the development of policies that prioritize global welfare and the universal provision of fundamental human rights. This could lead to stronger support for international aid, more equitable trade agreements, and enhanced cooperation on global issues like climate change and health crises. Cosmopolitanism advocates for the reform of global institutions such as the United Nations and the World Bank, making them more representative and effective in addressing global inequality. While a realist approach tends to prioritize national security and economic interests over global ethical considerations. This perspective may lead to more guarded policies regarding international aid and less enthusiasm for global redistributive efforts that do not align with national benefits. Realists would argue for maintaining strong state sovereignty and would be cautious about transferring powers to supranational bodies.

Under cosmopolitanism, humanitarian interventions are justified when they protect basic human rights and serve global justice. This approach would support interventions in cases of severe human rights violations, such as genocide or ethnic cleansing, irrespective of national boundaries. The rationale is that the global community has a responsibility to protect (R2P) individuals from grave injustices, regardless of where they occur. From a realist perspective, humanitarian interventions are viewed through the lens of national interest and strategic gains. Walzer suggests that interventions are justified only to counteract acts of aggression or gross violations of human rights but always with consideration for the political consequences. Realists would generally oppose interventions that risk national security or involve substantial commitments without clear benefits to the state.

John Rawls offers a nuanced view that can be seen as a bridge between cosmopolitanism and realism. In ***"The Law of Peoples,"*** Rawls extends his theory of justice to the international domain but limits his egalitarian principles to liberal and *'decent'* peoples, rejecting a fully cosmopolitan model of global justice. He argues for respect for human rights and fair trade but does not endorse extensive global redistribution. Rawls supports humanitarian duties but within the limits of what can be reasonably expected from sovereign states.

Choosing between cosmopolitan and realist approaches has far reaching implications for global governance and the conduct of international relations. A cosmopolitan approach pushes for deeper global integration and a broader moral community, promoting policies that aim for global welfare. In contrast, realism advocates for a more fragmented world system where state interests and sovereignty are paramount, potentially leading to more isolationist and protectionist policies. Ultimately, the choice between these frameworks influences how international laws are formulated and enforced, how humanitarian interventions are justified and carried out, and how global institutions are structured and operate. Each approach offers valuable insights, but also poses challenges in addressing the complexities of global justice in an interconnected yet diverse world.

Global challenges such as migration crises and international conflicts test the strengths and expose the weaknesses of both cosmopolitan and realist theories of global justice. By examining these theories in the context of contemporary issues, we can derive philosophical insights into which framework might provide more just and effective solutions to the pressing problems facing the global community today.

I. Migration Crises

COSMOPOLITANISM VIEWS migration crises as a responsibility that transcends national borders, emphasizing the duty to protect and assist individuals regardless of their nationality. According to cosmopolitan theorists, barriers to migration often reflect unjust global inequalities and a failure to recognize the basic rights and dignity of all humans as equal moral persons. A cosmopolitan approach advocates for open borders or at the very least, more generous and less restrictive migration policies, arguing that such measures are essential for rectifying global inequalities and fulfilling moral obligations to those displaced by economic hardship, conflict, or environmental disasters.

Realism approaches migration from the standpoint of national interest and security. Realists are likely to prioritize the control of borders to protect economic interests and maintain social stability. From this viewpoint, migration policies are crafted based on the benefits and risks to the nation-state, often leading to stricter immigration controls. Realists may argue that unregulated migration can strain a country's resources, disrupt social cohesion, and potentially introduce security threats, thus justifying rigorous controls and limited acceptance of refugees and migrants.

The cosmopolitan approach to migration is ethically appealing as it champions universal human rights and global solidarity. However, it often faces practical and political challenges in implementation, particularly in gaining the support of local populations in host countries. In contrast, while realism may offer more politically feasible solutions that preserve state sovereignty and security, it frequently does so at the expense of ignoring broader ethical responsibilities and humanitarian needs.

II. International Conflicts

IN DEALING WITH INTERNATIONAL conflicts, cosmopolitans emphasize the importance of international law and institutions to mediate and resolve disputes justly. They advocate for global governance mechanisms that can enforce peace and facilitate fair solutions, often supporting international interventions sanctioned by global consensus to prevent atrocities. Cosmopolitanism calls for a stronger role for international courts and multilateral organizations in conflict resolution and upholding the rule of law across borders.

Realists view international conflicts through the lens of power politics and national interest. They are generally skeptical of international interventions and the efficacy of global institutions, arguing that such entities reflect the interests of powerful states rather than any genuine moral consensus. For realists, the primary means of managing conflicts involve bilateral or regional power balances, deterrence strategies, and occasionally, military interventions when vital national interests are at stake.

While cosmopolitan solutions align closely with ideals of global justice and the universal application of moral principles, they may overlook the complex realities of political power and the often-parochial interests of states. Realist strategies, though perhaps more pragmatic and attuned to the geopolitical landscape, risk perpetuating injustice by prioritizing state interests over the welfare of individuals and disregarding the moral imperatives of global human rights.

Given these assessments, neither framework is entirely sufficient on its own to address all aspects of global challenges justly. A more nuanced approach, possibly integrating elements of both theories, might be necessary:

122

Developing a framework that combines the realist acknowledgment of state interests and power dynamics with the cosmopolitan commitment to universal moral values and human rights could lead to more effective and just solutions. This might involve crafting international policies that are both ethically informed and politically feasible. Tailoring responses to specific contexts and challenges can help balance ethical imperatives with practical considerations. For instance, in migration policy, this might mean combining the protection of refugee rights with measures that ensure the social and economic integration of migrants in ways that are sensitive to the capacities and concerns of host communities. Additionally, enhancing the legitimacy and effectiveness of international institutions to make them more responsive and equitable can also help bridge the gap between cosmopolitan ideals and realist pragmatics. This could involve reforming voting structures, increasing transparency, and ensuring that these bodies are genuinely representative of the global population.

While no single theoretical framework offers a panacea for global challenges, a philosophically informed approach that synthesizes the strengths of both cosmopolitanism and realism might provide a more robust and just basis for addressing the complex issues of our interconnected world.

III. *John Rawls' Bridging Framework in "The Law of Peoples"*

JOHN RAWLS' WORK IN "*The Law of Peoples*" provides a compelling philosophical approach that seeks to mediate between the broad ethical aspirations of cosmopolitanism and the pragmatic concerns of realism within the sphere of international relations. By extending his seminal theory of justice into the international domain, Rawls crafts a nuanced framework that accommodates the principles of liberal and 'decent' societies, while setting boundaries that respect state sovereignty and the diversity of cultural and political organizations globally.

Rawls differentiates between "*liberal peoples*," who govern according to democratic norms and respect individual rights, and "*decent peoples*," whose political structures may not be liberal but still adhere to principles of justice and respect human rights. His approach introduces a tiered system of international engagement, where interactions and expectations are adjusted based on the nature of the political entities involved. I've distributed the essence into the following bullets for an easier understanding of the core principles for the reader:

- Rawls advocates for a baseline respect for human rights that all societies, liberal or decent, should uphold. This respect forms the foundation of international law and order, ensuring that despite differing internal policies, all states adhere to certain universal standards that protect human dignity. Concurrently, he supports the principle of fair trade, arguing that economic interactions on the global stage should be conducted in a manner that respects the sovereignty of participating nations and seeks mutual benefit, avoiding exploitative practices that have historically marred international trade relations.

- Unlike more radical cosmopolitan theories that demand extensive global redistribution to achieve economic equality, Rawls proposes a more moderate approach. He acknowledges the importance of aiding less fortunate societies but frames this aid as a matter of ethical duty rather than a coercive obligation. This stance strikes a balance, aiming to alleviate severe poverty and support the development of political and civil institutions without imposing overwhelming economic demands on more affluent nations.

- Rawls supports the concept of humanitarian duties, but he insists that these duties must be feasible and not overly burdensome. He emphasizes that while wealthier nations should assist poorer ones, particularly in times of crisis, the extent of this assistance must be calibrated to what can reasonably be expected without compromising the assisting nation's own stability and priorities.

Rawls' framework effectively bridges the gap between cosmopolitanism's idealistic global ethics and realism's focus on state interest and sovereignty. By establishing a principled yet flexible approach to international relations, Rawls allows for 'Ethical Engagement,' encouraging states to engage ethically on the global stage, promoting policies that respect human rights and fair trade without requiring the relinquishment of national sovereignty or cultural identity. He also advocates for a practical morality that recognizes the complexities of international politics, where ethical goals must be pursued within the constraints of what is politically feasible and culturally respectful. Finally, recognizing the legitimacy of different types of political entities and cultural arrangements, Rawls widens the scope of international cooperation and dialogue. His approach offers several key philosophical insights for handling contemporary global challenges:

- **Flexibility in Application:** His framework's flexibility allows it to be applied to a variety of international issues, from migration crises to environmental policies, adapting ethical principles to fit the real-world context.

- **Moral and Political Balance:** It maintains a balance between moral obligations and political realities, ensuring that the pursuit of justice does not undermine the practical governance and security needs of individual states.

- **Inclusivity in Global Dialogue:** By recognizing the validity of various political and cultural entities, Rawls' theory fosters a more inclusive global dialogue that respects the autonomy of different societies while promoting a shared commitment to universal principles of justice.

In essence, John Rawls' "The Law of Peoples" presents a coherent and viable philosophical model that offers more just solutions to global problems by harmonizing ethical imperatives with the practical demands of international relations. This model provides a framework for understanding and addressing global challenges that respect both the diversity of the world's peoples and the shared human values that unite them.

3.2 State Sovereignty

Globalization has profoundly reshaped the traditional concept of state sovereignty, initiating a significant shift in power dynamics from national governments to international bodies and global markets. This transformation challenges the long-standing Westphalian notion of sovereignty, which emphasizes territorial integrity, political independence, and the legal equality of states. Established in the seventeenth century, this framework has served as the cornerstone of international relations, but the complex forces unleashed by globalization necessitate a reevaluation of these foundational principles.

The rise of international organizations and supranational entities marks a notable shift towards a global governance system that demands some degree of sovereignty cession. For instance, EU member states are required to align certain domestic laws with broader EU directives, which can supersede national legislation in critical areas like trade, immigration, and environmental regulations, reflecting a significant surrender of national legislative autonomy in favor of a collective regional interest.

Simultaneously, economic globalization has created an unprecedented level of integration in global markets, empowering MNCs to operate across borders with an efficiency that often circumvents or undermines national regulatory frameworks. This empowerment of MNCs and the influence of global financial markets challenge traditional state sovereignty by constraining the ability of governments to control economic activities within their territories. National policies intended to benefit the local economy can be significantly influenced or obstructed by external economic pressures and the strategic interests of global corporate actors.

This evolving landscape has prompted a shift from a strictly territorial view of sovereignty to a more in-depth, functional perspective, where sovereignty is increasingly seen in terms of a state's capacity to regulate and manage activities within its borders effectively. This includes addressing modern challenges such as cyber security, environmental protection, and economic regulation that require extensive international cooperation. The notion of shared sovereignty has also emerged, reflecting a pragmatic adaptation where states collaborate and share governance on issues of common global concern, such as climate change and international crime, through treaties and multinational agreements.

Moreover, the global emphasis on human rights often conflicts with the Westphalian model, which traditionally prioritizes the rights of states over those of individuals. The international community's interventions in instances of severe human rights abuses pose significant ethical and legal challenges to the non-interventionist stance that is a hallmark of Westphalian sovereignty. Additionally, the rise of powerful non-state actors, including terrorist organizations and multinational corporations, along with the importance of cyberspace as a realm of both conflict and cooperation, further complicates traditional notions of state control and governance.

Effectively, globalization has not merely challenged the traditional understanding of sovereignty but has necessitated its transformation to accommodate the realities of an interconnected global environment. As states navigate this new world, *sovereignty is increasingly characterized by the ability to effectively participate in and contribute to a global system that balances national interests with global responsibilities.* This ongoing evolution in the concept of sovereignty highlights the need for philosophical, legal, and political innovation to address the complexities of a world where borders are both physically porous and digitally dissolvable, requiring a redefined approach to sovereignty that is fit for the twenty-first century.

I. Bodin and Hobbes: Authority of Nation-States

JEAN BODIN introduced the concept of sovereignty in the late 16th century as the absolute and perpetual power of a state, a concept that was revolutionary in framing the modern understanding of nation-state governance. Bodin's assertion that sovereign power must be undivided and unrestricted within the confines of the state provides a baseline for discussing how globalization affects state authority. In parallel, Thomas Hobbes later reinforced this view in his portrayal of the sovereign as an absolute authority that prevents societal regression into chaos and war, as described in his seminal work, "***Leviathan***."

Transitioning to the modern era, the processes of globalization have challenged these traditional notions of sovereignty. The rise of MNCs, international non-governmental organizations, and supranational entities suggest that sovereignty is no longer exclusively or predominantly the domain of individual nation-states. Instead, sovereignty has become more diffused, shared among various actors on the global stage, which often operate across national borders and sometimes in conflict with national laws. This diffusion raises critical questions about the erosion of state authority as posited by Bodin and Hobbes. For example, the ability of international bodies to influence national policies on trade, environmental standards, and human rights often comes into tension with national laws and interests, suggesting a limitation on the absolute nature of state sovereignty.

Contemporary political philosophers have grappled with these issues, debating whether globalization ultimately enhances or undermines state authority. Some argue that globalization, through the spread of democratic values and international human rights norms, enhances state authority by promoting governance structures that are more transparent, accountable, and aligned with global standards. Others contend that globalization undermines state sovereignty by imposing external constraints on domestic decision-making processes and prioritizing global interests at the expense of national priorities. Philosophers like ***Jurgen Habermas*** and ***David Held*** offer perspectives that seek a middle ground, advocating for a cosmopolitan model of governance where sovereignty is re-conceptualized to include multiple layers of authority that operate both within and beyond the nation-state. This model suggests that sovereignty can be expanded rather than diminished, with states participating in a broader network of governance that enhances their legitimacy and efficacy in solving global problems.

The philosophical challenge lies in balancing the realities of global interdependence with the traditional value placed on national autonomy. This balance requires a rethinking of sovereignty not as a barrier to external influence but as a framework for engagement in the global arena. It involves states asserting their authority not through isolation but through strategic cooperation and engagement in international systems that respect their sovereignty while addressing global challenges like climate change, international trade, and cybersecurity.

Consequently, the question of whether globalization enhances or undermines the authority of nation-states does not have a straightforward answer but depends on how sovereignty is defined and exercised in an increasingly interconnected world. *The philosophical discourse suggests that a reconfigured understanding of sovereignty, one that accommodates the realities of globalization while respecting the autonomy of nation-states, may offer the most promising path forward.* This approach requires an ongoing dialogue among philosophers, policymakers, and global citizens to continually adapt and refine our concepts of governance and sovereignty in response to the evolving global landscape.

II. The EU and State Sovereignty

THE EU STANDS AS A paramount example of supranational governance and its complex interaction with the sovereignty of its member states. As an entity that integrates several nations into a cohesive political and economic union, the EU challenges traditional notions of sovereignty through shared governance and law-making mechanisms. This deep integration impacts member states' sovereignty particularly in the areas of trade, immigration, and legal systems.

First, the EU's common trade policy is a significant area where the sovereignty of member states is both enhanced and limited. By negotiating as a single bloc, EU countries benefit from stronger bargaining power on the global stage, which can lead to more favorable trade agreements and access to larger markets than any single member could achieve independently. This collective power is evident in trade deals such as the Comprehensive Economic and Trade Agreement (CETA) with Canada, which was negotiated by the EU on behalf of its members, offering them extensive economic benefits. However, individual member states lose the ability to negotiate bilateral trade agreements that might better suit their own economic contexts or priorities. They must conform to the trade policies and tariffs set by the EU, which are designed to benefit the Union as a whole but may not always align with the specific needs or desires of individual countries. This loss of control over national trade policies is a significant concession of sovereignty that member states make upon joining the EU.

In the context of immigration, the EU's Schengen Area abolishes internal borders, allowing for passport-free movement of people across most member states. This arrangement enhances the freedom of movement for EU citizens and reflects a shared commitment to open internal borders. However, it also requires a collective approach to external border controls and asylum policies, which can be contentious. The sovereignty of individual member states is impacted by EU directives and regulations that dictate common standards and procedures for handling asylum seekers and migrants. The 2015 migration crisis illustrated the challenges of this shared sovereignty, as the sudden influx of refugees tested the EU's external borders and challenged the internal cohesion among member states regarding how best to handle the crisis. Countries like Hungary and Poland resisted EU plans to distribute asylum seekers among member states, citing national sovereignty and security concerns, which highlighted the tension between national prerogatives and collective EU policies.

Lastly, the impact of EU law on the legal systems of member states is perhaps the most direct influence on national sovereignty. EU law has primacy over national laws, meaning that in cases of conflict between EU law and the law of a member state, EU law generally prevails. This principle is enshrined in the Treaty on the Functioning of the European Union and has been upheld by the European Court of Justice, the EU's highest judicial authority. This arrangement ensures uniformity and consistency in the application of EU law across all member states, which is crucial for the functioning of the single market and the enforcement of EU-wide policies and regulations. However, it also means that member states must sometimes alter or override their domestic laws, including those passed by democratically elected national parliaments, to comply with EU legislation and court decisions. This can be seen as a significant encroachment on national legal sovereignty and has been a point of contention in areas such as environmental regulation, consumer protection, and labor laws.

Analyzing the European Union reveals the balance between the benefits of supranational governance and the compromises on national sovereignty that such an arrangement requires. The EU model illustrates how sovereignty can be reconfigured to meet collective goals and challenges, but it also underscores the ongoing tension between upholding national interests and committing to a shared, supranational legal and political framework. This balance is continually negotiated and renegotiated as the dynamics within the Union evolve, reflecting the complex realities of modern governance in an interconnected world.

As discussed, this relationship produces significant tensions and advantages, highlighted vividly in events like Brexit and the EU's handling of the migration crisis. These instances provide critical insights into the practical implications of supranational governance on national sovereignty and the internal dynamics of the Union.

Brexit, the United Kingdom's decision to leave the European Union, serves as a pivotal case study in the tensions inherent in supranational governance. The pro-Brexit campaign was heavily predicated on the notion of "***taking back control***" of British laws, borders, and money, emphasizing a perceived loss of national sovereignty to EU institutions. This sentiment was driven by various factors, including EU regulations perceived as onerous or ill-suited to the UK's interests, and contributions to the EU budget which some British critics argued offered inadequate returns.

The benefits of EU membership, such as access to the single market, freedom of movement, and a strong voice in one of the world's largest trading blocs, were often overshadowed in public discourse by concerns about the democratic deficit and the bureaucracy of the EU. Brexit highlighted the challenge of aligning national sovereignty with obligations to a supranational body, showing that while the EU aims to foster unity among its members, it can also provoke strong nationalist and separatist sentiments. However, the aftermath of Brexit also highlights the challenges of disentangling from the EU's integrated systems. Trade disruptions, economic uncertainty, and the complex issue of the Northern Ireland border illustrate the difficulties and potential economic downsides of reclaiming national sovereignty in such an interconnected environment.

The EU's handling of the migration crisis in 2015 further illustrates the tensions within supranational governance, particularly in the areas of border control and immigration policy. The Schengen Agreement, which allows for passport-free movement across most of the EU, was put under tremendous pressure as member states grappled with unprecedented inflows of refugees and migrants. Countries like Greece and Italy, where many migrants first arrived, felt abandoned by other member states as they struggled to handle the influx. The crisis highlighted the limitations of the Dublin Regulation, which mandates that asylum claims be processed in the first country of entry, placing disproportionate pressure on these front-line nations.

In response, the EU proposed quotas to redistribute asylum seekers across the Union, but this was met with resistance from several member states that viewed the quotas as an infringement on their national sovereignty. Countries like Hungary and Poland opposed the scheme, citing security concerns and the right to control their own borders. This resistance showcases the friction between national interests and collective EU policies, revealing deep divides over solidarity and responsibility-sharing within the Union.

These examples illustrate that while supranational governance can bring economic benefits, increased security, and collective bargaining power, it also poses challenges to national sovereignty and traditional notions of state autonomy. The tension between collective action and national prerogatives can lead to significant discord and inefficiencies within the Union. The benefits of supranational governance, such as maintaining peace, facilitating economic integration, and collectively addressing global issues like climate change, are substantial. Yet, the challenges, particularly in reconciling diverse political, economic, and cultural perspectives within a unified legal framework, are equally formidable.

Critically, the future of supranational governance in the EU and similar bodies will depend on their ability to balance these benefits and tensions effectively. Enhancing mechanisms for democratic participation, ensuring fair and equitable policy impacts, and maintaining flexibility in integration levels may provide pathways to mitigate these tensions while preserving the advantages of a united approach to complex global challenges.

III. Balance of Power: Federalism and Confederalism

THE EU IS A UNIQUE and ambitious form of supranational governance that blends elements of *federalism* and *confederalism*, offering a distinctive model that might serve as a blueprint for other regions. The philosophical implications of this model, particularly in the context of its recent challenges and developments such as Brexit and the migration crisis, provoke a thought-provoking discourse on the nature of sovereignty, governance, and international cooperation.

The EU incorporates aspects of both federalism and confederalism, creating a hybrid system that maintains national sovereignty while pooling certain powers at a supranational level. Federalism typically involves a strong central authority governing a collection of states that relinquish some degree of sovereignty to achieve greater collective benefits. In contrast, confederalism is a loose arrangement where sovereign states voluntarily cooperate on common issues but retain more control over their internal affairs.

The EU's structure allows for collective decision-making in areas like trade, agriculture, and competition law, which are governed by EU institutions such as the European Commission, the European Parliament, and the European Court of Justice. These institutions have substantial authority to make and enforce laws that member states must comply with, reflecting a federalist approach. However, member states retain significant powers, especially in key areas such as foreign policy and defense, which aligns more closely with confederalist principles.

The blending of federalism and confederalism raises enticing philosophical questions about the nature of sovereignty and the right balance between local autonomy and collective action. The tension between these can be seen in the debates within the EU about how much power should be centralized and how member states can protect their own interests within a larger political entity. From a philosophical standpoint, the EU challenges traditional Westphalian notions of sovereignty, which emphasize absolute state control over territory and internal affairs. The EU model suggests a post-sovereign order where sovereignty is not abolished but transformed, shared among multiple levels of governance in ways that are meant to benefit all members.

This transformation is consistent with the ***principles of subsidiarity***, a key element in both federalist and confederalist theories, which holds that decisions should be made as closely as possible to the citizens they affect. The EU strives to apply this principle, though its implementation is often contested, particularly when member states feel that the EU is overreaching.

Considering the EU as a blueprint for other regions requires assessing both its successes and its shortcomings. The EU has undoubtedly achieved significant accomplishments, including the promotion of peace, the creation of a single market, and the facilitation of free movement for work and study, which have contributed to the prosperity and stability of the region. However, the EU's struggles with issues like the migration crisis and the rise of Euroscepticism highlight the challenges of maintaining unity in diversity. These challenges underscore the need for continual adaptation and reform to address disparities and discontent within the Union.

For other regions considering similar integration efforts, EU model provides valuable lessons:

- **The Importance of Flexibility:** Adapting the level of integration to the needs and circumstances of member states is crucial. The EU's experiences suggest that overly rigid structures or policies that do not account for diverse national contexts can lead to tensions and resistance.

- **Democratic Participation:** Enhancing mechanisms for democratic participation and ensuring that citizens feel represented at the supranational level can help mitigate feelings of detachment from the decision-making process.

- **Economic Convergence:** Efforts to balance economic disparities within the union are vital for its stability and legitimacy. The EU's cohesion policies aimed at reducing regional disparities can serve as a model for other integrated areas.

In effect, while the EU model is not without its flaws, its hybrid approach to federalism and confederalism offers a compelling framework for regions seeking deeper integration. Philosophically, it proposes a rethinking of sovereignty and governance that could be increasingly relevant in an interconnected global environment. By drawing on the lessons from the EU, other regions might find ways to design their own integrated systems that respect both diversity and the need for effective collective action.

3.3 Democratic Deficit

Global governance presents unique challenges to democratic principles, primarily through issues of representation and accountability in international organizations. These challenges can often result in what is termed a "***democratic deficit***," where the structures and processes of global governance fail to meet the standards of democratic legitimacy that are expected in national contexts. Analyzing these challenges requires an exploration into the mechanisms of global governance and the philosophical underpinnings of democracy.

One of the primary challenges in global governance is the issue of representation. International organizations often struggle with representing their member states equitably. The principle of sovereign equality, while nominally upheld, does not always translate into equal influence. For example, in the UN Security Council, the veto power held by the five permanent members (China, France, Russia, the United Kingdom, and the United States) can lead to situations where the interests of smaller or less powerful nations are overlooked or overridden, as recently witnessed in the Israel-Hamas conflict.

Moreover, the method of representation often does not adequately reflect the global population. Most international organizations are state-based, where governments represent the interests of their people. However, this raises questions about how well these governments represent their citizens in international forums, especially in non-democratic or partially democratic countries. Furthermore, global civil society, comprising NGOs, advocacy groups, and citizens, often finds itself without a direct voice in these organizations, even though the decisions made can have a significant impact on global civil society.

Closely tied to the issue of representation is the challenge of accountability. International organizations are typically accountable to their member states rather than directly to the citizens of those states. This indirect accountability can lead to a detachment of the organizations' policies and decisions from the preferences and interests of the global populace. The processes within many international bodies lack transparency, making it difficult for citizens to understand and influence what is decided on their behalf. For instance, negotiations in the WTO and treaty formations in the IMF are often conducted behind closed doors, with limited input from or disclosure to the public. This lack of transparency can contribute to a democratic deficit by obscuring the decision-making process and diminishing the ability of citizens to hold these organizations to account through democratic means.

The concept of a democratic deficit in global governance refers to the gap between the democratic credentials that these organizations are expected to have and what they actually possess. This deficit can undermine the legitimacy of international organizations and their decisions, especially when those decisions have far-reaching implications for national policies and individual rights.

One prominent example is the EU, which has often been criticized for its own democratic deficit. Critics argue that the decision-making processes within EU institutions are too removed from direct democratic control. The European Commission, which has significant executive powers, is composed of members appointed by national governments rather than directly elected by EU citizens. While the European Parliament does have elected representatives, it historically had limited legislative powers, although this has improved with successive treaties.

From a philosophical perspective, addressing the democratic deficits in global governance involves *rethinking the concepts of sovereignty, democracy, and legitimacy* on a global scale. Political philosophers like **Jürgen Habermas** have suggested ways to enhance the democratic legitimacy of international organizations, including increasing transparency, fostering greater public participation in international decision-making, and strengthening the roles of transnational parliaments and assemblies. To mitigate the issues of representation and accountability, international organizations could implement more inclusive decision-making processes that involve a broader array of stakeholders, including non-governmental actors, increase transparency by opening up meetings and negotiations to the public or by providing more comprehensive reporting on activities and decisions, and strengthen the role of international judicial bodies, such as the International Court of Justice, in overseeing the actions of international organizations to ensure they comply with international law and uphold democratic principles.

While global governance is crucial for addressing international issues that no single nation can manage alone, it must evolve to overcome significant challenges related to democratic principles. Enhancing representation and accountability within international organizations is critical to reducing the democratic deficit and increasing the legitimacy and effectiveness of global governance. To critically assess these mechanisms of accountability and propose ways global governance can be restructured to better align with democratic ideals, we must dive into the specifics of how these entities operate and their impact on global politics and economics.

I. World Bank and IMF

THE WORLD BANK AND IMF, often referred to as the *Bretton Woods Institutions*, are integral in managing global economic stability and development. However, their decision-making processes have been criticized for a lack of transparency and unequal voting power. Votes in these institutions are not distributed equally but are instead weighted based on financial contributions. As a result, wealthier nations, particularly the United States and other Western countries, wield disproportionate influence over the policies and priorities of these institutions. This arrangement undermines the principle of democratic equality and often leads to policies that reflect the interests of the most powerful countries at the expense of smaller or less wealthy nations.

- **Equal Representation:** Implementing a more equitable voting system that reduces the disparity in influence between rich and poor countries could help democratize these institutions. One proposal is the "one country, one vote" system, or at least adjusting the current system to increase the voice of developing nations.

- **Transparency and Engagement:** Increasing transparency in decision-making processes and enhancing the engagement of all stakeholders, including civil society and affected communities, could improve the legitimacy and effectiveness of the IMF and World Bank's initiatives.

- **Accountability Mechanisms:** Establishing stronger mechanisms for accountability, such as independent oversight bodies that can review and assess the impact of their policies on development and human rights, is crucial.

II. Transnational Corporations (TNCs)

TNCS HAVE ECONOMIC power that rivals that of states, influencing global trade, investment, and labor markets. The governance of these corporations is typically centered around shareholder interests, with minimal input from other stakeholders affected by their operations, such as workers, local communities, and the environment. This corporate governance model often leads to decisions that maximize profits at the expense of broader social and environmental concerns.

- **Stakeholder Involvement:** Expanding the governance structures of TNCs to include representatives from a broader range of stakeholders could help balance profit motives with social and environmental responsibilities.

- **Regulatory Frameworks:** Enhancing international regulatory frameworks to hold TNCs accountable for the social and environmental impacts of their operations worldwide. This could include mechanisms for enforcing international labor rights and environmental standards.

- **Corporate Transparency:** Increasing the transparency of TNC operations, including supply chains and financial transactions, to allow stakeholders and regulators to hold corporations accountable.

To align global governance structures with democratic ideals, a comprehensive restructuring is necessary. This restructuring should aim to reduce the dominance of powerful countries and corporations, enhance the representativeness and inclusiveness of international institutions, and increase their accountability to the global public.

- **Enhanced Multilateralism:** Strengthening multilateral institutions to ensure they are more representative and capable of managing global issues cooperatively. This involves reforming voting and decision-making processes to ensure fairer representation of different countries and stakeholders.

- **Global Legal Frameworks:** Developing and enforcing global legal frameworks that can oversee and regulate international economic activities to protect human rights and the environment.

- **Public Participation:** Creating mechanisms for greater public participation in global governance, such as global forums or referenda on significant international policies and agreements.

Essentially, while the mechanisms of global decision-making in entities like the World Bank, IMF, and transnational corporations have facilitated international cooperation and economic development, they also exhibit significant democratic deficits. Restructuring these mechanisms to enhance fairness, accountability, and transparency is imperative to ensure that global governance aligns with democratic ideals and effectively addresses the challenges of a complex, interconnected world.

3.4 The United Nations (UN)

The UN, established in the aftermath of World War II, serves as a central pillar in global governance, tasked with upholding international peace and security, promoting human rights, and cultivating social and economic development. Its role as a global governing body is complex and multifaceted, subject to ongoing scrutiny and debate regarding its effectiveness and legitimacy. Evaluating the UN involves examining its significant achievements against its notable limitations, which reveal the inherent challenges of managing global issues through an international framework.

The UN has marked several successes, notably in peacekeeping and conflict resolution. It has deployed numerous peacekeeping missions worldwide, playing a central role in stabilizing regions post-conflict and preventing further escalation of disputes. Successful interventions in Liberia, Sierra Leone, and the Balkans highlight the organization's capacity to manage complex operations under challenging conditions. Furthermore, the UN has been instrumental in coordinating humanitarian relief efforts in response to natural disasters, famines, and conflicts. Agencies such as the United Nations Children's Fund (UNICEF) and the World Food Programme (WFP) have efficiently delivered aid, underscoring the UN's critical role in global humanitarian efforts.

Another significant achievement is the advancement of human rights, anchored by the Universal Declaration of Human Rights in 1948. Through its various councils and committees, the UN has actively worked to promote and protect human rights across the globe. However, the organization faces substantial challenges that impact its effectiveness. It is often criticized for its bureaucratic inefficiencies and slow response times, which can impede its ability to act decisively. The structure of the UN, requiring consensus among its members, particularly within the Security Council, can lead to prolonged deliberations and stasis. The veto power held by the five permanent members often results in gridlocks, particularly visible in situations like the Syrian conflict where conflicting interests of major powers thwart collective action.

Moreover, the UN's limited enforcement capabilities, relying on member states for troop contributions and adherence to resolutions, further complicates its operational efficacy. This dependency dilutes its ability to enforce mandates robustly, often leading to compromised execution of its objectives.

The UN's legitimacy is derived from several sources, including its universal membership and the legal authority of the UN Charter. Representing nearly all sovereign states lends the organization a broad mandate, reinforcing its position as a universal platform for international cooperation. The legal frameworks established under the UN Charter provide a structured basis for international law and norms, bolstering its role as a guardian of global order.

However, the UN's legitimacy is not without challenges. The representation within its key bodies, particularly the Security Council, is often criticized for not reflecting contemporary global power dynamics. The permanent membership and veto power are seen as anachronistic, favoring post-World War II realities that no longer align with today's geopolitical landscape. This misalignment raises questions about the fairness and equity of the UN's decision-making processes.

Furthermore, the organization's interventions in sovereign nations are sometimes perceived as infringements on national sovereignty, complicating its legitimacy, especially when such actions are seen as serving the interests of powerful member states rather than broader international justice.

Enhancing both the effectiveness and legitimacy of the UN may require substantial reforms. Revising the Security Council's composition and veto privileges could render it more representative and functional. Improving transparency and accountability mechanisms within UN agencies and their operations could address inefficiencies and enhance performance. Moreover, broadening the involvement of non-state actors, NGOs, civil society, and the broader public, could democratize its processes, making the organization more reflective of global public opinion and thus bolster its legitimacy.

The UN is structured to address a wide array of global issues through its various organs and agencies, each designed with specific roles and responsibilities. Central to its structure are the General Assembly, the Security Council, the Economic and Social Council, the International Court of Justice, and the UN Secretariat. These bodies collectively strive to facilitate cooperation and address international issues such as peace and security, economic development, social progress, human rights, and international law. However, the effectiveness of these bodies often varies due to structural and operational challenges.

I. The General Assembly

THE GENERAL ASSEMBLY is the main deliberative body of the UN and is composed of all 193 member states, each with an equal vote, embodying the principle of sovereign equality among large and small states alike. It serves as a forum for multilateral discussion of the full spectrum of international issues covered by the Charter. The General Assembly passes non-binding resolutions that reflect member states' opinions and direct actions towards major general issues like development, peace and security, and international law. While its resolutions are not legally binding, they have a strong impact on normative behaviors and provide a foundation for international law.

II. The United Nations Security Council (UNSC)

THE SECURITY COUNCIL is arguably the most powerful body within the UN, charged with maintaining international peace and security. It has 15 members, including five permanent members (China, France, Russia, the United Kingdom, and the United States) who hold veto power, allowing them to block any substantive resolution. This structure is intended to reflect the power dynamics of the post-World War II international order but has often been criticized as outdated given the contemporary geopolitical landscape. The Council's ability to make decisions that are legally binding and enforceable gives it significant power to influence international relations, manage conflicts, and authorize peacekeeping missions, military actions, and economic sanctions.

The veto power of the five permanent members is the most significant challenge, often leading to paralysis within the body, particularly when the interests of these members clash. For example, resolutions on the Syrian conflict have been repeatedly vetoed by Russia and China, preventing international action. This has led to criticisms of the Council as being ineffective and unrepresentative, prompting calls for reform, such as expansion of the membership or modifications to the veto process to better reflect the current global power structure and to enhance its legitimacy and functionality.

III. The Economic and Social Council (ECOSOC)

ECOSOC SERVES AS THE central platform for discussing international economic and social issues and formulating policy recommendations addressed to member states and the UN system. It is responsible for promoting higher standards of living, full employment, and economic and social progress; identifying solutions to international economic, social and health problems; facilitating international cultural and educational cooperation; and encouraging universal respect for human rights and fundamental freedoms. Its broad mandate under the UN Charter enables it to initiate studies and reports on various issues, and to host forums where stakeholders can discuss global economic and social issues.

IV. The International Court of Justice

THE INTERNATIONAL COURT of Justice, located in The Hague, serves as the judicial arm of the UN. It settles disputes between states in accordance with international law and gives advisory opinions on international legal issues referred to it by the General Assembly or Security Council. While its rulings are binding, enforcement remains challenging if countries do not accept its jurisdiction or comply with judgments, undermining its effectiveness in resolving international disputes.

V. The UN Secretariat

THE UN SECRETARIAT, headed by the Secretary-General, provides studies, information, and facilities needed by the UN for its meetings and the execution of its functions. The Secretariat's role is primarily administrative, but the Secretary-General can bring to the attention of the Security Council any matter that, in their opinion, may threaten international peace and security. The effectiveness of the Secretariat often depends on the charisma and leadership qualities of the Secretary-General, as well as their ability to navigate complex political dynamics among member states.

The UN's structure is uniquely positioned to address a multitude of global issues through its various organs. However, the effectiveness of these bodies is frequently constrained by geopolitical realities, the non-binding nature of General Assembly resolutions, the veto power within the Security Council, and the challenges of enforcement at the International Court of Justice. Reforming these structures and mechanisms to better reflect the current global order and to enhance their effectiveness and responsiveness remains an ongoing debate among member states and global governance scholars.

VI. Veto Power

CENTRAL TO THE CRITICISM of the UN, is the veto power held by the five permanent members of the Security Council (P5): the United States, Russia, China, France, and the United Kingdom. This power, along with perceived political biases and the overall capacity of the UN to enforce its mandates, raises significant ethical and philosophical questions concerning justice, legitimacy, and governance.

The veto power allows any one of the P5 to block any substantive Security Council resolution, even if it has broad international support.

Philosophically, this raises questions about the principle of justice and equality among nations. In theory, the UN is an international body that represents the interests of all sovereign states equally. However, the veto power contradicts this principle by granting disproportionate influence to five member states, often at the expense of smaller or less powerful nations. This imbalance can lead to a perception of the UN as an inequitable institution where power dynamics, rather than justice or moral right, dictate international law and order.

Instances such as the veto of resolutions aimed at stopping the Syrian civil war, the Israel-Hamas conflict, or addressing the crisis in Ukraine highlight how veto power can be used in service of national interest rather than global justice. These actions bring to light the ethical dilemma posed by the veto, while it was originally intended to prevent the UN from taking actions that could lead to major power conflicts, it has also been used to shield allies from international scrutiny or intervention, often leading to prolonged human suffering.

The UN's effectiveness is also hampered by political biases that can influence its actions and decisions. These biases are often a reflection of the dominant geopolitical influences within its key bodies, particularly the Security Council. For instance, the influence of major powers in the Security Council can lead to a selective approach to international law enforcement, where some violations are addressed more vigorously than others. This selectivity undermines the UN's legitimacy, as it appears to apply principles of international law inconsistently.

Philosophical discussions about the legitimacy of such an institution often hinge on its adherence to principles of impartial justice, as articulated by philosophers like John Rawls. Rawls' theory suggests that for an institution to be considered legitimate, it must operate under a veil of ignorance, where decisions are made without considering the interests of specific people or groups. However, the evident biases in the UN's operations challenge its legitimacy under these criteria.

Reforming the veto power has been a subject of ongoing debate. Proposals range from completely abolishing it to limiting its use to vital national security issues. Philosophically, these reforms aim to realign the UN with the ethical principles of equality and justice among nations, enhancing its moral authority and legitimacy. For instance, introducing a majority override of the veto, as suggested by some scholars and international diplomats, could help mitigate the unilateral blocking of resolutions that have widespread international support. Enhancing the transparency of the Security Council's deliberations could also address issues of bias and legitimacy. By making proceedings more open, the international community could hold permanent members accountable for their use of the veto, potentially curbing its use in protecting national interests at the expense of broader international justice.

The criticisms of the UN related to veto power, political biases, and its capacity to enforce international law are deeply intertwined with philosophical considerations of justice, legitimacy, and ethical governance. Addressing these criticisms requires not only structural reforms but also a recommitment to the foundational ethical principles that should guide international relations. By reassessing the distribution of power within its institutions and striving for greater impartiality and fairness, the UN can better fulfill its role as a truly international body dedicated to maintaining global peace and advancing the common good.

3.5 Globalization and International Conflict

In the contemporary world, the emergence of global terrorism, cyber warfare, and international conflicts represents some of the most pressing challenges to global security and governance. These phenomena stretch the capacities of traditional political frameworks and demand a reevaluation of international law and security strategies. Engaging with these issues through the lenses of moral and political philosophy provides a deeper understanding of their ethical dimensions and helps frame appropriate responses.

Global terrorism has fundamentally challenged the concepts of national security and international peace. Terrorist acts, such as those perpetrated by al-Qaeda, ISIS, and other extremist groups, not only cause immediate harm but also seek to instigate widespread fear and disrupt societies. Philosophically, terrorism raises profound ethical questions about the balance between security and civil liberties. From a utilitarian perspective, the primary concern is the greatest good for the greatest number, which could justify extensive surveillance and stringent security measures. However, from a deontological standpoint, such measures often clash with individual rights and the intrinsic value of privacy and freedom, emphasizing that actions themselves must adhere to moral laws irrespective of outcomes.

The response to global terrorism must also consider the ethical implications of counter-terrorism measures, including military interventions and drone warfare. These responses often result in civilian casualties and can exacerbate the conditions that foster terrorism, such as social injustice and political oppression. Ethically, this cycle of violence challenges the just war theory, which holds that warfare must be morally justifiable through its causes, goals, and methods. Philosophers like **Michael Walzer** have examined these dilemmas, arguing for a moral framework that respects both the security of states and the rights of individuals, even in conflict zones.

Cyber warfare represents a new frontier in international conflict, involving state and non-state actors engaging in digital attacks that can cripple critical infrastructure, steal sensitive information, and spread disinformation. The anonymity and reach of cyber tactics pose unique challenges to traditional concepts of warfare and responsibility. Ethically, cyber warfare blurs the lines between civilian and military targets, raising significant concerns under the principles of distinction and proportionality in international humanitarian law. The philosophical debate surrounding cyber warfare involves assessing the moral status of cyber attacks compared to physical acts of war. *Are attacks that disable electrical grids or financial systems, potentially leading to loss of life and economic chaos, morally equivalent to traditional acts of war?* Philosophers like **Thomas Nagel** argue that the intentionality behind these acts, as well as their foreseeable consequences, play crucial roles in their ethical assessment.

International conflicts, whether territorial disputes, resource conflicts, or ideological confrontations, often reflect deeper issues of global injustice and inequality. Theories of global justice, such as those proposed by **Thomas Pogge**, suggest that many conflicts have roots in historical injustices and unequal distributions of resources. Pogge's approach calls for a restructuring of global institutions and relationships to address these fundamental inequities, proposing a cosmopolitan framework where individuals, not just states, are the primary subjects of global justice. Philosophical discussions on international conflict also involve the concept of sovereignty and the rights of states versus the rights of individuals or oppressed groups. The principle of non-intervention is challenged by situations where human rights are grossly violated, as seen in cases like Rwanda or Bosnia. Here, the responsibility to protect (R2P) doctrine emerges as a philosophical and practical response, arguing that the international community has a moral obligation to intervene when national governments fail to protect their citizens from atrocities.

Addressing the issues of global terrorism, cyber warfare, and international conflict requires an integrated approach that combines ethical reasoning, international law, and practical politics. Philosophically, this approach must navigate the delicate balance between respecting state sovereignty and fulfilling obligations to protect human rights globally. It must also critically assess the ethical implications of new forms of warfare and the global responses they necessitate. By fostering a discourse that is both ethically informed and pragmatically effective, we can hope to develop strategies that not only mitigate the impacts of these global challenges but also advance a more just and peaceful international order.

3.6 A Pragmatic View: The Syria Conflict

The Syrian conflict provides a compelling case study to examine how globalization has reshaped international conflicts and alliances. This section will utilize composite frameworks previously employed in discussions to dissect the layers of this crisis, considering the effects of international interests, humanitarian concerns, and the evolving nature of state sovereignty.

The Syrian conflict, which began as part of the Arab Spring uprisings in 2011, quickly escalated from a domestic civil war into a webbed international conflict involving multiple global powers and non-state actors. This conflict highlights how globalization has facilitated the rapid spread and escalation of local conflicts into global crises. The involvement of various countries, including Russia, the United States, Turkey, and Iran, as well as entities like ISIS, showcases the interconnected nature of contemporary geopolitical struggles, where local conflicts attract global attention and intervention.

From a cosmopolitan viewpoint, the international community's response to the Syrian crisis is a test of global moral obligations. Cosmopolitan ethics, which advocate for global justice and universal moral concern, would demand a concerted and humane international response aimed at protecting civilians and restoring peace. However, the realist perspective, which prioritizes national interest and power politics, often leads to interventions that are more about strategic interests than humanitarian needs, as seen in the proxy battles between different global powers on Syrian soil.

The intervention by various international actors in Syria poses significant ethical dilemmas related to sovereignty and the responsibility to protect (R2P). While globalization has enabled greater international cooperation and intervention in theory, in practice, it often complicates sovereignty issues. For example, the Syrian government's legitimacy has been questioned, yet it retains formal recognition at the United Nations. This situation challenges traditional notions of sovereignty and non-intervention, as articulated by philosophers like Jean Bodin and Thomas Hobbes, who emphasized the absolute authority of sovereign states over their territories.

Furthermore, the application of R2P in Syria has been contentious. Philosophically, R2P is supported by deontological ethics, which prioritize the duty to protect human life irrespective of national boundaries. However, the selective application of R2P, influenced by political interests rather than consistent ethical principles, has led to accusations of hypocrisy and ineffectiveness. This inconsistency undermines the moral authority of international law and global institutions, as they appear to be swayed by power politics rather than the principles of justice and human rights.

The humanitarian crisis in Syria, characterized by massive displacement, widespread casualties, and destruction, calls for a global response that transcends political interests. Utilitarian ethics, which advocate for actions that maximize well-being for the greatest number, would support robust humanitarian interventions. However, the actual global response has often fallen short, hindered by political disagreements and concerns over national security, particularly regarding the resettlement of refugees and the fight against terrorism. Marxist critiques of the situation might focus on how global capitalist interests influence the conflict, particularly in terms of arms sales and the geopolitical strategies of major powers seeking to control energy resources and trade routes in the region. This perspective sheds light on the underlying economic factors that perpetuate the conflict, suggesting that solutions must address these systemic issues to achieve lasting peace.

In the context of globalization, the Syria conflict also exemplifies the role of technology in modern conflicts. Cyber warfare and information wars have played significant roles, with various actors using digital platforms to influence public opinion, recruit fighters, and conduct cyber-attacks. The ethical governance of such technologies becomes a critical issue, as they can be used both to perpetuate violence and to facilitate peacekeeping and humanitarian efforts.

The Syria conflict, as examined through the prism of globalization, presents an array of international alliances, ethical dilemmas, and human suffering. Philosophical reflections on the conflict urge a reevaluation of how global justice, ethical intervention, and sovereignty are understood and implemented in an interconnected world. The case of Syria underscores the need for a global governance framework that is not only responsive and effective but also grounded in ethical principles that prioritize human dignity and global peace over national interests and power politics. The conflict acts as a microcosm of the broader challenges posed by globalization to international conflicts and alliances. It calls for a pragmatic yet ethically informed approach that can navigate the intricate dynamics of global interdependence, power politics, and human rights. This case study not only reflects the theoretical discussions in previous chapters but also provides a concrete instance of how globalization has transformed the global stage of international relations and conflict resolution.

3.7 A Pragmatic Response:

In response to the Syrian conflict, a pragmatic approach that aligns with the discussions on globalization's impact on international conflicts and alliances must be multifaceted. This approach should consider the roles of various international players, the underlying humanitarian crises, and the challenges posed to traditional concepts of state sovereignty and international law.

The conflict, exacerbated by the involvement of multiple global powers including Russia, the United States, Turkey, and Iran, alongside non-state actors like ISIS, highlights the need for a coordinated international strategy. This strategy should focus on de-escalating the conflict through diplomatic channels rather than unilateral or divisive actions that serve national interests over global peace. A cosmopolitan approach, advocating for a global responsibility to protect and uphold human rights, should guide these efforts. However, this must be balanced with a realistic understanding of the geopolitical landscape, ensuring that actions taken are not only ethical but also practical and effective in bringing about lasting peace.

The conflict challenges traditional notions of sovereignty, as the international community grapples with the Syrian government's legitimacy and the broader implications for international law. A pragmatic response would involve a renewed commitment to the principles of the United Nations and international law, particularly the Responsibility to Protect (R2P) doctrine. This doctrine needs to be applied consistently and impartially, ensuring that interventions are justified ethically and legally, not merely on strategic grounds. Moreover, the international community must address the limitations of current international frameworks in dealing with cases where state sovereignty is used as a shield for gross human rights violations.

Given the vast humanitarian crisis resulting from the conflict, including massive displacement and loss of life, a pragmatic approach necessitates a robust humanitarian response. Utilitarian ethics would dictate maximizing the well-being of the greatest number of people, which in this context means enhancing and expanding humanitarian aid, securing safe passages, and ensuring adequate resources for refugees and displaced persons. Moreover, international efforts must be made to rebuild war-torn regions, facilitate the safe return of refugees, and ensure that all parties respect and protect civilian populations.

Understanding the economic foundations of the conflict from a Marxist perspective involves recognizing how global capitalist interests, including arms sales and control over energy resources, have influenced the dynamics of the war. Addressing these underlying factors is crucial for resolving the conflict and ensuring that economic gains do not perpetuate warfare. A pragmatic solution would involve transparent discussions about these economic interests and seeking ways to mitigate their impact on the ongoing conflict.

A pragmatic response to modern warfare would involve the ethical governance of such technologies, ensuring they are used to promote peace and security rather than exacerbate conflict. This includes international agreements on cyber warfare, controls on the spread of misinformation, and the use of technology in monitoring ceasefires and humanitarian interventions.

The Syrian conflict requires a pragmatic yet ethically informed approach that navigates the web of international interests, humanitarian needs, and evolving legal norms. By integrating the philosophical insights discussed in previous chapters, particularly those related to globalization, sovereignty, and global justice, the international community can strive towards a more effective and humane resolution to the conflict. This approach would not only address the immediate needs arising from the conflict but also set a precedent for future international cooperation in a globalized world, ensuring that global governance structures are capable of addressing such crises more effectively and ethically.

I. Sovereignty and Intervention

IN THE REALM OF GLOBAL politics, the concept of sovereignty and the justification for international intervention represent crucial issues shaped profoundly by the forces of globalization. This complex dynamic challenges the Westphalian notion of sovereignty, which has traditionally emphasized the supremacy of the nation-state, free from external interference in its domestic affairs. However, as global interdependencies deepen, the sanctity of this principle is increasingly tested by international laws and norms that advocate for broader human rights protections and ethical responsibilities transcending national borders.

The principle of sovereignty, as enshrined since the *Treaty of Westphalia* in 1648, posits that each state has exclusive authority over its territory and domestic affairs. This concept has been a bedrock of international relations, ensuring stability and predictability among states. However, the advent of globalization has introduced a plethora of challenges to this framework. Economic integration, communication technology, and environmental issues are but a few arenas where the actions within one state can have significant repercussions beyond its borders, thereby necessitating some form of international oversight or intervention.

The tension between respecting state sovereignty and the need for international intervention is particularly pronounced in situations of human rights abuses and humanitarian crises. Philosophical and ethical debates arise around the conditions under which international entities, such as the UN or regional alliances, should intervene in the internal affairs of a sovereign state. This discourse often references ***just war theory***, which traditionally governs the moral justification for war but has been adapted to address the ethics of humanitarian intervention. The doctrine of the Responsibility to Protect (R2P), endorsed by the UN in 2005, further articulates this ethical imperative, stipulating that the international community has a responsibility to prevent and stop genocides, war crimes, ethnic cleansing, and crimes against humanity when national governments fail to protect their citizens.

The ethical arguments surrounding sovereignty and intervention are deeply rooted in philosophical discussions about the nature of state responsibility and the moral obligations of the international community. On one hand, a strict adherence to traditional sovereignty can hinder effective responses to gross human rights violations, potentially allowing atrocities to occur unchecked. On the other hand, unchecked intervention can undermine legitimate governments, destabilize regions, and lead to abuses of power under the guise of humanitarian aid.

These dilemmas prompt a reevaluation of how sovereignty is conceptualized and practiced in an interconnected world. The philosophical challenge lies in balancing respect for state autonomy with the imperative to protect human dignity and prevent suffering, crafting a nuanced approach that recognizes the rights of states alongside the ethical obligations of the global community. This balance requires a careful assessment of each situation, considering the potential benefits and risks of intervention, the motives of intervening states, and the long-term implications for international law and order.

By engaging with these philosophical issues, the discourse on sovereignty and intervention aims to develop frameworks that can guide the international community in making ethical, effective decisions about when and how to intervene in the affairs of sovereign states. This involves not only legal and political considerations but also a deep moral reflection on the values that should guide global interactions in the 21st century

II. Global Democratic Governance

THE ASPIRATION FOR Global Democratic Governance is a cornerstone in the discourse on the political dimension of globalization. This theme addresses the urgent need for more democratic processes within international bodies such as the UN, the World Bank, and the IMF. These institutions play critical roles in shaping global policies and thus, the push for reforms to make their decision-making processes more representative and equitable is both necessary and complex.

The challenge lies in the inherent structure of these organizations which often reflects the geopolitical realities of their founding eras, where economic and political power was concentrated in a few states. This historical context has led to governance models in global institutions that do not necessarily align with contemporary principles of democratic representation. For example, the veto power held by the permanent five members of the United Nations Security Council or the weighted voting systems in the IMF and World Bank, where voting power is determined by financial contributions, are often criticized for perpetuating unequal power dynamics.

Engaging with political philosophy, particularly theories of deliberative democracy and cosmopolitan democracy, provides a rich framework for rethinking how global governance can be restructured. Deliberative democracy emphasizes the importance of inclusive, participatory decision-making processes where the justification of policies occurs through reason and public argument among equals. Applying this to global governance suggests a model where all affected by certain global policies have a voice in the process, regardless of national borders.

Cosmopolitan democracy extends this concept further, proposing a system of governance that transcends national limitations and views all individuals as part of a global polity. This model advocates for the creation of new forms of political communities and structures that reflect the interdependent realities of our globalized world. It pushes for reforms that would allow these institutions to act not only as mediators of state interests but as stewards of the global common good, with accountability mechanisms that mirror those found in democratic nations.

Practically, this could involve the introduction of more transparent, participatory, and accountable mechanisms within international organizations. Proposals have included the establishment of a ***UN Parliamentary Assembly***, which would serve as a directly elected body to complement the existing UN framework, providing a voice to populations currently underrepresented in global decision-making. Similarly, reforms in financial institutions like the IMF could involve altering voting structures to ensure that decisions are not disproportionately influenced by economically dominant countries.

These philosophical and practical explorations aim to bridge the gap between the democratic ideals we uphold within national borders and the governance practices in the international arena. By advocating for structures that better represent the global citizenry, the discourse on Global Democratic Governance seeks to enhance the legitimacy and efficacy of international institutions. This would not only strengthen their ability to address global challenges more effectively but also ensure that their actions are grounded in the principles of democratic accountability and inclusivity, reflecting a true representation of the diverse global community they aim to serve

III. Political Accountability and Transparency

THE PRINCIPLE OF POLITICAL Accountability and Transparency is crucial in the context of globalization, where the actions of MNCs and international organizations significantly impact global communities. This principle underscores the necessity for these powerful entities to operate not only transparently but also ethically, adhering to high standards that ensure their contributions to society are beneficial and not detrimental.

In an era marked by complex global interactions, the activities of MNCs and international bodies can have far-reaching consequences on environmental, economic, and social levels. Therefore, establishing robust frameworks for accountability and transparency is essential to ensure that these entities are held responsible for their actions. The discussion about political accountability and transparency is deeply rooted in ethical theories that prioritize justice and the moral obligations of power. From a philosophical standpoint, the theories of distributive justice provide a foundational basis for understanding the ethical obligations of MNCs and international organizations. These theories argue that justice is not only a matter of fairness in distribution but also how institutions engage in practices that affect individuals' lives globally. Thus, ensuring that these entities operate transparently and are held accountable is not just a regulatory necessity but a moral imperative.

The principle of transparency is crucial because it allows stakeholders, including global citizens and governments, to have insight into the operations and decisions of these powerful entities. Transparency is not merely about making information available but ensuring that it is accessible and understandable, enabling effective oversight and public participation in governance processes. This visibility is essential for fostering trust and ensuring that the actions of MNCs and international organizations align with global ethical standards and contribute positively to societal welfare.

Accountability mechanisms play a critical role in this framework. They ensure that there are checks and balances in place to monitor the actions of these entities and provide recourse when their actions violate ethical norms or legal standards. This can include international regulatory frameworks, independent auditing bodies, and legal systems that can prosecute malfeasance or negligence. For example, the implementation of global standards like the United Nations Guiding Principles on Business and Human Rights offers a blueprint for how MNCs should respect human rights and remedy violations.

The ethical theories that emphasize the moral obligations of powerful entities to act responsibly suggest that MNCs and international organizations have a duty to contribute to the public good. This extends beyond mere compliance with laws, ethical corporate and organizational governance requires proactive engagement in practices that enhance the global community's welfare. This includes not only avoiding harm but actively doing good, a concept that aligns with the philosophical views of Emmanuel Kant, where actions are evaluated based on their conformity with moral law and their capacity to serve as a universal good.

The principle of Political Accountability and Transparency in global politics is about ensuring that the significant power wielded by multinational corporations and international organizations is matched by an equally robust system of ethical governance. By grounding their operations in principles of justice, transparency, and accountability, these entities can better align their strategies with the expectations and needs of a globalized world, ensuring their power is used responsibly and for the collective benefit of the global community. This approach not only fulfills their ethical obligations but also secures a more stable and just global political environment.

IV. Peace and Security in a Globalized World

THE PRINCIPLE OF "*Peace and Security in a Globalized World*" dives into the exchange between global interconnectivity and international conflicts, seeking strategies to achieve sustainable peace through collaborative international efforts. This principle is underpinned by the rich philosophical traditions of peace and conflict studies, which provide critical insights into both the causes of war and the foundations of peace, particularly in a globalized context where conflicts can have far-reaching impacts.

Globalization has undeniably transformed the landscape of international relations, making conflicts no longer isolated to specific geographical locations but rather capable of affecting global stability. The interconnected nature of today's world means that the ripples of conflict in one region can lead to waves of disruption globally, influencing economic markets, international migration, and global political stability. Therefore, understanding the dynamics of peace and security in this context requires a nuanced approach that considers both the direct and indirect effects of conflicts.

One of the central elements of this principle is the role of international peacekeeping forces, which are often deployed under the auspices of global institutions like the United Nations. These forces play a pivotal role in conflict zones, aiming to maintain ceasefires, protect civilians, and assist in building conditions for sustainable peace. Philosophically, the justification for international peacekeeping ventures into just war theory and the ethics of intervention, which debate the moral grounds for crossing national borders to maintain or restore peace. These theories also wrestle with the implications of sovereignty and the ethical considerations that should guide the international community's response to state-led violence or failure to protect its citizens.

Moreover, the effectiveness of global treaties in mitigating conflicts is another critical aspect of this principle. Treaties such as the Treaty on the Non-Proliferation of Nuclear Weapons (NPT) and various disarmament agreements aim to reduce the likelihood of escalated conflicts by controlling the spread of arms and fostering transparency among states. From a philosophical perspective, the effectiveness of these treaties can be analyzed through the lens of contract theory, which examines the conditions under which states enter into and adhere to agreements. This analysis includes considerations of trust, reciprocity, and mutual benefit—key elements that influence the success of treaties in achieving long-term peace and security.

Additionally, theories from peace and conflict studies emphasize the importance of understanding the root causes of conflicts, which often include issues like resource scarcity, ethnic tensions, and historical grievances. Globalization can exacerbate these conflicts by intensifying competition for resources and amplifying cultural and social tensions. However, it also offers tools for conflict resolution, such as enhanced communication technologies, international diplomatic and economic pressure, and cross-border civil society movements that advocate for peace.

To advance peace and security in a globalized world, it is essential to foster an international environment where cooperation and dialogue are prioritized over confrontation. This involves strengthening international institutions and mechanisms that facilitate peaceful dispute resolution and encouraging states to comply with international law and norms that promote peace and justice. Philosophical reflections on these strategies might draw upon cosmopolitan theories, which argue for global governance structures that protect human rights and secure peace as universal values transcending national interests.

In essence, the principle of "Peace and Security in a Globalized World" calls for a multidimensional approach to understanding and resolving conflicts in today's interconnected environment. By integrating the philosophical insights of peace and conflict studies with practical strategies for international cooperation and treaty enforcement, this principle seeks to build a framework that not only addresses the symptoms of conflicts but also targets their underlying causes, paving the way for a more peaceful and secure global community

V. Ethical Implications of Global Power Dynamics

THIS PRINCIPLE EXAMINES the complex and often contentious distribution of power on the international stage, a core aspect of globalization that shapes global relations and impacts nations both large and small. This discussion incorporates insights from realism and cosmopolitan ethics, two philosophical approaches that offer contrasting perspectives on how power should be understood and exercised in a global context.

Realism, grounded in the premise that international relations are a struggle for power among self-interested states, provides a framework for understanding the actions of major powers within global institutions. Realists argue that states act primarily in their own interest and view the accumulation and display of power as essential for securing national security and objectives. This perspective helps explain why powerful nations often seek to influence international institutions and how these institutions can become arenas for power plays rather than purely altruistic endeavors. Realism starkly portrays the ethical challenges posed by such power dynamics, highlighting the potential for exploitation and coercion by stronger states against weaker ones.

Conversely, cosmopolitan ethics offers a critique of this realist worldview by advocating for a global moral community where every individual's rights and dignity are respected, regardless of their state's power. Cosmopolitan thinkers argue for the establishment of global norms and institutions that not only prevent the abuse of power but also redistribute power more equitably among nations. This approach emphasizes justice, equality, and mutual respect in international relations, proposing that power should be exercised in ways that advance global welfare rather than merely national interests.

The current global power imbalances, where a few nations wield disproportionate influence over international policies and decisions, raise significant ethical concerns. These imbalances can lead to a world order that reflects the interests of powerful nations at the expense of weaker ones, often sidelining the needs and voices of smaller countries in major global decisions. Such dynamics challenge the principles of democratic governance and equitable participation, which are vital for the legitimacy and effectiveness of global governance.

Philosophically informed strategies to address these power imbalances include advocating for reforms in how international institutions are structured and governed. Proposals may include more inclusive decision-making processes that allow for greater representation and voice for smaller or developing nations. Additionally, the principle of subsidiarity, which suggests that decisions should be made at the most immediate level possible to those affected, could guide the restructuring of global governance to ensure that local needs and perspectives are not overshadowed by global agendas.

Moreover, building ethical leadership and promoting transparency in international relations are crucial for mitigating the negative impacts of power disparities. Ethical leadership involves leaders of powerful nations and global institutions committing to principles of fairness and justice, even when these may conflict with narrow national interests. Transparency, on the other hand, reduces the opportunities for covert power plays and increases the accountability of powerful actors on the global stage.

The principles of global ethics invite a deep reflection on how power is distributed and exercised globally. It challenges the realist acceptance of power politics as a given and instead advocates for a cosmopolitan approach that seeks to reform global governance in favor of a more just, ethical, and equitable world order. This principle not only critiques the status quo but also offers a visionary outlook on how global power dynamics could be transformed to foster a truly global community where power is wielded responsibly and for the common good.

These points are designed to provide a brief philosophical framework that not only addresses current political issues but also anticipates future challenges in globalization. They integrate ethical considerations with practical political analysis, aiming to foster a more equitable, democratic, and peaceful global system.

3.8 Future Developments in Global Politics

For the political dimension of globalization, a forward-looking analysis can encapsulate the evolving landscape of international politics, emphasizing emerging issues and trends that will shape future governance. This section would explore the anticipated developments that require an adaptive and proactive philosophical and policy approach to effectively manage the complexities of global political dynamics.

I. The Rise of Non-State Actors and Decentralized Networks

THE INCREASING PROMINENCE of non-state actors, such as multinational corporations, non-governmental organizations, and decentralized digital platforms like blockchain and cryptocurrencies, represents a significant shift in the traditional landscape of global politics. These entities operate across national borders, exert substantial economic and social influence, and often fill roles traditionally held by state governments. This evolution prompts a philosophical reevaluation of sovereignty and authority, challenging the Westphalian model that has dominated international relations theory for centuries. As these non-state actors continue to rise, questions about their legitimacy, their role in global governance, and their accountability become increasingly pertinent. Ethical considerations surrounding these entities focus on their impact on global inequality, their commitment to sustainable and humane practices, and their role in promoting or undermining democratic values and human rights.

II. Cybersecurity and Digital Sovereignty:

IN THE DIGITAL AGE, cybersecurity has become a paramount concern for states, shaping a new domain of sovereignty that intersects with traditional notions of territorial integrity. The global dependency on digital infrastructure for economic, political, and social operations has made cybersecurity a key area of national security. Philosophical debates in this realm explore the tension between maintaining state sovereignty in cyberspace and participating in a globally interconnected digital world that demands openness and shared norms. Issues such as data privacy, surveillance, and the ethical implications of digital monitoring raise significant questions about individual rights versus collective security. These discussions are further complicated by the transnational nature of cyber threats, which often blur the lines between domestic and international policy domains.

III. Global Environmental Governance:

THE URGENCY OF ENVIRONMENTAL challenges such as climate change, biodiversity loss, and pollution has highlighted the inadequacies of current global environmental governance structures. As the impacts of environmental degradation transcend national borders, the need for a cohesive international response becomes critical. This situation presses for an expanded philosophical discourse on global justice, specifically concerning who is responsible for addressing environmental damages and who is entitled to participate in the decision-making process. Ethical discussions focus on climate justice—addressing how the burdens and benefits of environmental policies are shared globally—and intergenerational equity, concerning the rights of future generations. The philosophical challenge lies in crafting governance structures that not only address the technical and economic aspects of environmental issues but also embody ethical principles that ensure fairness, responsibility, and respect for all life.

IV. Reforming International Institutions:

THE EFFECTIVENESS AND fairness of international institutions like the United Nations, the World Bank, and the International Monetary Fund are increasingly under scrutiny. Critiques often focus on these institutions' democratic deficits, such as unequal voting powers, lack of transparency, and the dominance of wealthy nations in decision-making processes. Reforming these bodies involves philosophical inquiries into the nature of global democracy and justice, exploring how global governance can be restructured to better reflect the diversity and plurality of the world's populations. This includes proposing mechanisms for more equitable representation and decision-making that ensure all nations have a voice in global affairs, regardless of their economic power. The goal is to create a global governance framework that is not only effective in managing international issues but also adheres to democratic principles and respects the sovereignty and dignity of all peoples.

V. Managing Global Health Challenges:

THE GLOBAL RESPONSE to health crises, highlighted by the COVID-19 pandemic, has brought to the forefront the need for an integrated approach to global health governance. Future strategies will likely emphasize strengthening the resilience of health systems and enhancing international cooperation to manage health emergencies effectively. Philosophical considerations in this domain involve debates over the ethical distribution of health resources, the right to health, and the responsibilities of states and international bodies to protect individuals' health without infringing on sovereignty or personal freedoms. These discussions also explore the balance between public health measures and individual rights, challenging policymakers to find solutions that respect both community safety and individual liberties.

These political developments call for a dynamic philosophical approach that is not only reactive but also anticipatory, recognizing and addressing the ethical, legal, and practical challenges posed by an increasingly interconnected world. Philosophers, policymakers, and political analysts must engage with these emerging issues, crafting frameworks that are robust enough to handle the uncertainties and complexities of future global politics. This approach should promote ethical standards that ensure political actions and policies contribute positively to global welfare, respecting the principles of justice, equity, and human dignity.

By proactively addressing these future developments, the discourse on global politics can evolve to better manage the challenges and opportunities presented by globalization. This not only enhances the effectiveness of global governance but also ensures that it is conducted in a manner that is just, equitable, and sustainable for all. As we continue to explore the political dimension of globalization, the insights derived from this analysis will provide a solid foundation for understanding and shaping the global political landscape in the years to come.

In this chapter, we have explored the political dimension of globalization, exploring the interrelationship between sovereignty, intervention, and the architecture of global governance. We've engaged with the dynamics of state power, the role of international organizations, and the philosophical debates surrounding global democratic governance and ethical power distribution. Our discussion has navigated the challenges of political accountability and transparency, the quest for sustainable global peace, and the deep ethical implications inherent in the power dynamics of globalization.

The rise of non-state actors and decentralized networks has prompted us to reconsider traditional notions of sovereignty and the ethical parameters of state intervention. This discourse has highlighted the tension between national autonomy and the global community's ethical obligations, especially in contexts involving human rights abuses and humanitarian crises. By examining theories such as just war theory and the Responsibility to Protect (R2P), we've critiqued the balance between respecting state sovereignty and intervening for the greater humanitarian good. Looking ahead, the path to managing the political challenges of globalization involves several forward-thinking strategies:

I. Strengthening Global Institutions: Reforming international bodies like the UN, the World Bank, and the IMF to ensure they not only respond effectively to global challenges but also operate in a manner that is transparent, accountable, and inclusive of all nations, particularly those historically marginalized.

II. Enhancing International Legal Frameworks: Developing and enforcing robust international laws that address new challenges such as cybersecurity, environmental protection, and human rights, ensuring these frameworks adapt to the evolving nature of global relations.

III. Promoting Ethical Leadership: Encouraging nations and global leaders to adopt ethical standards that prioritize human dignity, peace, and sustainability over narrow national interests or geopolitical strategies.

IV. Fostering Global Solidarity: Building a sense of global community that transcends national boundaries, emphasizing cooperation and mutual respect to tackle common challenges such as climate change, migration, and international conflict.

V. Cultivating Civic Engagement: Enhancing public participation in global governance through education and technology, ensuring that citizens worldwide are informed, engaged, and capable of influencing international policies.

As globalization continues to reshape the political landscape, it presents both profound challenges and transformative opportunities. By adopting a reflective and critical approach to its political dimension, we can aspire to craft a global order that is not only more just and equitable but also robust enough to handle future challenges. This requires a concerted effort among governments, international organizations, civil society, and individuals to reconfigure the global political architecture. Such efforts will ensure that globalization acts as a force for building up global peace, justice, and cooperation, promoting a political environment where all nations and peoples can thrive. As we move forward to explore the philosophical conundrums of globalization in subsequent chapters, the insights from this political analysis will enhance our understanding of globalization's broader impacts on society, culture, and the ethical landscape.

Concluding Part 1: Understanding Globalization

Globalization, in its essence, presents an interconnected web of economic, cultural, and political interrelations that redefine the modern world. This holistic examination synthesizes the insights from our previously studied dimensions, economic, cultural, and political, into a unified discourse, providing a deeper understanding of globalization's pervasive influence and the philosophical underpinnings necessary for navigating its pathways.

As studied, the economic dimension of globalization encompasses the interconnectedness of global markets and the impact of MNCs and international trade on local economies. This economic integration has facilitated a dramatic increase in wealth and access to goods and services worldwide but has also exacerbated inequalities and exposed vulnerabilities in global supply chains. Philosophically raising questions about justice, equity, and the ethical obligations of wealth redistribution. The economic narrative is interwoven with the cultural considerations, where the global flow of goods is paralleled by an exchange of ideas, media, and cultural practices. As digital platforms diminish distances and barriers, they create spaces for cultural interaction that challenge traditional identities and promote new global norms. This cultural exchange, however, also poses risks of cultural homogenization, necessitating a balance between embracing a global culture and preserving local traditions and values.

Politically, globalization challenges the sovereignty of states and reshapes governance through the rise of supranational entities such as the UN and the EU. These bodies attempt to address global issues that transcend national borders, like climate change, human trafficking, and pandemics, demanding cooperation beyond traditional political frameworks. This leads to a philosophical inquiry into the nature of sovereignty in the global age: *how can or should the nation-state evolve in response to the requirements of global governance?* Moreover, the political aspect of globalization highlights the need for democratic representation in international decision-making, ensuring that global governance structures do not merely serve the powerful but are responsive and accountable to all stakeholders involved.

At the core of this discourse is the need for a robust philosophical framework that can address the ethical challenges presented by globalization. This includes debates on global justice, the responsibilities of powerful nations and corporations towards less powerful ones, and the rights of individuals and communities to participate in decisions that affect them. Utilizing philosophical theories from cosmopolitanism, which advocates for global moral obligations, to realism, focused on power and security, this discourse navigates the ethical canvas of a globalized world. These philosophical reflections help us understand and critique the power dynamics at play and explore ways in which global solidarity and ethical governance can be promoted.

By integrating these economic, cultural, and political insights, we can approach globalization not just as a series of economic transactions or cultural exchanges, but as a dynamic, interconnected phenomenon that impacts nearly every aspect of human life. The interactions between these dimensions suggest that changes in one area, such as economic policies or technological advancements, inevitably influence the others, impacting cultural expressions and political structures. This integrated perspective underscores the importance of a multidisciplinary approach in developing policies and strategies that are not only effective but also just and sustainable.

As we move forward, the combined insights from the economic, cultural, and political analyses of globalization equip us to better anticipate and respond to its evolving challenges. A comprehensive understanding of globalization necessitates an ongoing, critical, and ethical engagement with its various dimensions, ensuring that the benefits of this global interconnection are shared equitably and sustainably. Embracing this multifaceted perspective allows policymakers, scholars, and global citizens to craft responses that respect the complexities of global interactions, promoting a future where globalization supports both global development and local flourishing. This approach not only enriches our understanding but also empowers us to shape a global community that upholds the dignity and welfare of all its members, guided by a committed and philosophically informed discourse.

From an exploration of globalization's economic, cultural, and political dimensions, it becomes apparent that the very interconnectivity that defines globalization also gives rise to profound ethical conundrums. These dilemmas are not confined to isolated aspects but span across all facets of globalization, challenging us to devise solutions that are as multifaceted as the problems themselves. The next part of our discourse dives into these ethical conundrums, proposing philosophical solutions that strive for a more just and sustainable global order.

We have briefly looked at one of the significant ethical issues is the exploitation of labor within global supply chains, a problem that touches on economic justice, cultural implications, and political regulation. Workers in developing countries often labor under harsh conditions for meager wages to produce goods for the global market. This issue raises questions about the balance of power in global economics and the responsibility of multinational corporations toward their workers. Philosophically, addressing this requires a blend of utilitarianism, to maximize the well-being of workers, and Kantian ethics, to treat these workers as ends in themselves rather than mere means to profit. Similarly, we have also briefly looked at issues from the other two dimensions like cultural homogenization and state-sovereignty.

Now, addressing these issues on a global scale demands addressing these conundrums in an integrated way that combines ethical theories and practical policies. For instance, nationalism emerges as a powerful interdimensional force in response to the perceived threats of globalization, impacting economic policies, cultural preservation, and political sovereignty. It can manifest as protectionist economic measures, a cultural retrenchment into traditional identities, and a political backlash against global governance structures. These protectionist policies can disrupt global supply chains and trade agreements, impacting global economic stability and development. Simultaneously, the resurgence in nationalist sentiments often promotes a singular cultural identity, which can suppress minority cultures and stifle the cultural exchange that enriches societies. And lastly, nationalism can lead to a rejection of international cooperation, impacting global issues like climate change, human rights, and peacekeeping.

Addressing an issue like nationalism will require a nuanced understanding of its roots and effects. Philosophically, a balance must be found between respecting individual national identities and promoting global solidarity. Theories of cosmopolitanism, which advocate for global citizenship and moral obligations beyond borders, can be counterbalanced with communitarian perspectives that emphasize the value of community and cultural integrity. By addressing these issues from a webbed perspective that considers all dimensions, we can develop more comprehensive and ethically grounded solutions. These solutions should not only tackle the immediate challenges but also anticipate future developments, ensuring that globalization evolves in a way that is equitable, sustainable, and respectful of diverse human values.

Part 2: Ethical Conundrums of Globalization

A s we conclude Part 1 and our exploration of the economic, cultural, and political dimensions of globalization, it becomes evident that these interconnected dimensions present not only opportunities but also profound challenges. The relationship between global trade, cultural exchange, and supranational governance has reshaped societies, markets, and governance structures worldwide. However, this transformation has not come without significant ethical conundrums that complicate the path toward a more inclusive and sustainable global society.

One of the most pressing challenges of globalization is the tension between nationalism and global integration. While globalization has built-up interconnectedness, it has also provoked a resurgence of nationalism. This nationalism manifests in economic protectionism, cultural preservation, and political sovereignty, often in direct opposition to global cooperation. Protectionist policies and trade barriers undermine the benefits of global trade, threatening economic growth and international partnerships. Nationalist movements frequently advocate for prioritizing local industries, which can destabilize global supply chains and reduce economic opportunities for developing nations. It also promotes a singular national identity, potentially marginalizing multicultural and minority communities. The desire to preserve national cultures sometimes clashes with the cosmopolitan ideals of diversity and inclusivity promoted by global integration. Additionally, supranational governance often faces resistance from nationalist movements prioritizing national sovereignty. This tension complicates the implementation of international treaties, human rights standards, and collaborative policies that require nations to compromise on their autonomy for the greater global good.

Similarly, the movement of people across borders is another critical issue that globalization has amplified, presenting ethical dilemmas surrounding migration and human rights. Global migration is driven by economic disparities, political instability, and environmental crises, leading to a diverse mix of migrants, refugees, and asylum seekers seeking safety and opportunity. Migrants often fill labor shortages in host countries, contributing positively to the economy through their work and remittances. However, they also face exploitation, discrimination, and precarious working conditions, highlighting the need for ethical labor practices. Migration also introduces cultural diversity to host societies, enriching them with new perspectives and traditions but it also raises questions of integration, assimilation, and multiculturalism, as well as resistance from nationalist groups opposed to increased immigration. Immigration policies often reflect national security concerns and domestic political pressures, sometimes at the expense of international human rights standards. The inconsistency between international commitments and national practices raises questions about the global community's commitment to protecting vulnerable populations across borders.

Simultaneously, environmental sustainability remains a crucial issue in the age of globalization, as economic growth and technological advancement often come at the expense of ecological balance. The global responsibility to protect the environment is increasingly critical, yet the economic and political interests of nations often impede progress. The pursuit of economic growth frequently leads to environmental degradation, particularly in developing countries seeking rapid industrialization. Striking a balance between development and sustainability requires innovative economic models that promote green economies and responsible resource management. Environmentalism has emerged as a global cultural movement, but local attitudes toward environmental protection vary significantly. Traditional practices, beliefs, and livelihoods can sometimes conflict with international environmental policies, necessitating culturally sensitive approaches to sustainability. International environmental agreements, such as the Paris Agreement, exemplify the potential for global cooperation but also reveal the challenges of aligning national interests with global commitments. Political will is crucial to implementing effective policies, yet nationalist agendas often hinder progress.

These issues intersect across all previously discussed dimensions, creating ethical challenges that require a nuanced philosophical approach such as balancing national sovereignty with global cooperation, which demands a comprehensive framework that reconciles national identity and autonomy with global responsibilities, addressing the rights and treatment of migrants, which necessitates a compassionate and just approach that respects human dignity while considering economic and security concerns, and navigating the ethical implications of environmental degradation, which requires a global commitment to sustainability that transcends political and economic interests.

This part of our discourse will dive deeper into these ethical conundrums, exploring the philosophical debates and practical solutions that can guide us toward a more ethical, equitable, and sustainable future. We will consider how moral and political philosophy can illuminate the path forward, ensuring that globalization enhances not only interconnectedness but also justice and sustainability. This section of our book will dissect these ethical challenges and provide insights into how to address them through informed and ethical approaches. It will emphasize the importance of moral and political philosophy in navigating the complexities of globalization, offering a comprehensive roadmap to resolving the conundrums facing our global society.

Moral and political philosophy provides the critical framework needed to navigate these complexities, offering insights that can help reconcile global integration with ethical considerations, ensuring a future that is not only interconnected but also just and sustainable. Philosophical frameworks like utilitarianism, deontology, and virtue ethics can clarify ethical dilemmas posed by globalization. For instance, *how do we balance economic growth with environmental sustainability, or national security with migrant rights?* Universal principles of justice and fairness could provide consistent standards for evaluating global practices, ensuring that international policies uphold human dignity and global solidarity. Similarly, Nationalism and global integration often seem at odds, but philosophers like Martha

Nussbaum and Kwame Anthony Appiah show us how to balance patriotic loyalties with cosmopolitan obligations.

A philosophical approach is crucial for crafting a harmonious and ethical framework that reconciles the forces of global integration with moral imperatives. Informed and ethical global policies are necessary to address issues like human rights and migration by developing immigration policies that uphold fundamental human rights while respecting national security concerns. Similarly, global environmental responsibility requires crafting international agreements that prioritize ecological sustainability and equitable resource distribution. Building a just and sustainable future involves developing a spirit of global solidarity that transcends national interests and prioritizes the well-being of humanity as a whole. Encouraging interdisciplinary collaboration can develop innovative solutions that address global issues holistically and ethically.

As we move further into Part 2 of this book, we will explore the ethical conundrums posed by globalization in detail, focusing on nationalism versus global integration, migration and human rights, and environmental sustainability. These chapters will explore the underlying philosophical foundations of these issues, highlighting how moral and political philosophy can guide us toward a more just and sustainable global future. By embracing a philosophical approach, we can illuminate a path forward that harmonizes global interconnectedness with ethical responsibility, ensuring a world where economic prosperity, cultural diversity, and political cooperation thrive together.

Chapter 4: Nationalism vs. Global Integration

The resurgence of nationalism in the age of globalization presents a paradox: as the world becomes more interconnected through economic, cultural, and political exchanges, nationalist movements gain strength in their call for insularity and preservation of national sovereignty. This chapter provides an analysis of how globalization has influenced the resurgence of nationalism and, in turn, how nationalist movements challenge global integration across economic, cultural, and political dimensions.

Historically, nationalism emerged as a powerful force in the wake of the French Revolution, representing a collective identity based on shared language, culture, and values. The Westphalian system established the concept of nation-states, cementing national sovereignty as a foundational principle of international relations. Nationalism and the nation-state concept developed alongside industrialization and colonialism, which structured global economic and political relationships. Globalization, particularly after World War II, significantly reshaped international relations. The Bretton Woods institutions, the UN, and subsequent trade agreements laid the groundwork for an interconnected world economy and a new era of political cooperation. The end of the Cold War further accelerated globalization, with the fall of communism leading to market liberalization and democratization in Eastern Europe and beyond. The formation of supranational entities and global financial institutions exemplified this new era of integration.

Despite the apparent benefits of globalization, such as increased economic growth and cultural exchange, nationalist movements have resurged in recent decades, challenging the assumption that global integration naturally leads to greater harmony among nations. This resurgence is driven by various factors across economic, cultural, and political dimensions.

Globalization has facilitated unprecedented levels of trade and investment across borders, leading to rapid economic growth in many parts of the world. However, the benefits have not been evenly distributed. In advanced economies, the outsourcing of manufacturing jobs to lower-cost regions, particularly in Asia, has led to deindustrialization, creating economic dislocation for workers, resulting in rising unemployment and a sense of economic insecurity. This dislocation contributed to the appeal of nationalist rhetoric, as politicians blamed global trade agreements for the loss of jobs. While globalization has lifted millions out of poverty in developing countries, it has also exacerbated inequality within and between nations. Nationalist movements often exploit this discontent by advocating protectionist policies to safeguard domestic industries and restore economic sovereignty.

The rise of supranational institutions like the EU has brought about significant economic integration, often requiring member states to adhere to strict fiscal rules and austerity measures. In the aftermath of the 2008 financial crisis, countries like Greece, Spain, and Portugal were forced to implement austerity measures in exchange for financial aid from the EU and IMF. These measures resulted in high unemployment rates, cuts to public services, and social unrest. Nationalist parties capitalized on this discontent by framing the EU as an institution that undermined national sovereignty and imposed economic hardships on ordinary citizens. Eurosceptics argued that the EU's trade policies and regulations restricted Britain's economic sovereignty, preventing it from independently negotiating trade deals and controlling immigration. The Brexit campaign emphasized the need to "take back control," resonating with those who felt left behind by globalization.

Similarly, the cultural factors leading to the rise of nationalism involve the movement of people across borders, leading to demographic shifts that challenge traditional notions of national identity. Immigration has become a flashpoint in nationalist politics, with many nationalist movements framing immigrants as threats to national identity, security, and economic stability. In Europe, the influx of refugees from the Middle East and North Africa during the Syrian conflict fueled fears of cultural dilution and social unrest.

Nationalist movements often advocate for exclusionary policies that prioritize the rights and interests of the "native" population, reinforcing ethnic, religious, and linguistic divisions, framing immigrants and minorities as "outsiders" who undermine national cohesion.

Nationalist movements resist the perceived cultural homogenization of globalization by emphasizing traditional values and cultural preservation. The dominance of Western media and consumer culture is often perceived as a form of cultural imperialism that undermines indigenous traditions. In Russia, for example, Vladimir Putin's administration has positioned itself as a defender of traditional Orthodox Christian values against the liberal norms of the West. Nationalist rhetoric frequently invokes a nostalgic vision of a past "golden age" when national identity was purer and life was simpler. This longing for the past resonates with those who feel disoriented by the rapid changes brought about by globalization, such as urbanization, technological advancement, and multiculturalism.

Politically, globalization has empowered supranational institutions and multinational corporations, often at the expense of national sovereignty. The EU, UN, WTO, and other institutions wield significant influence over national policies. The EU, for example, requires member states to adhere to common regulations on trade, immigration, and fiscal policy. Nationalist movements perceive these requirements as infringements on national sovereignty, advocating for a return to self-governance. Moreover, MNCs often wield significant power in shaping national policies through lobbying and investment decisions. This influence can undermine democratic processes and lead to policies that favor corporate interests over national welfare.

Nationalist movements exploit this sentiment by portraying themselves as champions of the "common people" against global elites. The rise of nationalism is often accompanied by populist rhetoric and a shift toward authoritarian governance. Nationalist movements frequently employ populist rhetoric, framing their struggle as one between the "common people" and a corrupt global elite. This rhetoric resonates with those who feel left behind by globalization and view international institutions as detached from their everyday concerns.

In many cases, nationalism leads to democratic backsliding and the erosion of checks and balances. Leaders like Viktor Orbán in Hungary and Recep Tayyip Erdoğan in Turkey have used nationalist rhetoric to justify restrictions on the press, judiciary, and civil society. So the rise of nationalism within the framework of globalization represents a significant challenge to global integration. The web between global economic policies, cultural exchanges, and political dynamics has created an environment where nationalist movements can thrive, exploiting economic discontent, cultural anxieties, and political disillusionment. Addressing these challenges requires a nuanced understanding of the root causes driving nationalist sentiments and a commitment to finding ethical solutions that balance national interests with global cooperation.

In effect, the rise of nationalism economically undermines international trade and disrupts global supply chains, politically challenges the legitimacy of supranational institutions, and culturally exacerbates identity politics and intolerance toward immigrants and minorities. In short:

- **Protectionism:** Nationalist movements often advocate for protectionist policies to safeguard domestic industries and jobs. Tariffs, import restrictions, and preferential treatment for local businesses are championed as measures to restore economic sovereignty.

- **Global Trade Tensions:** The rise of nationalism disrupts global supply chains and international trade agreements. Trade wars between major economies and the questioning of multilateral trade agreements like NAFTA highlight the fragility of global economic cooperation.

- **Identity Politics:** Nationalists often emphasize ethnic, religious, or linguistic identity to unite their base. Immigration and multiculturalism are seen as threats to cultural cohesion and are thus opposed by nationalist movements.

- **Cultural Preservation:** The protection of "traditional values" becomes a rallying cry against perceived external influences. Populist rhetoric often portrays globalization as a force that undermines national traditions, leading to cultural backlash.

- **Sovereignty Concerns:** Nationalist movements reject supranational governance that overrides national decision-making. The EU is often criticized for eroding the sovereignty of member states, particularly on issues like immigration and fiscal policy.

- **Populism and Authoritarianism:** Nationalist movements often align with populist rhetoric, portraying themselves as defenders of "the people" against globalist elites. This rhetoric frequently leads to the erosion of democratic norms and the rise of authoritarian leaders who justify their power through nationalism.

The resurgence of nationalism presents a significant challenge to global integration across the globe. Globalization's promises of prosperity and cultural exchange are undermined by rising inequality, cultural tensions, and political fragmentation. As nationalist movements disrupt supranational cooperation and advocate for protectionist policies, the philosophical debate between nationalism and cosmopolitanism becomes increasingly relevant. The following sections will venture into the theoretical perspectives on nationalism, case studies of its impact, and potential solutions for balancing national interests with global cooperation.

4.1 Impact of Nationalism on the Economic Dimension

Globalization's economic dimension has significantly contributed to the rise of nationalist movements across the world. By facilitating unprecedented levels of trade and investment across borders, globalization has driven economic growth but also created disparities and disruptions. Understanding how these economic shifts have fueled nationalist sentiments requires a deep dive into the consequences of global trade policies, economic integration, and structural changes in labor markets.

One of the most significant economic factors leading to the rise of nationalism is the deindustrialization of advanced economies. The relocation of manufacturing jobs to lower-cost regions, particularly in Asia, has led to economic dislocation for workers in the United States and Europe. This trend created rising unemployment rates and economic insecurity in regions previously dependent on manufacturing industries.

- **Deindustrialization in the United States:** The Rust Belt, a region known for its manufacturing industries, experienced severe job losses due to factory closures and outsourcing. The decline of manufacturing hubs like Detroit and Pittsburgh left many workers unemployed and created a pervasive sense of economic despair. Politicians blamed global trade agreements like NAFTA for the loss of jobs, and nationalist rhetoric capitalized on this discontent. Donald Trump's 2016 presidential campaign, which emphasized protectionism and criticized NAFTA, resonated with many who felt left behind by globalization.

- **European Deindustrialization:** Similarly, in Europe, the outsourcing of manufacturing jobs to Eastern Europe and Asia led to deindustrialization in countries like the UK, France, and Germany. The decline of traditional industries resulted in significant job losses and economic dislocation. In the UK, the Leave campaign exploited this sentiment, arguing that the European Union's trade policies and regulations restricted Britain's economic sovereignty, preventing it from independently negotiating trade deals and controlling immigration. The campaign's slogan "Take Back Control" resonated with those who felt economically marginalized by globalization.

In developed economies, the benefits of globalization have largely accrued to capital owners, leading to wage stagnation for many workers and widening the wealth gap. Nationalist movements often exploit this discontent by advocating protectionist policies to safeguard domestic industries and restore economic sovereignty

- **Rising Inequality in Developed Economies:** In countries like the United States and the UK, the benefits of globalization have not been evenly distributed. High-income earners have seen significant gains, while middle- and low-income workers have experienced wage stagnation. This growing inequality has created fertile ground for nationalist movements, which argue that global trade agreements and international institutions prioritize corporate interests over those of ordinary citizens.

- **Protectionist Policies and Economic Sovereignty:** In response to rising inequality and economic dislocation, nationalist movements advocate for protectionist policies such as tariffs, import quotas, and subsidies for domestic industries. These policies aim to protect jobs and industries from foreign competition and restore economic sovereignty. However, such measures often lead to trade disputes and can hinder global economic growth. The trade war between the United States and China under the Trump administration exemplifies how protectionist policies can disrupt global trade flows and escalate tensions between nations.

The rise of supranational institutions has also brought about significant economic integration, often requiring member states to adhere to strict fiscal rules and austerity measures. As mentioned above, countries like Greece, Spain, and Portugal were forced to implement austerity measures in exchange for financial aid from the EU and IMF in the aftermath of the 2008 financial crisis. These measures resulted in high unemployment rates, cuts to public services, and social unrest.

- **Eurozone Crisis and Austerity:** The Eurozone crisis exposed the vulnerabilities of the European monetary union, particularly for weaker economies like Greece and Portugal. Austerity measures imposed by the EU and IMF led to severe economic hardships, with unemployment rates soaring above 25% in Greece and Spain. Nationalist parties like Golden Dawn in Greece and Podemos in Spain capitalized on this discontent by framing the EU as an institution that undermined national sovereignty and imposed economic hardships on ordinary citizens.

- **Brexit and Economic Sovereignty:** The UK's decision to leave the EU was significantly influenced by economic concerns. Eurosceptics argued that the EU's trade policies and regulations restricted Britain's economic sovereignty, preventing it from independently negotiating trade deals and controlling immigration. The Brexit campaign emphasized the need to "take back control," resonating with those who felt left behind by globalization. The result was a narrow victory for the Leave campaign, leading to the UK's withdrawal from the EU and raising questions about the future of European integration.

The rise of nationalism within the economic framework of globalization represents a significant challenge to global integration. The web between global trade policies, economic integration, and structural changes in labor markets has created an environment where nationalist movements can thrive, exploiting economic discontent and advocating protectionist policies. Addressing these challenges requires a nuanced understanding of the root causes driving nationalist sentiments and a commitment to finding ethical solutions that balance national interests with global cooperation.

4.2 Impact of Nationalism on the Cultural Dimension

Globalization's cultural dimension has also played a crucial role in fueling nationalist movements across the world. As globalization intensifies cross-border exchanges of goods, information, and people, it has given rise to concerns about identity preservation, cultural homogenization, and societal stability. Understanding how cultural factors contribute to the rise of nationalism requires analyzing identity politics, the role of the media, and fears surrounding immigration and cultural dilution.

One of the central cultural factors leading to the rise of nationalism is the intensification of identity politics. Globalization has facilitated the movement of people and ideas across borders, creating multicultural societies that often struggle to balance the preservation of national identity with cultural inclusivity. This tension has resulted in a resurgence of identity politics, where nationalist movements emphasize the protection of traditional values and cultural heritage.

Identity Politics in Multicultural Societies: The increased movement of people across borders has led to demographic shifts that challenge traditional notions of national identity. Immigration has become a flashpoint in nationalist politics, with many nationalist movements framing immigrants as threats to national identity, security, and economic stability. In Europe, the influx of refugees from the Middle East and North Africa during the Syrian conflict fueled fears of cultural dilution and social unrest. Nationalist movements like France's National Rally and Germany's Alternative for Germany (AfD) have advocated for exclusionary policies that prioritize the rights and interests of the "native" population, reinforcing ethnic, religious, and linguistic divisions.

Cultural Preservation and Traditional Values: Nationalist movements resist the perceived cultural homogenization of globalization by emphasizing traditional values and cultural preservation. The dominance of Western media and consumer culture is often perceived as a form of cultural imperialism that undermines indigenous traditions. In Russia, for example, Vladimir Putin's administration has positioned itself as a defender of traditional Orthodox Christian values against the liberal norms of the West. Similarly, Hindu nationalist groups in India advocate for the preservation of Hindu culture against perceived Westernization. Nationalist rhetoric frequently invokes a nostalgic vision of a past "golden age" when national identity was purer and life was simpler. This longing for the past resonates with those who feel disoriented by the rapid changes brought about by globalization, such as urbanization, technological advancement, and multiculturalism.

Populist Rhetoric and Ethnic Nationalism: Nationalist movements often employ populist rhetoric, framing their struggle as one between the "common people" and a corrupt global elite. This rhetoric resonates with those who feel left behind by globalization and view international institutions as detached from their everyday concerns. Ethnic nationalism plays a significant role in this narrative, as nationalist movements advocate for policies that favor the ethnic majority and exclude minority groups. In Hungary, Viktor Orbán's government has embraced ethnic nationalism, framing the country as a bastion of Christian values against the influx of Muslim immigrants. This rhetoric has led to the passage of strict immigration laws and the erosion of minority rights.

Globalization has also brought about concerns over cultural homogenization, where the dominance of Western media and consumer culture threatens to erode local traditions and identities. The global reach of digital media has amplified these concerns, as nationalist movements exploit social media platforms to spread their messages and mobilize supporters.

Western Media and Cultural Imperialism: The dominance of Western media and consumer culture is often perceived as a form of cultural imperialism that undermines local traditions and values. American movies, music, and fashion trends have a global reach, influencing the cultural tastes of young people across the world. This phenomenon has led to fears that globalization is eroding unique cultural identities and replacing them with a homogenized global culture. Nationalist movements often advocate for protectionist policies that limit the influence of foreign media and promote local content. For instance, France has long implemented cultural protectionism through quotas that ensure a significant portion of films shown in cinemas are of French origin.

Social Media and Echo Chambers: The rise of social media has also contributed to the resurgence of nationalism by creating echo chambers where people are exposed primarily to views that reinforce their preexisting beliefs. Nationalist movements have capitalized on social media platforms to spread their messages, often using disinformation and inflammatory rhetoric to stoke fears about immigration, cultural dilution, and economic insecurity. Algorithms that prioritize engagement over accuracy can exacerbate these issues by promoting sensationalist content that polarizes public opinion. In Myanmar, for instance, disinformation campaigns on Facebook fueled ethnic tensions that contributed to the persecution of the Rohingya Muslim minority.

Digital Nationalism and the Internet: The internet itself has become a battleground for nationalist movements, leading to the rise of digital nationalism. In countries like China and Russia, governments have sought to control the flow of information online by creating national intranets that limit access to foreign websites and social media platforms. The "Great Firewall" of China, for example, restricts access to Western platforms like Google and Facebook, enabling the Chinese government to control the digital narrative. Similarly, Russia has passed legislation requiring internet service providers to store user data on servers within the country, giving authorities greater control over online activities. Digital nationalism reflects the broader desire of nationalist movements to assert control over cultural narratives and protect national identity in the digital age.

Immigration has become a central issue in nationalist politics, as nationalist movements frame immigrants as threats to national identity, security, and economic stability. The influx of refugees and migrants from conflict regions like Syria, Afghanistan, and North Africa has fueled fears of cultural dilution and social unrest.

Refugee Crisis and Cultural Tensions: The Syrian refugee crisis, which began in 2011, saw millions of refugees fleeing conflict and seeking asylum in Europe. The influx of refugees strained social services and heightened cultural tensions, particularly in countries like Germany and Sweden, which accepted large numbers of asylum seekers. Nationalist movements exploited these tensions by framing refugees as threats to national security and cultural cohesion. In Germany, the AfD capitalized on public fears of cultural dilution by advocating strict immigration controls and opposing Angela Merkel's "open-door" refugee policy. Similarly, in Sweden, the Sweden Democrats gained support by campaigning against immigration and emphasizing the need to preserve Swedish culture.

Immigrant Integration and Assimilation: Nationalist movements often emphasize the importance of integrating immigrants into the dominant culture, arguing that assimilation is necessary for social cohesion. This view contrasts with multiculturalist approaches that advocate for the coexistence of diverse cultural identities within a society. Nationalist parties in Europe frequently oppose multiculturalism, arguing that it undermines national identity and fosters division. In France, the National Rally (formerly the National Front) has long criticized multiculturalism and called for a strict assimilation policy that requires immigrants to adopt French values and customs.

Islamophobia and Religious Nationalism: Immigration has also led to the rise of religious nationalism and Islamophobia. In India, the Bharatiya Janata Party (BJP), led by Prime Minister Narendra Modi, has promoted a form of Hindu nationalism that frames Muslims as threats to the nation's Hindu identity. The BJP's policies, such as the Citizenship Amendment Act, have been criticized for discriminating against Muslim immigrants. In Europe, nationalist movements often portray Muslim immigrants as incompatible with Western values and a threat to national security. This rhetoric has contributed to the rise of anti-Muslim sentiment and the adoption of policies that restrict religious freedoms, such as bans on face veils and minarets.

The rise of nationalism within the cultural framework of globalization represents a significant challenge to global integration. The interplay between identity politics, cultural homogenization, and immigration has created an environment where nationalist movements can thrive, exploiting fears of cultural dilution and societal instability. Addressing these challenges requires a nuanced understanding of the root causes driving nationalist sentiments and a commitment to finding ethical solutions that balance cultural preservation with inclusivity.

In the following sections, we will investigate the political factors driving nationalism, examine case studies that illustrate its impact across dimensions, and explore potential solutions for reconciling national identity with global solidarity. Ultimately, the goal is to develop a comprehensive framework that allows us to navigate the complexities of nationalism and globalization in a way that promotes both unity and diversity in an interconnected world.

4.3 Impact of Nationalism on the Political Dimension

Globalization has altered the nature of political power and governance, creating tensions between traditional nation-state sovereignty and the increasing influence of supranational entities. The rise of nationalist movements can be traced back to concerns about the erosion of national sovereignty, the effectiveness of global governance, and the legitimacy of international law. Additionally, the politics of national security, electoral strategies, and historical grievances further fuel nationalist sentiments.

Globalization has led to the emergence of supranational organizations that challenge traditional notions of sovereignty. Institutions such as the EU, UN, WTO, and IMF increasingly influence domestic policies, often prompting nationalist backlash.

European Union and National Sovereignty: The EU represents one of the most ambitious attempts at supranational governance, yet it has become a focal point of nationalist opposition. Critics argue that EU policies undermine national sovereignty by imposing regulations that member states must adhere to, even if they conflict with domestic interests. For instance, the EU's fiscal rules, immigration policies, and judicial decisions often override national legislation. This perceived loss of control was a significant factor in the Brexit referendum, where the Leave campaign capitalized on slogans like "Take Back Control," highlighting concerns about the erosion of British sovereignty. Similar sentiments fuel anti-EU parties across the continent, including France's National Rally, Italy's League, and Hungary's Fidesz.

United Nations and International Law: The UN embodies the principles of international cooperation and peacekeeping but has often been criticized for infringing on national sovereignty. The concept of the Responsibility to Protect (R2P), which allows international intervention to prevent atrocities, has been met with resistance by nationalist governments wary of foreign interference. Russia and China, both permanent members of the UN Security Council, have repeatedly vetoed resolutions authorizing intervention in Syria, citing respect for national sovereignty. Additionally, international law mechanisms like the International Criminal Court (ICC) face opposition from countries like the United States, which withdrew from the ICC due to concerns over the prosecution of American soldiers.

World Trade Organization and Global Trade Rules: The WTO has been instrumental in promoting global trade liberalization, but its dispute resolution mechanism is perceived as limiting national trade policies. Nationalist movements often frame WTO rules as favoring global corporations at the expense of domestic industries. In the United States, the Trump administration criticized WTO rulings and imposed tariffs on China, the EU, and other trading partners to protect American industries. This protectionist approach, justified by invoking national security concerns, marked a departure from the U.S.'s traditional role as a promoter of free trade.

National security concerns have also played a prominent role in the rise of nationalism. Globalization has increased the movement of people and goods across borders, raising fears of terrorism, organized crime, and uncontrolled immigration.

Immigration and Border Security: Immigration is often framed as a national security issue by nationalist movements, which advocate for strict border controls and immigration policies. The United States, under the Trump administration, sought to build a border wall with Mexico to curb illegal immigration and implemented a travel ban on several Muslim-majority countries, citing national security concerns. In Europe, the refugee crisis prompted countries like Hungary to erect fences along their borders and implement strict asylum policies to prevent the influx of migrants. Nationalist parties frequently link immigration to terrorism and crime, reinforcing fears that open borders compromise national security.

Terrorism and Islamophobia: Terrorist attacks in Western countries, such as the 9/11 attacks in the U.S. and the 2015 Paris attacks, have fueled

Islamophobia and contributed to the rise of nationalist movements. In France, the National Rally has called for a crackdown on radical Islam, while the AfD in Germany has advocated for banning minarets and burqas. These parties capitalize on public fears of terrorism to justify exclusionary policies and position themselves as defenders of national security.

Cybersecurity and Digital Nationalism: Globalization has also expanded the digital frontier, with cybersecurity becoming a critical national security concern. Cyberattacks attributed to state actors like Russia and China have prompted nationalist movements to call for greater digital sovereignty. The EU's General Data Protection Regulation (GDPR) reflects this trend, emphasizing data protection and privacy. In Russia and China, governments have sought to control the flow of information online, restricting access to foreign websites and social media platforms.

Nationalist movements often gain traction through populist rhetoric that resonates with voters who feel marginalized by globalization. Electoral strategies and historical grievances play significant roles in mobilizing support for nationalist parties.

Populist Mobilization: Populist rhetoric frames the political struggle as one between the "common people" and a corrupt global elite. Nationalist movements often exploit economic and cultural insecurities by promising to restore national pride and prioritize the interests of the "native" population. In Italy, Matteo Salvini's League leveraged anti-immigrant sentiment to win over working-class voters, while in the U.S., Trump's "Make America Great Again" slogan resonated with those who felt left behind by globalization. Populist movements frequently undermine trust in mainstream media and institutions, portraying them as tools of the global elite.

Historical Grievances and National Identity: Nationalist movements often tap into historical grievances to strengthen their narratives. In Russia, Vladimir Putin has invoked the legacy of the Soviet Union and the Great Patriotic War to foster national pride and justify foreign policy actions like the annexation of Crimea. Similarly, the BJP in India emphasizes the historical oppression of Hindus under Mughal and British rule to promote

Hindu nationalism. In Turkey, President Erdogan's government frames its actions in the context of Ottoman history, appealing to nationalist sentiments.

Electoral Strategies and Polarization: Nationalist parties often employ divisive electoral strategies that polarize societies along ethnic, religious, or regional lines. Gerrymandering, voter suppression, and disinformation campaigns are used to sway public opinion and secure electoral victories. In the U.S., strict voter ID laws and purges of voter rolls disproportionately affect minority groups, while in Hungary, electoral reforms by the Fidesz government have entrenched its dominance. Polarization undermines democratic norms and erodes trust in political institutions, making it challenging to build consensus around global integration.

The rise of nationalism within the political framework of globalization presents a complex challenge to global integration. Concerns about national sovereignty, security, and identity have created an environment where nationalist movements can thrive. Addressing these challenges requires a nuanced understanding of the political factors driving nationalist sentiments and a commitment to finding ethical solutions that balance national interests with global cooperation.

4.4 Theories of Nationalism: Primordialism and Modernism

Nationalism, as both an ideology and a movement, has been studied extensively within political philosophy and sociology. The philosophical underpinnings of nationalism are often explored through two primary theoretical perspectives: *primordialism and modernism.* Understanding these theories provides insight into the origins and nature of nationalism, particularly in the context of globalization.

Primordialism

PRIMORDIALISM VIEWS nations as natural and ancient phenomena rooted in shared characteristics like ethnicity, language, and culture. This perspective suggests that nations predate modern states and that nationalist sentiments are deeply ingrained in human nature.

Ethnic and Cultural Foundations: Primordialists argue that nations are founded on immutable ethnic and cultural ties. *Clifford Geertz* describes primordial attachments as "givens" of social existence, rooted in blood relations, language, region, and custom. According to this view, individuals naturally identify with those who share the same ethnic or cultural background, fostering a strong sense of solidarity and loyalty.

Perennialism and Eternal Nations: Some primordialists, often referred to as perennialists, extend this concept by arguing that nations are eternal, predating modernity. *Anthony D. Smith*, for instance, argues that modern nations have ancient roots in pre-modern ethno-symbolic communities, which provided the cultural foundation for contemporary nationalism.

Nationalism and Authenticity: Primordialism tends to emphasize the authenticity of national identities, viewing them as organic expressions of historical and cultural continuity. In this framework, nationalism becomes a moral imperative to preserve and defend the cultural essence of the nation against external threats.

Modernism

IN CONTRAST TO PRIMORDIALISM, modernism views nationalism as a product of modernity, emerging in the context of socio-political changes like industrialization, capitalism, and the rise of the modern state.

Benedict Anderson and Imagined Communities: Benedict Anderson's concept of "imagined communities" is foundational to modernist theories. He argues that nations are socially constructed communities, imagined by individuals who perceive themselves as part of a larger group. Print capitalism, facilitated by the proliferation of newspapers and novels in vernacular languages, played a critical role in creating these imagined communities by fostering a shared consciousness among diverse populations.

Ernest Gellner and Industrial Society: Ernest Gellner argues that nationalism is a byproduct of industrial society, which required a culturally homogenous workforce to ensure economic productivity and social cohesion. The modern state promoted standardized education and a common language to create a unified national identity that could mobilize and manage the industrial workforce.

Eric Hobsbawm and Invented Traditions: Eric Hobsbawm highlights the role of "invented traditions" in shaping national identities. He suggests that many national symbols, rituals, and myths were deliberately crafted by elites to forge a sense of national unity and loyalty. For example, national holidays, anthems, and monuments often have recent origins but are presented as ancient traditions to legitimize the modern nation-state.

Nationalism as Political Legitimacy: Modernists view nationalism as a tool for political legitimacy, used by emerging states to mobilize populations and establish authority. Nationalist movements often seek to create a congruence between political and national boundaries, leading to demands for self-determination and the establishment of nation-states.

Cosmopolitan Responses to Nationalism

COSMOPOLITANISM OFFERS a contrasting philosophical perspective that emphasizes global citizenship and the moral equality of all individuals, regardless of national affiliation. In responding to nationalism, cosmopolitan theories advocate for ethical principles that transcend national borders and promote global integration.

Immanuel Kant and Perpetual Peace: Immanuel Kant's essay "Perpetual Peace: A Philosophical Sketch" laid the groundwork for cosmopolitan thought. Kant envisioned a world where individuals are treated as citizens of a universal community governed by principles of justice and morality. He argued for a federation of free states that would ensure peace and protect human rights globally.

Peter Singer and Global Ethics: Peter Singer's concept of "expanding the moral circle" reflects a cosmopolitan ethic that extends moral consideration to all humans. He argues that nationalism arbitrarily restricts moral obligations and that we should act to alleviate suffering and promote well-being globally. Singer's utilitarian framework prioritizes actions that maximize happiness and reduce suffering, regardless of national boundaries.

Global Justice and Rawlsian Approaches: John Rawls, in "The Law of Peoples," extends his theory of justice to the international sphere but stops short of advocating full cosmopolitanism. He argues for a society of liberal and decent peoples governed by principles like human rights, self-determination, and non-intervention. However, Thomas Pogge criticizes Rawls for failing to address global inequalities and advocates for a more egalitarian global order.

Martha Nussbaum and Patriotism vs. Cosmopolitanism: Martha Nussbaum challenges the primacy of national identity in her essay "Patriotism and Cosmopolitanism," arguing that we should prioritize our roles as global citizens. She proposes an education system that promotes cosmopolitan values and empathy, fostering a sense of shared humanity.

David Held and Global Governance: David Held advocates for cosmopolitan democracy, which seeks to democratize global governance institutions like the United Nations. He argues that globalization has eroded the effectiveness of nation-states in addressing global challenges like climate change and inequality. Cosmopolitan democracy aims to create accountable and inclusive global institutions that represent the interests of all people.

The tension between nationalism and cosmopolitanism raises several moral and ethical considerations regarding the coexistence of diverse national identities within a globally integrated world.

Self-Determination and Cultural Preservation: Nationalist movements often emphasize the moral right to self-determination and the preservation of distinct cultural identities. For marginalized communities, nationalism can be a source of empowerment and resistance against cultural imperialism. However, when nationalism turns exclusionary or xenophobic, it can justify discrimination and violence against outsiders.

Ethnocentrism and Moral Particularism: Nationalism is often criticized for promoting ethnocentrism and moral particularism, prioritizing the interests of one's own nation over universal moral obligations. This can lead to policies that exclude or marginalize minorities and justify the neglect of global responsibilities.

Global Justice and Equity: Cosmopolitanism seeks to establish a framework for global justice that ensures fair treatment and opportunities for all individuals. However, implementing global distributive justice remains challenging due to differences in political will and economic capabilities among states.

Diverse Identities and Global Integration: While cosmopolitanism advocates for global integration, it must also recognize and respect diverse national identities. The challenge lies in creating a global order that balances universal moral principles with the right to cultural self-determination.

Democratic Deficit and Accountability: Cosmopolitan governance faces the challenge of addressing the democratic deficit in global institutions.

Critics argue that supranational organizations like the UN and EU are often unaccountable and lack legitimacy, highlighting the need for inclusive and democratic global structures.

Reconciling nationalism and cosmopolitanism requires a nuanced approach that acknowledges the moral imperatives of both perspectives. While nationalism provides a sense of belonging and cultural continuity, cosmopolitanism emphasizes universal moral obligations and global cooperation. A balanced framework would:

- **Promote Inclusive Nationalism:** Encourage forms of nationalism that are inclusive and embrace diversity, avoiding exclusionary and xenophobic tendencies.

- **Advance Global Solidarity:** Build global solidarity through education and policies that promote empathy and shared humanity, addressing global challenges like poverty.

- **Strengthen Democratic Global Institutions:** Reform global institutions to ensure greater representation and accountability, to enable effectively addressing global issues.

- **Respect Cultural Diversity:** Recognize and protect diverse national identities while ensuring that they align with universal human rights principles.

In wandering the coexistence of diverse national identities within a globally integrated world, moral and political philosophy plays a crucial role in guiding policies that are both inclusive and ethically sound. By blending the moral insights of nationalism and cosmopolitanism, we can work towards a future that respects both local identities and global responsibilities.

4.5 Solutions to the Challenges of Nationalism in Global Integration

The resurgence of nationalism poses significant challenges to global cooperation, necessitating nuanced philosophical and practical solutions. Here, we explore strategies that balance national interests with global integration, while also considering the role of international organizations and treaties in mitigating the adverse effects of nationalism.

I. Inclusive Nationalism and Civic Patriotism

INCLUSIVE NATIONALISM, as discussed earlier, seeks to maintain national identity while embracing diversity. Civic patriotism, a form of nationalism rooted in shared values rather than ethnicity, can promote inclusivity. ***Jürgen Habermas*** argues for a form of *national identity based on constitutional values like democracy and human rights*, rather than ethnic or cultural ties. This form of civic nationalism prioritizes shared political principles over exclusionary cultural markers. Similarly, in "*Thick and Thin: Moral Argument at Home and Abroad*," **Michael Walzer** distinguishes between thick, culturally specific moral norms and thin, universal principles. Applying this concept, nations can cultivate a thick moral identity while embracing thin cosmopolitan principles like human rights and global cooperation. This can be done by:

- **Promoting Civic Education:** Governments should invest in civic education that emphasizes democratic values, human rights, and global citizenship. This education should cultivate respect for diversity and counter exclusionary nationalist narratives.

- **Inclusive National Symbols and Narratives:** National symbols and narratives should reflect the multicultural nature of modern nations. Public campaigns and cultural projects can highlight contributions from diverse communities to national identity.

II. Global Solidarity and Cosmopolitan Cooperation

GLOBAL SOLIDARITY, rooted in cosmopolitan principles, calls for cooperation that transcends national borders to address common challenges. *Thomas Pogge*, in "World Poverty and Human Rights," advocates for global cooperation to reduce poverty and inequality. *Immanuel Kant's* vision of a federation of free states in "Perpetual Peace" provides a philosophical framework for cosmopolitan cooperation. States should respect human rights and work towards global peace through mutual agreements. *Peter Singer's* concept of effective altruism emphasizes the moral obligation to address global suffering. This approach advocates for targeted efforts that maximize positive global impact. This can be practically implemented by:

- **Supporting Global Development Goals:** Nations should commit to global development goals like the UN's Sustainable Development Goals (SDGs), aligning national policies with global welfare.

- **Transnational Advocacy Networks:** Support transnational networks that advocate for global issues like climate change, poverty reduction, and human rights. These networks can influence international organizations and mobilize grassroots support.

III. Reforming International Organizations and Treaties

INTERNATIONAL ORGANIZATIONS and treaties play a crucial role in promoting global cooperation, but they need reform to be more inclusive and effective. *David Held's* concept of cosmopolitan democracy calls for global governance structures that represent global citizens and are accountable to them. As explored extensively earlier, *John Rawls'* framework emphasizes that international cooperation should be based on shared principles like human rights and non-aggression. Here are some consideration for practical Implementation:

- **UN Security Council Reform:** Expand the Security Council's membership to include more countries from Africa, Latin America, and Asia.

- **Voting Rights in International Financial Institutions:** Adjust voting rights in the IMF and World Bank to reflect current global economic realities.

- **Paris Agreement Implementation:** Nations should commit to reducing emissions and support developing countries in their climate adaptation efforts.

- **Trade Agreements with Labor and Environmental Standards:** Embed labor rights and environmental protections in international trade agreements.

IV. Responsible Sovereignty and the Responsibility to Protect (R2P)

THE CONCEPT OF RESPONSIBLE sovereignty suggests that states should prioritize the well-being of their populations and respect international norms. Former UN Secretary-General ***Kofi Annan's*** Responsibility to Protect (R2P) doctrine emphasizes the duty of states to protect their populations from genocide, war crimes, and other atrocities. Simultaneously, Martha Nussbaum's approach emphasizes the need to enhance individual capabilities globally, aligning with the concept of responsible sovereignty. R2P Framework can be strengthened through early warning systems, for instance, by establishing international early warning systems to identify potential atrocities or support regional organizations in developing peacekeeping capacities.

Similarly, promoting Capabilities-Oriented Development through International Development Programs (IDP) by aligning them with

Nussbaum's capabilities approach, focusing on education, health, and gender equality can be an integral initiative in the long-run.

V. Bridging Dialogue and Cultural Exchange

DIALOGUE AND CULTURAL exchange can mitigate nationalist sentiments by developing mutual understanding and respect. In "Power & Ethics," this approach is highlighted as essential for conflict resolution. Hans-Georg Gadamer's *'hermeneutics of understanding'* argues that understanding between different cultures can be achieved through dialogue that seeks to find common ground. Similarly, Kwame Anthony Appiah's concept of rooted cosmopolitanism emphasizes the need to embrace both local and global identities through dialogue. To practically achieve this, governments should invest in exchange programs that allow students, artists, and professionals to engage with different cultures and support initiatives that promote interfaith and intercultural dialogues, creating platforms for understanding and cooperation.

In essence, addressing the challenges of nationalism in the context of global integration requires a multi-faceted approach rooted in both philosophical principles and practical measures. By balancing national interests with global cooperation, reforming international organizations, and fostering dialogue, we can build a world where diverse national identities coexist within a framework of ethical global integration.

In doing so, the principles of inclusive nationalism, cosmopolitan cooperation, responsible sovereignty, and global solidarity can guide us toward a more just and peaceful global society, ensuring that nationalism serves as a unifying force rather than a divisive one. The role of moral and political philosophy is crucial in shaping policies and narratives that align with these principles, providing a coherent framework to traverse the sophistications of nationalism in a globalized world.

Synthesis

In this chapter, we explored how the resurgence of nationalism intersects with the processes of globalization, resulting in a multifaceted and challenging landscape. By analyzing the economic, cultural, and political factors contributing to the rise of nationalism, we have uncovered the deep-seated anxieties and aspirations that fuel nationalist sentiments worldwide.

We explored the impact of nationalism on the three dimensions of globalization like how trade liberalization has led to economic displacement and growing inequality, creating fertile ground for protectionist policies. The decline of traditional industries due to globalization has caused widespread job losses, prompting nationalist calls to revive local economies. Similarly, rapid cultural exchanges have led to fears of cultural erosion and identity loss, resulting in identity politics and movements aimed at preserving cultural uniqueness. Moreover, the influx of migrants has heightened concerns over cultural integration, fueling xenophobia and resistance to multicultural policies. And finally, supranational entities like the EU challenge traditional notions of sovereignty, provoking nationalist reactions against perceived external control. Populist leaders have exploited nationalist sentiments to rally support against global institutions, portraying them as threats to national sovereignty.

We discussed how the challenge of balancing nationalism with global interdependence requires a nuanced philosophical and practical approach. The resurgence of nationalism reflects genuine concerns that must be addressed without compromising the ideals of global cooperation and ethical governance.

Firstly, the concept of ethical nationalism emphasizes pride in one's nation without denigrating others. By fostering inclusive national identities that embrace diversity, nations can maintain social cohesion while respecting multiculturalism. Civic patriotism, as advocated by Jürgen Habermas, promotes a sense of belonging based on shared democratic values rather than ethnicity, allowing for inclusive and multicultural national identities.

Secondly, David Held's cosmopolitan democracy provides a framework for enhancing global governance, making it more representative and accountable. Thomas Pogge and Peter Singer advocate for global solidarity, emphasizing the moral obligation to alleviate global inequality and protect human rights.

Finally, responsible sovereignty, aligned with the Responsibility to Protect doctrine, calls for states to protect their citizens while respecting international norms. Reforming international organizations and treaties to be more inclusive and representative can strengthen global cooperation and mitigate nationalist tensions.

Implications for the Future of Global Politics, Economy, and Culture

GLOBAL POLITICS: Reforming supranational institutions to be more democratic and transparent can enhance their legitimacy and reduce nationalist backlash. Addressing the root causes of populism requires inclusive policies that address economic inequality and cultural integration.

Global Economy: Trade agreements should include labor and environmental standards to ensure fair competition and protect vulnerable communities. Economic policies must support local industries and provide retraining programs to help workers adapt to the changing global economy.

Global Culture: Promoting intercultural dialogue and education can foster mutual understanding and reduce xenophobia. International organizations should support cultural diversity through policies that protect indigenous and marginalized cultures.

Overall, the resurgence of nationalism in the context of globalization poses significant challenges to global cooperation and integration. However, by embracing inclusive nationalism, cosmopolitan ethics, and responsible sovereignty, we can find a balance between national interests and global cooperation. This balance will require the collective efforts of governments, international organizations, and civil society to address economic inequality, cultural anxieties, and political instability.

The future of global politics, economy, and culture depends on our ability to reconcile nationalism with the principles of global solidarity and ethical governance. By doing so, we can build a world where diverse national identities coexist within a framework of mutual respect, cooperation, and justice, ensuring that globalization becomes a force for good in an interconnected world.

Chapter 5: Migration and Human Rights

———

Migration has become one of the defining phenomena of the 21st century, characterized by unprecedented global mobility and an intricate web of human rights challenges. In today's interconnected world, migration transcends national boundaries, weaving together economies, cultures, and societies in complex ways. Globalization, with its vast networks of economic opportunities and technological advancements, has facilitated the movement of people across borders in search of better livelihoods, safety, and new beginnings. However, this freedom of movement is met with significant challenges, revealing glaring ethical dilemmas and human rights violations along migration routes.

Globalization has influenced migration patterns in various ways. Trade liberalization and economic integration have created opportunities for labor migration as economies seek to attract talent and fill gaps in their labor markets. Conversely, economic disparities between and within regions have pushed millions to seek better prospects abroad. Conflicts, environmental degradation, and political instability have also driven massive displacement, resulting in refugee crises that strain international cooperation and challenge the moral responsibilities of host nations.

Amid these dynamics, ethical issues emerge around the rights and treatment of migrants. The promises of globalization are often marred by harsh realities: dangerous journeys, discriminatory immigration policies, human trafficking, and exploitation in informal economies. Migrants, particularly refugees and asylum seekers, face discrimination and exclusion in host societies, with their basic rights often violated. Moreover, the rise of nationalism and populist politics has led to stricter immigration policies and xenophobic rhetoric that undermine international cooperation on migration.

This chapter will explore these interconnections between global migration trends and human rights challenges through the lens of moral and political philosophy. We will delve into the ethical theories underpinning migration, such as care ethics and justice as fairness, to understand the moral obligations of individuals, societies, and governments toward migrants. The philosophical implications of human rights philosophy will be examined in the context of migration, particularly the universality of rights versus state sovereignty.

In analyzing the impact of migration across economic, cultural, and political dimensions, we will assess the effects on labor markets, remittances, and global development, as well as the challenges of integration, multiculturalism, and political representation. Case studies like the Syrian refugee crisis and shifting U.S. immigration policies will illustrate the ethical dilemmas and policy implications. Finally, we will propose philosophical and practical solutions to uphold migrant rights, considering strategies for global cooperation, the role of international organizations, and ethical frameworks that can guide migration management.

By the end of this chapter, we will have an understanding of how globalization shapes migration and the resulting human rights challenges. Our goal is to identify pathways toward a more ethical approach that ensures the rights and dignity of migrants are respected within a global context, reinforcing the broader moral responsibilities that globalization demands.

5.1 Global Migration

Migration, in its broadest sense, refers to the movement of people from one place to another, often across international borders, in search of better living conditions, safety, or economic opportunities. Historically, migration has been a constant in human societies, driven by exploration, trade, conquest, colonization, and escape from persecution or economic hardship. Today, globalization has intensified migration patterns, creating intricate networks of economic migrants, refugees, and asylum seekers. Migration can be voluntary or forced, temporary or permanent, and its significance lies in how it shapes demographics, economies, and socio-political landscapes.

Refugees are individuals who have been forced to flee their home countries due to persecution, conflict, violence, or other forms of human rights violations. The 1951 Refugee Convention and its 1967 Protocol, the foundational international legal instruments for refugee protection, define a refugee as someone who *"owing to a well-founded fear of being persecuted for reasons of race, religion, nationality, membership of a particular social group, or political opinion, is outside the country of his nationality and is unable or, owing to such fear, is unwilling to avail himself of the protection of that country."*

Historically, the refugee concept emerged prominently during World War II and its aftermath, when millions were displaced across Europe. The United Nations High Commissioner for Refugees (UNHCR) was established in 1950 to address the crisis and later became the lead international agency for refugee protection. Refugees are entitled to specific rights under international law, particularly the principle of non-refoulement, which prohibits their return to a country where their life or freedom would be threatened.

Simultaneously, asylum seekers are individuals who have crossed international borders in search of protection but whose claims for refugee status have not yet been evaluated. According to international law, anyone has the right to seek asylum in another country. However, this process involves legal verification of whether the individual's circumstances meet the criteria outlined in the 1951 Refugee Convention. Asylum seekers are often in precarious situations, facing lengthy legal processes, detention, and inadequate living conditions while awaiting decisions on their applications.

The concept of asylum has ancient roots, dating back to Greek and Roman times when cities and temples offered sanctuary to those seeking refuge. Modern asylum law, however, developed after World War II, with the 1951 Refugee Convention setting the standards for determining refugee status. Today, asylum seekers play a critical role in global human rights discourse as their treatment and protection reflect the commitments of states to international humanitarian norms.

In the modern era, migration has become a defining feature of globalization. Millions of people are on the move, driven by a combination of economic opportunities, environmental changes, political instability, and conflict. The most pressing issues involve the movement of refugees and asylum seekers, which have reached unprecedented levels in recent years. According to the United Nations High Commissioner for Refugees (UNHCR), as of 2023, there are over 35 million refugees and 5 million asylum seekers worldwide. Key global migration trends include:

- **Displacement due to Conflict and Persecution:** The Syrian conflict has led to over 6.8 million Syrian refugees, primarily hosted in Turkey, Lebanon, Jordan, Iraq, and Egypt. Conflicts in Afghanistan, South Sudan, Myanmar, and Venezuela have also resulted in significant refugee movements, straining neighboring countries' resources.

- **Climate-Induced Migration:** Climate change has increasingly become a driver of migration. Extreme weather events, rising sea levels, and desertification have forced millions to leave their homes. In regions like the Sahel in Africa and the Pacific Islands, climate change-related displacement is a growing concern.

- **Economic Migration:** Economic disparities continue to fuel migration, with millions moving for better employment opportunities. Major migration corridors include South-South movements (e.g., within Africa or Asia) and South-North movements (e.g., from Latin America to the U.S. or from Africa to Europe).

- **Mixed Migration Flows:** The distinction between refugees and economic migrants has become blurred, leading to mixed migration flows. In Latin America, the Venezuelan crisis has resulted in mixed movements of refugees, asylum seekers, and economic migrants across the region.

Migrants, particularly refugees and asylum seekers, face significant human rights challenges:

- **Perilous Journeys and Smuggling:** Refugees often take dangerous routes and rely on smugglers to reach safety, facing risks of exploitation, abuse, and death. In the Mediterranean Sea and along the U.S.-Mexico border, thousands have died attempting to cross.

- **Discriminatory Immigration Policies:** Restrictive immigration policies in many developed countries have resulted in discriminatory practices, prolonged detention, and family separations. Travel bans and pushbacks at borders violate international refugee and human rights law.

- **Lack of Access to Asylum:** Many countries have made it increasingly difficult to access asylum procedures, leaving refugees stranded in unsafe conditions. In Libya, refugees and migrants intercepted at sea by the Libyan Coast Guard face detention, abuse, and exploitation.

- **Exploitation and Labor Rights Violations:** Migrants often work in low-wage, informal sectors, where they face exploitation and poor working conditions. Lack of legal protection and documentation makes them vulnerable to abuse and trafficking.

- **Integration and Xenophobia:** Refugees and migrants often face difficulties integrating into host societies due to language barriers, lack of employment opportunities, and xenophobia. Anti-immigrant sentiment has led to violence, discrimination, and exclusion in many countries.

Global migration trends and the associated human rights challenges have profound implications for global governance and international law.

- **International Refugee Law and Non-Refoulement:** The 1951 Refugee Convention and its 1967 Protocol establish the principle of non-refoulement, prohibiting the return of refugees to countries where they face persecution. However, inconsistent application and lack of ratification by some countries undermine its effectiveness.

- **Global Compacts on Migration and Refugees:** The Global Compact for Safe, Orderly, and Regular Migration (GCM) and the Global Compact on Refugees (GCR) aim to improve international cooperation on migration and refugee protection. Their non-binding nature and differing national interests have limited their impact.

- **Role of International Organizations:** The UNHCR and International Organization for Migration (IOM) play critical roles in coordinating humanitarian responses and advocating for migrant rights. However, their efforts are often constrained by funding shortages and political opposition.

- **National Sovereignty vs. Global Responsibility:** States prioritize sovereignty and border control, often conflicting with international obligations to protect migrants. This tension undermines the universality of human rights and highlights the need for stronger global governance mechanisms.

Current global migration trends reveal a complex interconnectivity between economic, environmental, cultural, and political factors. Refugees and asylum seekers are particularly vulnerable, facing significant human rights challenges that demand urgent attention. The implications for global governance and international law underscore the need for a more cohesive and ethically grounded approach to migration management. Balancing national sovereignty with global responsibility remains a crucial challenge in upholding the rights and dignity of migrants in today's interconnected world.

5.2 Impacts of Migration

Again, migration is one of the most significant phenomena of our time, influencing various dimensions of global society. Its impacts on labor markets, cultural dynamics, and political policies are far-reaching, often sparking debates about economic integration, cultural identity, and national security. A philosophical analysis of these impacts sheds light on the broader ethical implications of migration and helps frame solutions that align with the principles of justice, fairness, and human dignity.

Migration profoundly affects global labor markets, both in host and origin countries. Host nations often benefit from the influx of migrant labor, which can fill skill gaps, contribute to economic growth, and increase productivity. Migrants are often willing to take on jobs that are in low demand among the native workforce, particularly in agriculture, construction, and domestic services. High-skilled migrants, on the other hand, bolster innovation and competitiveness in technology and healthcare sectors.

From an economic perspective, migration often improves overall economic efficiency by reallocating labor where it's most needed. This aligns with the utilitarian principle of maximizing overall happiness, as economic growth and productivity benefit both the host society and the migrants who gain employment.

However, migration also presents challenges. Critics argue that migrants can drive down wages or displace native workers, particularly in low-skilled sectors. Additionally, migration can strain public services like healthcare, education, and housing in host countries, leading to social tensions. Philosophically, this raises questions about distributive justice and how to balance the interests of migrants with those of native populations. John Rawls' theory of justice as fairness offers a perspective here, suggesting that economic policies should be designed to ensure that the least advantaged members of society are not disproportionately affected by migration.

In countries of origin, migration often leads to brain drain, where the emigration of skilled professionals hampers economic development. Conversely, remittances sent back by migrants can significantly bolster the economies of developing nations, providing a vital source of income for millions of families and promoting investment in education and healthcare. This interplay of benefits and drawbacks requires a nuanced understanding of the ethical responsibilities of both host and origin countries in managing migration.

Culturally, it reshapes cultural dynamics in both sending and receiving societies. In host countries, migrants bring diverse languages, religions, and traditions, contributing to the cultural mosaic of multicultural societies. This cultural exchange can enhance social cohesion by fostering understanding and appreciation of different cultures. It aligns with cosmopolitan ethics, which advocate for a global society where cultural diversity is celebrated, and individuals are seen as citizens of the world.

However, cultural integration is often met with challenges. The influx of migrants can lead to identity politics and the perception that national cultures are under threat, sparking nationalist sentiments and anti-immigrant policies. This raises questions about how to balance the preservation of cultural identity with the values of inclusivity and diversity. Charles Taylor's concept of the "politics of recognition" is relevant here, emphasizing the importance of recognizing and valuing cultural differences as a means of ensuring equality and respect.

Multiculturalism, as a policy framework, seeks to promote the coexistence of multiple cultures within a single society. However, it is often criticized for encouraging cultural segregation rather than integration. Philosophers like Will Kymlicka advocate for a "liberal multiculturalism" that recognizes group rights while ensuring that all citizens have equal access to opportunities and public resources. This approach seeks to balance the cultural rights of migrants with the need for a cohesive national identity.

Politically, migration challenges traditional notions of sovereignty and citizenship. Host countries often face dilemmas in developing immigration policies that balance national security concerns with humanitarian obligations. The rise of right-wing populism in many countries is partly attributed to fears about uncontrolled immigration and its perceived impact on national identity and security.

These political reactions often result in stricter immigration policies and border controls, which can undermine the rights of migrants and asylum seekers. For instance, the European Union's approach to migration, particularly during the Syrian refugee crisis, highlighted the tension between national sovereignty and international obligations. The principle of non-refoulement, a cornerstone of international refugee law, was frequently compromised due to concerns about security and social cohesion.

Philosophically, this raises questions about the ethical basis for restricting migration. Michael Walzer, in his book Spheres of Justice, argues that nations have the right to control their borders to preserve cultural and political communities. However, he also acknowledges that this right is not absolute and should be balanced against the moral duty to help those in dire need.

On the other hand, cosmopolitan thinkers like **_Joseph Carens_** advocate for open borders, arguing that restricting migration is inherently unjust and perpetuates global inequality. Carens compares immigration controls to feudal privilege, suggesting that birthplace should not determine one's life chances. This view challenges the legitimacy of exclusive national citizenship in an interconnected world.

In the context of international relations, migration has also prompted changes in global governance structures. The Global Compact for Safe, Orderly and Regular Migration (GCM) and the Global Compact on Refugees (GCR) represent attempts to develop comprehensive international frameworks for managing migration. However, these initiatives face challenges due to the differing interests of nation-states.

Migration's multifaceted impacts highlight the need for a philosophical approach that addresses the ethical challenges it poses. Justice as fairness, care ethics, and cosmopolitanism provide valuable frameworks for understanding the rights and responsibilities of states and migrants.

A just migration policy must reconcile the legitimate interests of host communities with the universal rights of migrants and refugees. This requires a global approach to burden-sharing, equitable integration policies, and the protection of vulnerable groups. Moreover, it demands a shift in perspective from seeing migrants as economic commodities or security threats to recognizing their intrinsic human worth and potential.

Ultimately, exploring the web of migration in a globalized world requires embracing diversity, upholding human dignity, and building international solidarity. Only through such an inclusive and ethical approach can we hope to address the challenges and opportunities that migration presents.

5.3 Ethical Theories: Care Ethics and Justice as Fairness

Care Ethics

Care ethics, a normative ethical theory that emphasizes relationships, empathy, and the moral significance of care in human interactions, offers a unique framework for understanding migration and the responsibilities of host countries toward migrants and refugees. This approach, rooted in the feminist philosophy of thinkers like Carol Gilligan and Nel Noddings, prioritizes moral obligations that arise from specific relationships and the needs of vulnerable individuals.

In the context of migration, care ethics demands a compassionate response to migrants and refugees, recognizing their vulnerability and the relational interdependence between individuals and communities. Unlike theories that emphasize abstract principles of justice or universal rights, care ethics stresses the moral imperative of responding to individuals' immediate needs and building empathetic connections.

Central to care ethics is the concept of relational responsibility. It emphasizes the moral duty between host countries and migrants, particularly refugees and asylum seekers who are fleeing violence, persecution, or environmental disasters. This responsibility extends beyond legal obligations to include a moral duty of care that prioritizes empathy and support for migrants' immediate needs, such as safety, shelter, and emotional well-being. In addition to emphasizing relational responsibility, care ethics brings attention to vulnerability. Migrants and refugees often face precarious and dangerous journeys to reach safety. Care ethics highlights their heightened vulnerability, urging host countries to provide tailored support that addresses their specific circumstances. For instance, children separated from their families or women who have faced sexual violence require particular forms of care that respect their unique vulnerabilities.

Furthermore, care ethics argues that fulfilling international legal obligations is insufficient if done without genuine empathy or concern for migrants' well-being. Host countries should not merely comply with refugee conventions but should actively create an environment where migrants can rebuild their lives with dignity. The inclusive nature of care ethics challenges exclusionary immigration policies that prioritize national interests over humanitarian concerns. Host countries should consider the moral implications of restrictive policies that exclude those in desperate need and strive to build inclusive societies that value and integrate migrants.

In summary, care ethics provides a compassionate and relational framework that encourages host countries to extend empathy, support, and protection to migrants and refugees. By emphasizing the moral significance of care, this theory challenges the impersonal and often exclusionary policies that characterize many contemporary immigration systems.

Justice as Fairness

JOHN RAWLS' THEORY of "justice as fairness," articulated in his seminal work *A Theory of Justice (1971)*, offers another significant framework for analyzing the rights and responsibilities of host countries towards migrants and refugees. Rawls' theory is grounded in the principles of equality and fairness, emphasizing that social and economic inequalities are only justifiable if they benefit the least advantaged members of society.

In his thought experiment, individuals in the "original position" are placed behind a "veil of ignorance," unaware of their social status, nationality, or personal attributes. This forces them to design a just society without bias. Applied to migration, the original position would lead to a framework where the rights and needs of migrants and refugees are considered impartially, ensuring fair treatment regardless of nationality.

From this starting point, Rawls derives two principles of justice as fairness. The first principle *calls for equal basic rights and liberties*, ensuring that all individuals, including migrants and refugees, are granted basic rights and freedoms, such as the right to freedom from persecution and the right to seek asylum. The second principle emphasizes *fair equality of opportunity*, asserting that migrants and refugees should have equitable access to opportunities in education, employment, and healthcare in host countries. Additionally, Rawls' "difference principle" stipulates that social and economic inequalities should benefit the least advantaged. In the context of migration, this principle implies that host countries should structure policies to uplift vulnerable migrant populations.

While Rawls initially limited justice as fairness to a single society, his later work The Law of Peoples extends these principles to the international sphere. Here, Rawls argues for "decent peoples" to ensure that their policies do not exacerbate global inequalities or violate human rights. In migration, this suggests that affluent nations have a moral duty to offer asylum and contribute to international efforts to aid refugees, balancing national interests with global responsibilities.

In practical terms, justice as fairness calls for non-discriminatory asylum procedures to ensure fair and non-discriminatory asylum processes that prioritize the safety and rights of all applicants. Furthermore, migrants and refugees should receive adequate support to access education, employment, and healthcare, ensuring fair opportunities for integration. At a global level, justice as fairness encourages host countries to cooperate internationally to share the burden of refugee protection and address the root causes of forced migration.

In essence, justice as fairness provides a robust ethical framework for host countries to design migration policies that are not only legally compliant but also morally just. By focusing on fairness, equality, and the rights of the least advantaged, this theory offers a principled guide for reconciling national sovereignty with global ethical obligations.

Combining the insights of care ethics and justice as fairness provides a comprehensive framework for understanding the rights and responsibilities of host countries toward migrants and refugees. While care ethics emphasizes the moral importance of empathy and relational responsibility, justice as fairness offers a principled structure for equitable policy-making.

Together, these theories encourage host countries to design migration systems that are both compassionate and just, ensuring that migrants and refugees are treated with the dignity and respect they deserve in an increasingly interconnected world.

5.4 Human Rights Philosophy and Migration

The philosophy of human rights provides a crucial framework for understanding the global ethical obligations toward migrants and ensuring their rights in the context of migration. Rooted in the principles of universal human dignity and equity, human rights philosophy emphasizes the inherent worth of every individual and the moral imperative to protect this worth through legal and ethical norms. In the realm of migration, this philosophy intersects with various ethical theories to advocate for the protection and fair treatment of migrants and refugees, regardless of their legal status or nationality.

The modern conception of human rights, as encapsulated in the Universal Declaration of Human Rights (UDHR) of 1948, serves as a foundational document in human rights philosophy. Article 14 of the UDHR explicitly recognizes the right to seek asylum from persecution, emphasizing the global community's responsibility to protect those fleeing violence and oppression. This declaration, along with subsequent international treaties like the 1951 Refugee Convention and its 1967 Protocol, establishes the principles of non-refoulement (prohibiting the forced return of individuals to countries where they face persecution) and the right to non-discrimination in refugee protection.

The UDHR's recognition of universal human dignity implies that all individuals, including migrants and refugees, possess inherent rights that transcend national borders. This idea is reinforced by the International Covenant on Civil and Political Rights (ICCPR) and the International Covenant on Economic, Social, and Cultural Rights (ICESCR), both of which underscore the duty of states to protect individuals within their jurisdictions, including migrants and asylum seekers.

The philosophy of human rights is closely aligned with ethical theories that emphasize universal moral obligations, such as deontology and consequentialism. Immanuel Kant's deontological ethics, with its categorical imperative to treat humanity as an end in itself, aligns with the principle of universal human dignity, urging nations to respect the rights of migrants and refugees unconditionally. Kant's concept of "cosmopolitan right" further supports the ethical duty to offer asylum and hospitality to strangers seeking refuge, regardless of their national origin.

Consequentialist theories, particularly utilitarianism, advocate for maximizing overall well-being and minimizing suffering. In the context of migration, this framework suggests that states should act to protect migrants and refugees because doing so reduces global suffering. Peter Singer's utilitarian arguments for global poverty alleviation, as articulated in his work The Life You Can Save, resonate with this perspective. Singer argues that affluent nations have a moral obligation to aid those in desperate need, which includes providing refuge and support to displaced populations.

Additionally, the capabilities approach, pioneered by Martha Nussbaum and Amartya Sen, provides a comprehensive framework for understanding the rights of migrants. This approach emphasizes the importance of enabling individuals to achieve core capabilities, such as health, education, and social participation. In the context of migration, it argues that host countries have a moral duty to ensure that migrants and refugees can access opportunities to realize their potential and live fulfilling lives.

The concept of global ethical obligations builds on these theoretical foundations to advocate for a shared responsibility in protecting migrants and ensuring their rights. This responsibility extends beyond the borders of individual nations to encompass a global framework where affluent countries assist those less equipped to handle migration crises.

A significant aspect of this obligation lies in the principle of equity. Equity, as distinct from equality, recognizes that different groups have different needs and requires policies tailored to address these differences. In migration, this translates to providing specific support for vulnerable groups like women, children, and the elderly, who may face unique challenges and risks during migration.

Furthermore, global ethical obligations require a fair distribution of the burden of refugee protection. The concept of "burden-sharing" is rooted in the notion that no single country should bear the full responsibility for protecting refugees. The New York Declaration for Refugees and Migrants (2016) and the Global Compact on Refugees (2018) emphasize the importance of international solidarity and cooperation in sharing this responsibility equitably.

Despite the philosophical and legal frameworks supporting migrant rights, numerous challenges persist in practice. Xenophobia, discrimination, and restrictive immigration policies often prevent migrants from accessing basic rights and opportunities. Refugees face prolonged periods in camps with inadequate living conditions, and asylum seekers encounter lengthy and uncertain asylum processes.

Moreover, irregular migrants, who lack legal documentation, are particularly vulnerable to exploitation and abuse. Their precarious status often excludes them from legal protection and basic services, highlighting the gap between human rights ideals and reality. The "deterrence policies" adopted by some nations, involving pushbacks at borders, detention of asylum seekers, and offshore processing, further undermine the principle of non-refoulement and violate international human rights norms.

To address these challenges, a philosophical approach to migration must advocate for policies that uphold the dignity and rights of migrants, grounded in universal human rights philosophy. This approach would emphasize comprehensive asylum procedures that prioritize human rights over national interests, ensuring fair treatment for all applicants.

Moreover, equitable global burden-sharing should be institutionalized through international agreements, with affluent nations providing financial and logistical support to countries hosting large refugee populations. Regional protection frameworks, like the European Union's Common

European Asylum System (CEAS), should be strengthened and expanded to offer consistent protection standards across regions.

Lastly, inclusive integration policies must be developed to ensure that migrants and refugees can access education, employment, and healthcare, enabling them to rebuild their lives with dignity. These policies should be guided by care ethics, justice as fairness, and the capabilities approach to ensure that the most vulnerable are prioritized and supported.

In effect, human rights philosophy provides a powerful framework for understanding and addressing the ethical challenges of migration. By emphasizing universal human dignity and equity, it calls for a global response that prioritizes the rights of migrants and refugees, ensuring that their humanity is recognized and respected in an increasingly interconnected world.

5.5 Philosophical and Practical Solutions

Addressing the ethical challenges posed by migration requires a multifaceted approach that considers philosophical frameworks while also implementing practical solutions. This necessitates collaborative efforts from international organizations, national governments, and non-governmental bodies to craft policies that protect migrant rights and welfare effectively. Below are comprehensive philosophical and practical solutions that can guide this endeavor.

1. Strengthening International Cooperation and Frameworks

THE CONCEPT OF GLOBAL justice, rooted in cosmopolitan ethics, underpins the idea that all individuals deserve equal moral consideration, regardless of nationality. Joseph Carens and Martha Nussbaum advocate for a cosmopolitan model where nation-states recognize their moral obligations to migrants as part of a shared humanity.

- **Ratifying International Conventions:** All nations should ratify and implement international conventions like the International Convention on the Protection of the Rights of All Migrant Workers and Members of Their Families (ICRMW). This would establish a minimum standard of rights and protection for migrants.

- **Strengthening International Organizations:** The United Nations should bolster the mandates of the International Organization for Migration (IOM) and the United Nations High Commissioner for Refugees (UNHCR) to monitor and advocate for migrant rights. A Global Migration Observatory could be established to collect data, track trends, and advise governments on policy.

- **Global Compacts Implementation:** Nations should fully implement the Global Compact for Safe, Orderly and Regular Migration (GCM) and the Global Compact on Refugees (GCR). These compacts emphasize shared responsibility, solidarity, and international cooperation, promoting policies that respect human rights and humane treatment of migrants.

II. Reforming National Immigration Policies

JOHN RAWLS' THEORY of justice as fairness emphasizes the need to protect the most vulnerable in society. Applying this to migration, national immigration policies should be crafted to ensure fair treatment and opportunities for all migrants.

- **Pathways to Citizenship:** Create clear and achievable pathways to citizenship or legal residency for migrants. This includes reducing bureaucratic barriers and ensuring that long-term migrants can eventually gain permanent residency or citizenship.

- **Regularization Programs:** Implement regularization programs for undocumented migrants, providing them with legal status and access to essential services like healthcare and education.

- **Balanced Immigration Quotas:** Establish balanced immigration quotas that reflect labor market needs while also prioritizing family reunification and humanitarian protection.

- **Non-Discriminatory Policies:** Enforce non-discriminatory immigration policies that ensure all migrants receive equal treatment, regardless of nationality, ethnicity, or religion.

- **Migrant Integration Programs:** Develop comprehensive integration programs that include language courses, employment assistance, and cultural orientation. These programs should be tailored to the specific needs of different migrant groups.

III. Protecting the Rights of Vulnerable Migrants

IMMANUEL KANT'S PRINCIPLE of universal human dignity dictates that all individuals must be treated as ends in themselves, not as means to an end. Migrants, especially the vulnerable, deserve full protection of their rights and dignity.

- **Special Protection for Women and Children:** Establish specialized programs to protect migrant women and children, who are often at higher risk of exploitation and abuse. This includes providing shelters, legal aid, and counseling services.

- **Anti-Trafficking Measures:** Strengthen anti-trafficking measures through international collaboration, focusing on the identification, rescue, and rehabilitation of victims.

- **Fair Labor Practices:** Enforce international labor standards for migrant workers through partnerships with the International Labour Organization (ILO). This includes ensuring fair wages, safe working conditions, and the right to organize.

- **Access to Justice:** Provide legal aid and support services to help migrants navigate the legal system and claim their rights. This includes creating migrant resource centers and hotlines for reporting abuse.

IV. Involving Non-Governmental Organizations (NGOs) and Civil Society

CIVIL SOCIETY INVOLVEMENT is crucial for fostering global solidarity and advocacy. The principle of subsidiarity, as discussed by Aristotle and Thomas Aquinas, emphasizes the importance of local and non-governmental bodies in addressing social issues.

- **Advocacy and Awareness Campaigns:** NGOs should lead advocacy campaigns to raise awareness of migrant rights and influence public opinion. Highlighting success stories can challenge negative stereotypes about migrants.

- **Public-Private Partnerships:** Foster partnerships between NGOs, governments, and private entities to support job training and placement programs for migrants.

- **Community Support Networks:** Establish community support networks that connect migrants with local volunteers, organizations, and services, fostering social cohesion and mutual understanding.

- **Research and Policy Development:** NGOs can contribute by conducting research on migration trends and challenges, providing data to inform more effective policy development.

V. Promoting Fair Trade and Sustainable Development

FAIR TRADE AND SUSTAINABLE development policies align with Marxist and postcolonial critiques of global inequality, emphasizing the need to address structural factors that drive migration.

- **Fair Trade Initiatives:** Support fair trade initiatives that ensure producers in developing countries receive fair compensation, reducing the economic pressures that drive migration.

- **Sustainable Development Programs:** Invest in sustainable development programs that address poverty, unemployment, and instability in migrants' home countries.

- **Corporate Social Responsibility:** Encourage multinational corporations to adopt corporate social responsibility (CSR) initiatives that support local communities and create employment opportunities.

- **Debt Relief and Aid:** Provide debt relief and development aid to poor countries to foster economic stability and reduce the root causes of migration.

The ethical challenges of migration demand comprehensive solutions that blend philosophical principles with practical action. By fostering international cooperation, reforming national policies, protecting vulnerable groups, involving civil society, and promoting sustainable development, we can ensure that migration policies align with global justice and human dignity. Such an approach not only addresses the immediate challenges of migration but also lays the groundwork for a more just and equitable global society.

5.6 Strategies for Safeguarding Migrant Rights

Addressing the rights of migrants requires comprehensive strategies that operate across legal, social, and economic dimensions, both locally and internationally. Ensuring their welfare is a moral imperative that aligns with global principles of justice and human rights. Below are strategies rooted in these frameworks.

In the legal sphere, safeguarding migrant rights necessitates bolstering international conventions and national laws while enhancing access to justice. One of the critical steps is encouraging all nations to ratify and implement conventions like the International Convention on the Protection of the Rights of All Migrant Workers and Members of Their Families (ICRMW). This would establish a universal standard for protecting migrant rights. Equally important is implementing the Global Compact for Safe, Orderly and Regular Migration (GCM) and the Global Compact on Refugees (GCR), which promote shared responsibility in protecting migrants.

At the national level, comprehensive immigration reforms should offer clear pathways to citizenship, fair asylum procedures, and protection against deportation for migrants who have established roots in the host country. Additionally, enacting and enforcing non-discriminatory laws is imperative to safeguard migrants from xenophobia, racism, and discrimination.

To ensure access to justice, governments must provide legal aid, helping migrants navigate complex immigration laws and claim their rights. Immigration courts with specialized judges should be established to fairly adjudicate cases with nuanced understanding. Further, policies and shelters should be developed to protect vulnerable groups like migrant women and children from trafficking and abuse. Upholding the principle of non-refoulement, which ensures that no refugee or asylum seeker is forcibly returned to a country where they could face persecution, is essential in protecting refugee and asylum rights.

Similarly, social frameworks are equally important in fostering the integration and protection of migrants. Programs that provide language courses and cultural orientation help migrants integrate into new societies, while mentorship programs that connect migrants with locals can offer valuable guidance and support. Community engagement should also be promoted through grassroots advocacy groups that foster understanding between migrants and locals, and public awareness campaigns to combat xenophobia and promote positive migration narratives.

Ensuring access to education is another critical aspect of migrant welfare. Universal education policies should guarantee that migrant children have access to free, quality education, regardless of their legal status. Vocational training and skill-building programs can further empower migrants economically. Healthcare access is crucial, with universal healthcare coverage extending to migrants, including mental health services and maternal care. Mobile clinics and outreach programs can serve migrant workers in remote areas, ensuring they receive essential medical care.

Economically, protecting migrant rights requires fair labor practices and inclusive social protection measures. Enforcing International Labour Organization (ILO) standards on wages, working conditions, and the right to unionize should be a priority, while regular workplace safety inspections ensure compliance with safety standards. Extending social security benefits like unemployment insurance and pensions to migrants, and creating migrant welfare funds that offer financial assistance during hardship, can provide a crucial safety net.

Regularization programs, which grant legal status to undocumented migrants who have established roots in the host country, and simplified work permit procedures, can enable more migrants to work legally. Additionally, economic empowerment initiatives such as microfinance opportunities, business grants, and financial literacy training can encourage migrant entrepreneurship and financial inclusion.

A global coalition of governments, NGOs, and international organizations should advocate for migrant rights and coordinate international responses. Annual forums where countries can share best practices and address emerging issues in migration can promote collaboration and learning. Multilateral agreements, such as bilateral labor agreements between countries, can ensure migrant workers receive fair treatment and protection. Regional cooperation can also address migration issues, like the European Union's Common European Asylum System.

Simultaneously, CSR plays a significant role in this regard. Companies should be encouraged to adopt ethical recruitment practices and avoid exploitative labor agencies. Audits that ensure supply chains do not exploit migrant workers are equally essential. Finally, research and data collection are crucial. Establishing a global migration observatory to collect data, track trends, and inform policy decisions can be a vital step. Partnering with academic institutions to conduct research on migration patterns and develop innovative policy solutions will also be instrumental.

Safeguarding the rights of migrants requires a comprehensive approach that integrates multiple frameworks. International cooperation, national policy reform, and grassroots advocacy must work in tandem to address the multifaceted challenges migrants face. By embracing these strategies, we can ensure that the principles of justice, equity, and universal human rights are upheld in migration policies worldwide.

5.7 Ethical Management of Migration: Policy Reforms

Effectively managing migration ethically requires a collaborative approach between global and local policies. As migration trends evolve due to economic disparities, conflicts, and climate change, policies must adapt to safeguard migrants' rights while addressing security and integration challenges. Here, we analyze the role of global and local policies and propose reforms in international law and national frameworks to better protect migrants and facilitate their integration.

Global Policies and International Law

INTERNATIONAL CONVENTIONS and frameworks lay the foundation for ethical migration management. The ICRMW, the GCM, and the GCR are pivotal in promoting a coordinated response. However, their effectiveness hinges on universal ratification and robust implementation. Therefore it is crucial to encourage all nations to ratify these conventions and establish a robust monitoring mechanism to ensure compliance. For example, the UN Committee on Migrant Workers could be empowered to investigate violations and recommend reforms.

Non-Refoulement and Refugee Protection

THE PRINCIPLE OF NON-refoulement, enshrined in the 1951 Refugee Convention, protects refugees from being returned to a country where they face persecution. However, its implementation is often inconsistent due to security concerns and xenophobia. Therefore it is imperative to create a unified, legally binding framework that mandates all signatories to adhere to non-refoulement principles. The framework should also establish a rapid response system to provide immediate protection for refugees fleeing persecution.

Global Coordination and Burden-Sharing

THE GCM AND GCR EMPHASIZE burden-sharing among nations, yet many countries resist hosting refugees and migrants due to economic or political concerns. To resolve this, we could establish a Global Migration Fund that provides financial incentives for nations hosting large numbers of refugees or migrants. Wealthier nations should contribute proportionally, and the fund should be managed transparently, ensuring that resources are used for migrant welfare and integration.

International Labour Standards

THE INTERNATIONAL LABOUR Organization (ILO) standards on fair wages, working conditions, and social protection are essential for protecting migrant workers. However, enforcement remains weak due to limited jurisdiction and varying national standards. To deal with this, it is crucial to strengthen the ILO's monitoring powers and introduce a Global Labour Certification System that incentivizes countries to comply with international labor standards. Companies sourcing labor internationally should be required to certify their supply chains as migrant-friendly, ensuring ethical recruitment practices.

Climate Migration and Internally Displaced Persons (IDPs)

CLIMATE CHANGE-INDUCED displacement creates new challenges for international law, as climate migrants often lack formal refugee status. Here, world governments could draft an International Convention on Climate Migrants that defines their rights and obligations. This convention should also establish a global fund for climate adaptation and support, prioritizing vulnerable regions prone to displacement.

Comprehensive Immigration Reform

NATIONAL IMMIGRATION policies often fail to address the nuanced needs of migrants and refugees, leading to precarious legal statuses and exploitation. Enacting comprehensive immigration reform that includes clear pathways to citizenship, humanitarian visa programs for climate migrants, and streamlined asylum procedures could help subside this issue. Regularization programs should be established for undocumented migrants who have established roots in the host country.

Inclusive Social Protection and Access to Services

MIGRANTS OFTEN FACE barriers in accessing healthcare, education, and social services due to legal status or discrimination. Countries could expand social protection schemes to include all migrants, regardless of status, ensuring access to healthcare, education, and social benefits. Create national migrant welfare funds that provide financial assistance during hardship, funded through contributions from employers and government subsidies.

Labor Market Integration and Skill Development

LABOR MARKET INTEGRATION is crucial for migrant self-sufficiency and social cohesion. However, barriers like credential recognition and language proficiency often hinder migrants. Nations could develop labor market integration programs that offer language training, vocational courses, and credential recognition pathways. Partnerships between governments, NGOs, and private sectors can create internship and apprenticeship opportunities for migrants.

Combating Xenophobia and Promoting Social Cohesion

XENOPHOBIA AND DISCRIMINATION undermine migrant integration and fuel social tensions. To fight this, implement nationwide public awareness campaigns that promote positive narratives around migration. Community engagement programs that connect migrants with locals through mentorship, cultural exchange, and sports can foster mutual understanding.

Decentralized Policy Implementation

CENTRALIZED MIGRATION policies often fail to address the unique challenges of different regions within a country. Decentralized migration policy implementation through the empowerment of local governments to tailor programs to their regional contexts could help alleviate the afflictions of this issue. Local authorities should have greater autonomy in managing migrant integration, with central governments providing technical and financial support.

Managing migration ethically requires a holistic approach that integrates global conventions with national policies and local frameworks. By advocating for reforms in international law and national strategies, we can establish a more just and inclusive system that upholds the dignity and rights of migrants. Collaboration between governments, NGOs, and international organizations is crucial in developing ethical migration policies that promote global solidarity, social cohesion, and sustainable development.

Synthesis

Throughout this chapter, we've explored the multifaceted ethical debates surrounding migration and human rights including, State Sovereignty vs. Universal Human Rights, Care Ethics vs. Justice as Fairness, Economic Contributions vs. Labor Exploitation, Cultural Integration vs. Identity Politics, and other such issues.

Looking ahead, global migration trends will continue to evolve, driven by economic disparities, conflicts, and environmental changes. As these trends unfold, several human rights challenges will need to be addressed such as climate change, which will displace millions, necessitating a comprehensive framework that recognizes and protects climate migrants. International cooperation is crucial in managing this challenge, ensuring that affected populations receive adequate assistance. Similarly, with the increasing use of digital technologies in border management, ethical concerns around surveillance, data privacy, and discriminatory practices will emerge. Transparent and rights-based frameworks are essential to prevent abuse.

Automation and the gig economy will reshape labor markets, potentially exacerbating migrant exploitation. Fair labor standards and social protection measures will be vital to safeguard migrant workers in this changing landscape. Geopolitical tensions will continue to fuel forced migration, necessitating stronger global governance and humanitarian frameworks. The international community must bolster efforts to protect refugees and resolve underlying conflicts.

Managing the integration of migrants into host societies will remain a challenge, particularly in regions experiencing rising nationalism. Inclusive social policies and public awareness campaigns are needed to promote mutual understanding and cohesion. At the same time, as migration flows increase, so will the risk of human trafficking and exploitation. Strengthening international cooperation and enforcement mechanisms is crucial to dismantling trafficking networks and protecting vulnerable migrants.

The ethical debates surrounding migration and human rights reflect a world grappling with the issues of globalization. Balancing the rights and responsibilities of nations and individuals remains a moral challenge, requiring philosophical and practical solutions. By embracing a framework that prioritizes human dignity, justice, and global solidarity, we can work towards migration policies that are both ethical and effective. The future of migration will demand innovative strategies that address the evolving trends and challenges in an interconnected world. As we move forward, policymakers, scholars, and global citizens must collaborate to uphold the fundamental rights of migrants while fostering a more inclusive and just global society. Closing this chapter on migration and human rights, we now turn to another pressing issue that transcends borders, environmental sustainability and global policies.

Chapter 6: Environmental Sustainability and Global Policies

In the modern era, environmental challenges have escalated to unprecedented levels, posing existential threats to humanity and the natural world. Globalization, while fostering economic growth and cultural exchange, has simultaneously magnified environmental degradation through unbridled industrialization, deforestation, and carbon emissions. The interplay between global economic activities, cultural practices, and political decisions has rendered environmental sustainability one of the most pressing ethical conundrums of our time. The growing consumption of resources, coupled with the unbalanced distribution of environmental burdens, makes this challenge a quintessential issue in understanding globalization's multifaceted impacts.

Globalization has exacerbated environmental issues by accelerating industrial activities, enabling mass consumption, and promoting resource-intensive lifestyles. This rapid economic growth, particularly in developing nations, has often come at the expense of environmental sustainability. Key environmental challenges shaped by globalization include *climate change, deforestation, biodiversity loss, plastic pollution, marine debris, water scarcity, contamination, air pollution, health risks, desertification, and soil degradation*. Climate change, for instance, has been significantly influenced by globalization through increased greenhouse gas emissions from industrial activities and extensive energy consumption. Deforestation and biodiversity loss, driven by global demand for commodities like timber, palm oil, and soy, have threatened biodiversity and disrupted ecosystems, particularly in the Amazon and Southeast Asia. Furthermore, the global proliferation of plastic products has resulted in severe plastic pollution, particularly in oceans, where marine debris is impacting marine life and coastal communities.

Water scarcity and contamination have also been exacerbated by industrial activities and large-scale agriculture, leading to water scarcity in several regions. Pollution from industries and agricultural runoff has contaminated freshwater resources, affecting both human populations and ecosystems. Additionally, rapid urbanization and industrialization have led to deteriorating air quality in many global cities, with adverse health effects on millions of people worldwide. Intensive agriculture, deforestation, and unsustainable land-use practices have caused desertification and soil degradation, threatening food security and rural livelihoods.

This chapter ventures into the ethical, economic, cultural, and political dimensions of environmental sustainability in the context of globalization. The discussion will be framed around key philosophical underpinnings of environmental ethics and global responsibility, providing a comprehensive analysis of the theoretical and practical aspects of sustainable development. The chapter will be organized into five sections, each focusing on different aspects of environmental sustainability and global policies.

The first section explores the philosophical underpinnings of environmental sustainability by examining environmental ethics and global responsibility through theories of sustainable development, ecological justice, and stewardship. It will analyze the moral obligations of states, corporations, and individuals towards environmental protection, highlighting the ethical frameworks that guide sustainable practices in a globalized world. This section will draw from philosophical concepts like the land ethic, deep ecology, and ecological citizenship to discuss the responsibilities of various stakeholders in protecting the environment.

The second section analyzes the impact of globalization on environmental sustainability across economic, cultural, and political dimensions. The economic impact will focus on the rise of green economies and sustainable development, exploring how globalization has influenced the transition to renewable energy and sustainable agriculture. The cultural impact will examine environmentalism as a cultural movement and the role of indigenous knowledge in promoting sustainable practices. The political impact will investigate the effectiveness of international environmental agreements and policies, such as the Kyoto Protocol and the Paris Agreement, in addressing global environmental challenges.

The third section presents detailed case studies that highlight the complexities and challenges of environmental sustainability in different global contexts. The first case study examines the achievements and shortcomings of the Paris Agreement in the fight against climate change, analyzing the commitments made by various countries and the challenges in implementing them. The second case study focuses on deforestation in the Amazon, exploring the local and global consequences of deforestation and the impact of international trade on the region's ecosystems. The third case study delves into the challenges of electronic waste disposal and recycling in developing countries, highlighting the environmental and health risks associated with improper e-waste management.

The fourth section proposes philosophical and practical solutions to environmental challenges by promoting global and local policies for environmental protection. It discusses innovations in technology and policy for sustainability, including global frameworks for ecological justice and equitable resource distribution, the role of technology in sustainable agriculture and renewable energy, and collaborative approaches between states, corporations, and civil society. This section emphasizes the importance of collective action and ethical governance in addressing environmental challenges, advocating for a multilateral approach to sustainable development.

The final section synthesizes the philosophical insights and challenges discussed throughout the chapter, offering a roadmap for sustainable practices in a globalized world. It highlights the critical need for collective action and ethical governance in addressing the environmental crisis, calling for a global commitment to sustainable development that balances economic growth with ecological preservation. By weaving together philosophical reflections with practical policy insights, Chapter 6 aims to provide a nuanced understanding of how we can navigate the ethical conundrums of environmental sustainability in an increasingly globalized world.

6.1 Environmental Ethics and Global Responsibility

In understanding environmental sustainability, we must ground our analysis in the field of environmental ethics, which probes the moral relationship between humans and the natural environment. Environmental ethics helps us discern the moral obligations of states, corporations, and individuals in protecting the environment, especially in the globalized world where interconnected economic and cultural activities transcend borders. Within this framework, the concepts of sustainable development, ecological justice, and stewardship become pivotal in outlining the ethical principles that underpin environmental sustainability.

Sustainable Development

SUSTAINABLE DEVELOPMENT has emerged as a cornerstone concept in discussions about environmental sustainability. *The Brundtland Commission's* landmark report *Our Common Future* defined sustainable development as development that meets the needs of the present without compromising the ability of future generations to meet their own needs. This definition encapsulates the ethical imperative to balance current economic growth with long-term environmental preservation, thus advocating for a holistic approach that integrates economic, environmental, and social dimensions.

Philosophically, sustainable development challenges the utilitarian calculus that prioritizes immediate economic benefits over long-term ecological health. Instead, it aligns with principles of justice as fairness, articulated by John Rawls, by emphasizing intergenerational equity and ensuring that future generations inherit an environment capable of sustaining life and prosperity. It requires that states and corporations internalize the environmental costs of their activities and prioritize sustainable practices that do not undermine ecological stability.

Ecological Justice

ECOLOGICAL JUSTICE extends the concept of justice to encompass the natural world, arguing that non-human entities have intrinsic value and deserve moral consideration. This idea expands beyond anthropocentric ethics to include biocentric and ecocentric perspectives. Biocentrism holds that all living beings have inherent worth, while ecocentrism values ecosystems as whole, emphasizing the interconnectedness of life forms and their environments.

The theories of ecological justice are particularly relevant in globalization, as global economic activities often lead to environmental degradation in less developed regions while benefiting more developed nations. This imbalance raises questions of distributive justice, especially regarding the disproportionate impact of environmental degradation on marginalized communities. Environmental philosopher **Robyn Eckersley** argues for "ecological citizenship," suggesting that individuals and states have global responsibilities to reduce environmental harm and promote sustainability. This notion aligns with Peter Singer's concept of "effective altruism," which advocates for maximizing positive global impact, particularly in addressing climate change and environmental degradation.

Stewardship and the Land Ethic

STEWARDSHIP REFLECTS the idea that humans are caretakers of the Earth, entrusted with the responsibility of preserving and enhancing the natural environment for future generations. This concept finds resonance in **Aldo Leopold's** land ethic, which asserts that humans are part of a larger biotic community and should act as responsible members rather than conquerors of the land. Leopold argues that ethical land use is rooted in a deep ecological understanding of the interdependence between humans and nature.

The stewardship model implies that states, corporations, and individuals have moral obligations to adopt sustainable practices that protect ecosystems, biodiversity, and natural resources. Corporations, for instance, should minimize their ecological footprint by adopting circular economy principles that reduce waste and promote recycling. Individuals, as consumers and citizens, should make lifestyle choices that align with ecological values, such as reducing consumption, supporting environmentally friendly businesses, and advocating for green policies.

Deep Ecology and Ecological Citizenship

DEEP ECOLOGY, A TERM coined by Norwegian philosopher *Arne Naess*, extends the ethical considerations of environmentalism to challenge the anthropocentric worldview that places humans above other forms of life. Instead, deep ecology promotes a holistic view of nature, recognizing the intrinsic value of all living beings and advocating for a radical transformation in how humans interact with the environment.

Naess proposed an eight-point platform for deep ecology, which includes the reduction of human population, decentralization of economic and political structures, and the promotion of biodiversity and ecological harmony. This platform aligns with the concept of ecological citizenship, which argues that individuals have ethical obligations to protect the environment not just locally but globally. Ecological citizenship emphasizes global solidarity and advocates for lifestyle changes that reflect a commitment to reducing one's ecological footprint.

Responsibilities of Stakeholders in Environmental Protection

GIVEN THESE PHILOSOPHICAL underpinnings, the responsibilities of various stakeholders become clearer. States have the responsibility to implement and enforce environmental regulations, promote renewable energy, and support international agreements that address global environmental issues. Corporations must prioritize CSR by internalizing environmental costs, reducing emissions, and adopting sustainable production practices. Individuals, as ecological citizens, should advocate for environmental policies, support sustainable businesses, and reduce their consumption of non-renewable resources.

In a globalized world where environmental degradation transcends borders, these ethical frameworks guide sustainable practices and emphasize the moral imperative of protecting the environment for current and future generations. By embracing principles of sustainable development, ecological justice, stewardship, and deep ecology, humanity can forge a path towards a more harmonious and sustainable relationship with the natural world.

6.2 Impact of Globalization on Environmental Sustainability

Global Transition to Renewable Energy

The global economy has undergone significant shifts due to globalization, particularly in transitioning towards greener, more sustainable practices. The global push towards renewable energy sources like wind, solar, and hydropower reflects the growing awareness of climate change's catastrophic effects and the moral imperative to reduce carbon emissions. This transition to renewable energy, often framed within the broader concept of sustainable development, has been accelerated by globalization through technological transfers, international funding, and policy cooperation.

Economic globalization has facilitated the proliferation of renewable energy technologies by enabling the rapid dissemination of innovations across borders. For instance, technological advancements in photovoltaic solar panels have reduced the cost of solar energy production, making it competitive with fossil fuels. China, the United States, and the European Union have emerged as leaders in solar and wind energy production, thanks to global trade networks that have enabled the mass production and export of these technologies. The global diffusion of renewable technologies exemplifies the potential of globalization to accelerate the transition to green economies.

Moreover, global institutions like the World Bank and the IMF have played pivotal roles in financing renewable energy projects in developing countries, facilitating their access to clean energy sources. The Green Climate Fund, established under the United Nations Framework Convention on Climate Change (UNFCCC), aims to mobilize $100 billion annually to help developing nations mitigate and adapt to climate change. This funding structure reflects an ethical commitment to ecological justice, ensuring that less developed nations can participate in the global transition to renewable energy.

Sustainable Agriculture and Fair Trade

GLOBALIZATION HAS ALSO influenced sustainable agricultural practices through the rise of fair trade and organic farming. Fair trade initiatives aim to ensure that farmers in developing countries receive fair prices for their products, enabling them to invest in sustainable farming practices. Organizations like Fairtrade International and the Rainforest Alliance have established certification systems that guarantee fair wages and environmentally friendly farming methods.

Sustainable agriculture, such as agroecology and permaculture, has gained traction globally as awareness of industrial farming's environmental impacts has grown. Global networks of environmental organizations, research institutions, and policymakers have facilitated the exchange of knowledge and best practices in sustainable agriculture. For example, agroecology emphasizes biodiversity, soil health, and water conservation, offering a holistic approach that aligns with the principles of ecological justice and stewardship.

However, the globalization of agriculture has also raised ethical concerns, particularly regarding the commodification of land and resources. Large-scale land acquisitions by multinational corporations, often termed "land grabbing," have led to the displacement of indigenous communities and the degradation of local ecosystems. This trend underscores the need for international regulations that promote sustainable land use and protect the rights of local populations.

Circular Economy and Waste Management

THE CONCEPT OF THE circular economy, which emphasizes reducing, reusing, and recycling resources to minimize waste, has gained prominence in recent years. Globalization has facilitated the adoption of circular economy principles through international collaborations and the standardization of waste management practices.

Countries like Japan and Germany have led the way in implementing circular economy strategies, reducing their reliance on virgin materials and promoting recycling. The European Union's Circular Economy Action Plan aims to make sustainable products the norm, reduce waste, and empower consumers to make environmentally friendly choices. These initiatives reflect a growing recognition of the need for systemic change in global economic practices to address environmental sustainability.

Environmentalism as a Global Cultural Movement

ENVIRONMENTALISM HAS evolved into a global cultural movement, driven by the interconnectedness of global media, advocacy networks, and grassroots activism. The environmental movement, which began with localized efforts to protect natural spaces, has expanded to address global issues like climate change, biodiversity loss, and pollution.

Globalization has played a significant role in spreading environmental awareness, with documentaries like An Inconvenient Truth and platforms like the United Nations' International Day for Biological Diversity reaching global audiences. Social media has enabled activists to mobilize support for environmental causes across borders, as seen in movements like Fridays for Future, led by Greta Thunberg, and Extinction Rebellion.

Environmental organizations like Greenpeace, the World Wildlife Fund (WWF), and Friends of the Earth have established global networks that advocate for stronger environmental policies and corporate accountability. These organizations often collaborate with indigenous communities and local activists, emphasizing the intersectionality of environmental issues with human rights, social justice, and cultural preservation.

Indigenous Knowledge and Sustainable Practices

INDIGENOUS KNOWLEDGE has gained recognition as a valuable resource for promoting environmental sustainability. Indigenous communities often possess intricate knowledge of local ecosystems and sustainable land management practices developed over centuries. Globalization has facilitated the integration of this knowledge into global environmental policies and practices.

For example, the concept of Buen Vivir, rooted in indigenous Andean cultures, emphasizes living harmoniously with nature and prioritizing community well-being over economic growth. This philosophy has influenced environmental policies in Ecuador and Bolivia, where the rights of nature have been enshrined in national constitutions. Similarly, the Maori concept of kaitiakitanga in New Zealand advocates for guardianship of the environment, reflecting a deep ecological understanding that aligns with the principles of stewardship and the land ethic.

The integration of indigenous knowledge into global environmental policies is not without challenges. The commodification of indigenous practices through eco-tourism and intellectual property rights often leads to cultural appropriation and exploitation. Furthermore, the displacement of indigenous communities due to resource extraction and infrastructure projects continues to threaten their traditional ways of life.

Effectiveness of International Environmental Agreements

GLOBAL ENVIRONMENTAL agreements like the Kyoto Protocol and the Paris Agreement represent collective efforts to address environmental issues through international cooperation. The Kyoto Protocol, adopted in 1997, was the first international treaty to set legally binding emission reduction targets for developed countries. However, its effectiveness was limited by the lack of participation from major emitters like the United States and developing nations like China and India.

The Paris Agreement, adopted in 2015, marked a significant milestone in global climate policy. Unlike the Kyoto Protocol, it set voluntary emission reduction targets (Nationally Determined Contributions) for all countries, emphasizing the principle of common but differentiated responsibilities. The agreement aims to limit global warming to well below 2°C above pre-industrial levels, with a target of 1.5°C.

Despite its ambitious goals, the Paris Agreement faces challenges in implementation. The voluntary nature of emission targets has led to criticisms of inadequate ambition and lack of enforcement mechanisms. Additionally, the withdrawal of the United States from the agreement under the Trump administration highlighted the fragility of international climate commitments. However, the subsequent rejoining by the Biden administration underscores the agreement's importance as a framework for global climate action.

National Environmental Policies and Globalization

NATIONAL ENVIRONMENTAL policies have been influenced by globalization, with many countries adopting regulations and standards that align with international agreements. The European Union's Emissions Trading System (ETS), the world's largest carbon market, reflects the integration of global climate goals into regional policies. Similarly, China's Belt and Road Initiative (BRI) has incorporated sustainability guidelines to mitigate the environmental impact of infrastructure projects in participating countries.

However, globalization has also led to regulatory challenges, as multinational corporations often exploit lax environmental regulations in developing countries to minimize costs. This practice, known as "pollution haven," highlights the need for stronger international regulations and corporate accountability. The United Nations Guiding Principles on Business and Human Rights provide a framework for corporations to respect human rights and environmental standards in their global operations, but their voluntary nature limits their effectiveness.

Role of Non-Governmental Organizations and Grassroots Movements

NON-GOVERNMENTAL ORGANIZATIONS (NGOs) and grassroots movements have emerged as influential actors in global environmental governance. NGOs like Greenpeace and WWF advocate for stronger environmental policies, conduct scientific research, and hold corporations accountable for their environmental impact. They often collaborate with international organizations like the United Nations and the World Bank to influence global environmental policies.

Grassroots movements, such as indigenous land defenders in the Amazon and anti-coal protests in India, highlight the intersection of environmental and social justice issues. These movements emphasize the need for environmental policies that prioritize marginalized communities and recognize the rights of indigenous peoples. Their activism often leads to policy changes, as seen in the halting of the Keystone XL pipeline in the United States and the protection of the Arctic National Wildlife Refuge.

The impact of globalization on environmental sustainability is multifaceted, influencing economic practices, cultural movements, and political policies. While globalization has facilitated the transition to renewable energy, sustainable agriculture, and circular economy principles, it has also led to environmental degradation and exploitation. Cultural movements like environmentalism and indigenous knowledge have gained prominence globally, advocating for ecological justice and stewardship.

International environmental agreements like the Paris Agreement and grassroots movements have shaped global environmental governance, emphasizing the need for collective action and ethical responsibility. However, the challenges of enforcement, corporate accountability, and cultural appropriation remain significant barriers to achieving global sustainability.

By integrating economic, cultural, and political dimensions, we can develop a comprehensive understanding of environmental sustainability and the ethical frameworks that guide global environmental policies. This understanding is crucial in navigating the complexities of globalization and forging a path towards a more just and sustainable relationship with the natural world.

6.3 Case Studies

The Paris Agreement

The Paris Agreement, adopted in 2015, represents a landmark moment in international climate policy. For the first time, almost all nations came together to establish a universal framework to combat climate change, aiming to limit global temperature rise to well below 2°C above pre-industrial levels, with an aspirational target of 1.5°C. This case study examines the achievements and shortcomings of the Paris Agreement, analyzing the commitments made by various countries and the challenges in implementing them.

The Paris Agreement was groundbreaking in securing the participation of nearly 200 countries, including major emitters like the United States, China, India, and the European Union. Unlike previous climate treaties, which often differentiated between developed and developing nations, the Paris Agreement adopted a more inclusive approach. All countries were encouraged to submit Nationally Determined Contributions (NDCs), representing their voluntary targets for reducing greenhouse gas emissions.

This inclusivity reflects a shared understanding of the principle of common but differentiated responsibilities, where all nations have a role in addressing climate change, but developed countries bear a greater historical responsibility. The participation of developing nations like India and China demonstrated a global recognition of the urgency of climate action.

The concept of Nationally Determined Contributions (NDCs), where each country voluntarily sets its emission reduction targets, was a significant innovation. This flexibility allowed countries to tailor their climate commitments according to their national circumstances, leading to broad participation. As of 2021, 191 parties have submitted their initial NDCs, with many pledging ambitious goals such as carbon neutrality by mid-century.

For example, the European Union committed to reducing emissions by at least 40% below 1990 levels by 2030. China pledged to peak its carbon dioxide emissions by 2030 and increase the share of non-fossil fuels in its energy mix to 20%. India aimed to reduce the emissions intensity of its GDP by 33-35% from 2005 levels and increase renewable energy capacity to 175 GW by 2022.

The Paris Agreement emphasized the importance of financial support for developing countries to help them mitigate and adapt to climate change. Developed countries reaffirmed their commitment to mobilize $100 billion annually by 2020 through the Green Climate Fund and other sources. This financial assistance was crucial for less developed nations to transition to renewable energy and build resilience against climate impacts.

In addition to public financing, the agreement also sought to mobilize private sector investment in climate action. Initiatives like the Climate Finance Leadership Initiative, led by Michael Bloomberg, and the Task Force on Climate-related Financial Disclosures (TCFD) aimed to align global financial markets with climate goals.

The Paris Agreement established a framework for transparency and review to hold countries accountable for their climate commitments. The "global stocktake," conducted every five years, assesses collective progress towards achieving the agreement's goals and informs the enhancement of NDCs. The Enhanced Transparency Framework requires countries to regularly report their greenhouse gas inventories and track their progress in implementing NDCs.

These mechanisms provide a level of accountability that was absent in previous climate treaties, fostering a culture of transparency and peer pressure that encourages countries to raise their climate ambitions.

Despite the ambitious goals of the Paris Agreement, the cumulative impact of current NDCs falls short of limiting global warming to 2°C, let alone

1.5°C. According to the United Nations Environment Programme (UNEP) Emissions Gap Report 2020, current NDCs would result in a temperature rise of around 3°C by 2100. This "ambition gap" reflects the voluntary nature of NDCs and the lack of stringent enforcement mechanisms.

Many countries have not updated their NDCs since their initial submissions in 2015, and some, like Brazil and Australia, have even rolled back their climate commitments. The lack of legally binding emission targets has made it challenging to hold countries accountable for their promises, leading to accusations of greenwashing.

While developed countries pledged to mobilize $100 billion annually for climate finance, actual disbursements have consistently fallen short. According to the Organisation for Economic Co-operation and Development (OECD), climate finance flows reached $79.6 billion in 2019, still below the target. Moreover, much of this funding has been in the form of loans rather than grants, raising concerns about debt sustainability in developing nations.

Equity issues also persist, with many least-developed countries (LDCs) and small island developing states (SIDS) receiving disproportionately low levels of climate finance despite their vulnerability to climate impacts. The adaptation finance gap remains particularly wide, as most funding has been directed towards mitigation efforts.

The withdrawal of the United States, the world's second-largest emitter, from the Paris Agreement under the Trump administration significantly undermined global climate efforts. Although the Biden administration has since rejoined the agreement, the episode highlighted the fragility of international climate commitments and the potential for domestic politics to disrupt global cooperation.

Non-compliance with reporting requirements and transparency mechanisms has also been an issue. Some countries have failed to submit their greenhouse gas inventories on time, and others have provided incomplete data, making it challenging to assess progress accurately.

The Paris Agreement relies heavily on voluntary compliance and peer pressure rather than legally binding enforcement mechanisms. While the Enhanced Transparency Framework and the global stocktake are intended to promote accountability, there are no penalties for countries that fail to meet their NDCs. This lack of enforcement mechanisms has led to concerns about the agreement's effectiveness in driving meaningful climate action.

Overall, the Paris Agreement represents a remarkable achievement in securing global consensus on climate action, emphasizing inclusivity, flexibility, and financial support for developing nations. Its emphasis on NDCs, transparency mechanisms, and climate finance reflects a pragmatic approach to international climate policy.

However, significant challenges remain in bridging the ambition gap, ensuring equitable financial support, and strengthening enforcement mechanisms. The voluntary nature of NDCs and the reliance on peer pressure have limited the agreement's ability to drive meaningful emissions reductions. To address these shortcomings, future climate negotiations must focus on enhancing ambition, securing financial commitments, and developing more robust accountability frameworks.

Despite its limitations, the Paris Agreement provides a valuable framework for global climate action, demonstrating that international cooperation is possible even in the face of diverse national interests. Its success ultimately depends on the willingness of countries to rise to the challenge, translating their commitments into concrete actions that align with the ethical imperatives of ecological justice and stewardship.

Deforestation in the Amazon

THE AMAZON RAINFOREST, often referred to as the "lungs of the Earth," plays a crucial role in regulating global climate and preserving biodiversity. However, deforestation in the Amazon has escalated in recent years due to the pressures of international trade, agricultural expansion, and lax environmental policies. This case study explores the local and global consequences of deforestation and examines the impact of international trade on the region's ecosystems.

The Amazon rainforest is home to an estimated 10% of the world's known species, making it one of the most biodiverse regions on the planet. Deforestation, however, poses a severe threat to this biodiversity. As vast swathes of forest are cleared for agriculture, logging, and mining, critical habitats are destroyed, leading to the displacement and extinction of countless species.

The International Union for Conservation of Nature (IUCN) estimates that over 50% of the Amazon's amphibians, reptiles, and mammals are now threatened due to habitat loss. Species like the jaguar, giant otter, and harpy eagle are among those facing significant risks. This biodiversity loss has cascading effects on ecosystem functions, reducing the rainforest's resilience and ability to regenerate.

The Amazon rainforest acts as a major carbon sink, absorbing an estimated 2 billion tons of carbon dioxide annually. However, deforestation and forest degradation are turning the region into a net carbon emitter. According to a study published in Nature, the Amazon released more carbon dioxide than it absorbed between 2010 and 2019, primarily due to forest fires and deforestation.

This shift has significant implications for global climate change. The carbon emissions resulting from deforestation and forest fires contribute to rising global temperatures and the acceleration of climate change. Moreover, the loss of forest cover reduces the Amazon's ability to regulate regional weather patterns, leading to changes in rainfall and temperature that affect agriculture and water availability.

Indigenous communities in the Amazon have long relied on the forest for their livelihoods and cultural practices. However, deforestation has displaced many of these communities and threatened their way of life. According to the World Bank, there are over 400 indigenous groups in the Amazon basin, many of whom are now facing increased violence and land grabs due to illegal logging and mining activities.

For instance, the Yanomami and Kayapo tribes have been actively resisting deforestation and mining on their ancestral lands. Despite international recognition of their rights, weak enforcement of environmental laws and political pressure have made it challenging to protect their territories.

Deforestation in the Amazon also contributes to soil degradation and desertification. The rainforest's nutrient-rich topsoil is held together by the dense network of tree roots. When these trees are removed, the soil becomes vulnerable to erosion and nutrient loss. This degradation reduces agricultural productivity and can lead to the transformation of once-fertile land into arid, unproductive desert-like areas.

The global demand for commodities like soybeans, beef, and palm oil has driven much of the deforestation in the Amazon. Brazil is one of the world's largest exporters of soybeans and beef, and vast areas of the rainforest have been cleared to make way for soybean plantations and cattle ranches. According to the World Wildlife Fund (WWF), over 80% of deforestation in the Amazon is due to cattle ranching.

The European Union and China are among the largest importers of Brazilian soybeans and beef, linking international trade directly to deforestation. Despite efforts to promote sustainable sourcing, such as the Soy Moratorium, illegal land clearing continues to expand into protected areas.

Illegal logging for timber and mining for gold and other minerals have also contributed significantly to deforestation. The demand for timber, particularly hardwoods like mahogany, has led to rampant illegal logging operations that destroy critical habitats. Mining activities, often carried out illegally, not only clear vast areas of forest but also pollute rivers and soil with toxic chemicals like mercury.

The global supply chains for timber and minerals are complex and often lack transparency, making it challenging to trace products back to their source.

This opacity allows illegally sourced timber and minerals to enter global markets undetected, fueling further deforestation.

Infrastructure projects, such as roads, dams, and pipelines, have opened up previously inaccessible areas of the Amazon to deforestation. Foreign investment in these projects, particularly from China and Europe, has facilitated their expansion. For instance, the planned construction of the BR-319 highway, which will connect Manaus to Porto Velho, has raised concerns about accelerating deforestation in the surrounding areas.

Similarly, the Belo Monte Dam, one of the world's largest hydroelectric dams, has displaced thousands of indigenous people and flooded large areas of forest. The dam's construction was funded by a consortium of Brazilian and international companies, highlighting the role of foreign investment in driving environmental degradation.

Deforestation in the Amazon presents a complex web of environmental, social, and economic challenges that transcend national borders. The local consequences of biodiversity loss, climate change, and indigenous displacement are compounded by global trade dynamics and foreign investment. International demand for agricultural commodities, timber, and minerals has incentivized illegal land clearing, while infrastructure projects have opened up new areas for exploitation.

Addressing deforestation requires a multifaceted approach that includes stronger enforcement of environmental laws, sustainable supply chain management, and the protection of indigenous rights. International cooperation is crucial, particularly in regulating global markets to prevent the trade of products linked to illegal deforestation.

Philosophically, the crisis in the Amazon underscores the need for ecological justice and stewardship, emphasizing humanity's moral obligation to protect critical ecosystems for future generations. It challenges us to rethink the ethical frameworks that govern international trade and development, advocating for policies that prioritize environmental sustainability and social equity over short-term economic gains.

Electronic Waste Disposal and Recycling in Developing Countries

ELECTRONIC WASTE, OR e-waste, has emerged as one of the fastest-growing waste streams in the world. With rapid technological advancements and the increasing demand for electronic devices, managing e-waste has become a significant global challenge. This case study examines the challenges of e-waste disposal and recycling in developing countries, highlighting the environmental and health risks associated with improper management.

According to the Global E-Waste Monitor 2020, the world generated a record 53.6 million metric tons (Mt) of e-waste in 2019, representing a 21% increase in just five years. This figure is projected to reach 74 Mt by 2030, driven by rising consumption of electronic devices, shorter product lifespans, and limited repair options.

Asia generates the largest amount of e-waste (24.9 Mt), followed by the Americas (13.1 Mt) and Europe (12 Mt). However, developing countries, particularly in Africa and Asia, often become dumping grounds for e-waste due to weak environmental regulations and limited recycling infrastructure.

E-waste encompasses a wide range of discarded electronic devices, including computers, mobile phones, televisions, refrigerators, and medical equipment. These devices contain valuable materials like gold, silver, copper, and platinum, making e-waste recycling a potentially profitable industry.

However, e-waste also contains hazardous substances such as lead, mercury, cadmium, and brominated flame retardants. If not managed properly, these substances can leach into soil and water, posing severe environmental and health risks.

Improper disposal of e-waste in open dumps and landfills leads to the leaching of hazardous chemicals into the soil and groundwater. For instance, lead from cathode ray tubes (CRTs) in old televisions and computers can contaminate soil, affecting plant growth and entering the food chain.

In areas where e-waste is burned to extract valuable metals, toxic fumes and ash can pollute the air and water. Studies in the Agbogbloshie e-waste dump in Ghana have found elevated levels of lead and cadmium in the soil, posing health risks to nearby communities.

In developing countries, e-waste recycling is often carried out by informal workers using rudimentary methods. They manually dismantle devices, burn cables to extract copper, and use acid baths to recover precious metals. These processes expose workers to hazardous chemicals and fumes without proper protective equipment.

Common health issues among informal recyclers include respiratory problems, skin disorders, and lead poisoning. A study by the World Health Organization (WHO) found that children living near e-waste dumps had higher levels of lead in their blood, impairing cognitive development and increasing the risk of anemia.

Despite international regulations like the Basel Convention, which restricts the transboundary movement of hazardous waste, significant amounts of e-waste continue to be illegally exported to developing countries. Developed nations often ship e-waste under the guise of "second-hand goods" or "reusable electronics," exploiting regulatory loopholes and weak enforcement.

In countries like Nigeria, India, and Pakistan, imported e-waste is often dismantled in informal recycling facilities, exacerbating environmental pollution and health risks. The lack of accurate data on e-waste trade makes it challenging to quantify the scale of illegal exports and hold exporters accountable.

Extended Producer Responsibility (EPR) is a policy approach that holds manufacturers responsible for the entire lifecycle of their products, including end-of-life disposal. EPR programs require producers to finance the collection, recycling, and safe disposal of e-waste.

In Europe, the Waste Electrical and Electronic Equipment (WEEE) Directive has made EPR mandatory for electronic producers, leading to higher e-waste collection and recycling rates. Similar programs in Japan and South Korea have also been successful in reducing illegal e-waste dumping.

Formalizing the e-waste recycling sector can improve environmental and health standards while creating economic opportunities. Governments can incentivize informal recyclers to join formal recycling facilities through training, financial support, and access to technology.

The Swiss-funded E-Waste Programme in Ghana is a successful example of formalizing the recycling sector. It has provided training and protective equipment to informal recyclers, helping them transition to safer recycling practices.

International cooperation is crucial in combating illegal e-waste exports and promoting responsible recycling practices. The Basel Convention's Ban Amendment, which prohibits the export of hazardous waste from developed to developing countries, came into force in 2019, providing a stronger legal framework.

The International Telecommunication Union (ITU) and the United Nations Environment Programme (UNEP) have also launched the Global E-Waste Statistics Partnership to improve data collection and transparency in e-waste management.

Educating consumers about the environmental impact of e-waste and promoting sustainable consumption can reduce the generation of e-waste. Campaigns encouraging consumers to repair or recycle their electronics, rather than discarding them, can extend product lifespans.

Manufacturers can also adopt sustainable design principles to make electronics easier to repair and recycle. Modular designs, standardized components, and the reduction of hazardous substances can significantly reduce the environmental footprint of electronic devices.

The challenges of electronic waste disposal and recycling in developing countries reflect the darker side of globalization, where the rapid consumption of electronics in wealthy nations leaves behind a trail of hazardous waste. The environmental and health risks associated with improper e-waste management highlight the urgent need for global cooperation and sustainable practices.

Addressing these challenges requires a multifaceted approach, from stricter international regulations and EPR programs to the formalization of the recycling sector and consumer education. Philosophically, the issue of e-waste disposal raises questions about environmental justice and the ethical responsibilities of producers, consumers, and governments in managing waste sustainably.

Globalization has interconnected markets and supply chains, making it imperative to adopt a holistic approach to e-waste management that prioritizes ecological stewardship and social equity. By integrating environmental ethics with practical policies, we can work towards a future where electronic waste is no longer a global burden but a source of sustainable innovation.

6.4 Philosophical and Practical Solutions

I. Ecological Justice

Ecological justice extends the concept of social justice to include non-human entities and the environment, emphasizing that all species and ecosystems have intrinsic value and deserve protection. It builds on Aldo Leopold's land ethic and Arne Naess's deep ecology, advocating for a relationship with nature that goes beyond exploitation and acknowledges our ethical responsibility towards other living beings. From this perspective, global environmental policies should prioritize:

- **Intergenerational Equity:** The current generation has a moral obligation to preserve natural resources and ecosystems for future generations. This principle aligns with John Rawls's theory of justice, which requires designing social institutions that benefit even the least advantaged members of future societies.

- **Intragenerational Equity:** Resources should be distributed equitably among nations and populations today. This requires fair access to clean water, air, and land, ensuring that vulnerable communities, often disproportionately affected by environmental degradation, receive their share of benefits and are shielded from harm.

Global Governance Structures

- **Paris Agreement:** Despite its shortcomings, the Paris Agreement remains a landmark in international climate cooperation. Moving forward, countries should be held to stricter emission reduction targets, backed by transparent monitoring systems. Developed nations must also fulfill their financial commitments to assist developing countries in transitioning to low-carbon economies.

• **United Nations Framework Convention on Climate Change (UNFCCC):** The UNFCCC should strengthen its role in coordinating global efforts by ensuring binding commitments on emission reductions. It should also facilitate knowledge-sharing between nations on best practices for adaptation and mitigation.

• **Global Environmental Fund (GEF):** The GEF provides crucial funding for environmental projects. Increasing its budget and focusing on projects that promote equitable resource distribution, such as community-based renewable energy initiatives, will enhance global ecological justice.

• **Convention on Biological Diversity (CBD):** Strengthening the implementation of the CBD's protocols is essential to preserving biodiversity. This includes the Nagoya Protocol on Access and Benefit-Sharing, which ensures that profits derived from genetic resources are fairly shared with indigenous and local communities.

• **International Environmental Court:** The establishment of an International Environmental Court, akin to the International Criminal Court, could hold states and corporations accountable for environmental crimes, providing legal recourse for affected communities.

Technological Innovations

• **Sustainable Agriculture:** Using GPS and data analytics to optimize crop yields and reduce pesticide use (precision farming). Combining modern agricultural science with traditional ecological knowledge to improve soil health and biodiversity (Agroecology).

- **Renewable Energy:** Increasing the efficiency of solar panels and wind turbines while reducing costs through mass production. Innovations in battery storage, such as lithium-ion and solid-state batteries, will address the intermittency of renewables. Developing hydrogen as a clean fuel source through electrolysis and storage technology.

- **Circular Economy:** Designing products for longevity, repairability, and recyclability to minimize waste. Implementing extended producer responsibility (EPR) policies, which mandate that manufacturers take back products at the end of their life cycle.

- **Sustainable Urban Development:** Integrating IoT and AI into city infrastructure to optimize energy use, waste management, and transportation (Smart Cities). Incorporating energy-efficient designs and materials in construction (Green Buildings).

Policy Innovations

- **Carbon Pricing:** Implementing carbon pricing through taxes or cap-and-trade systems provides economic incentives to reduce emissions. Successful examples include the European Union Emissions Trading System (EU ETS) and British Columbia's carbon tax.

- **Subsidy Reform:** Phasing out subsidies for fossil fuels and reallocating funds towards renewable energy and sustainable practices.

- **Ecosystem-Based Management:** Adopting holistic management approaches that recognize the interdependence of ecosystems, as seen in marine spatial planning and integrated water resources management.

- **Payments for Ecosystem Services (PES):** Compensating landowners for maintaining forests, wetlands, and other ecosystems that provide crucial services such as carbon sequestration and water purification.

- **Sustainable Public Procurement:** Governments can lead by example by prioritizing environmentally friendly products and services in their procurement processes.

- **Legally Binding Treaties:** Strengthening legally binding treaties like the Montreal Protocol for ozone depletion and expanding them to cover new issues, such as microplastics pollution.

State-Level Collaboration:

- **Regional Agreements:** Regional agreements like the EU's Green Deal can set ambitious environmental standards that transcend national boundaries. Similar initiatives in Latin America (Amazon Cooperation Treaty Organization) and Africa (African Union's Agenda 2063) have the potential to tackle region-specific challenges.

- **Bilateral Agreements:** Bilateral partnerships can accelerate the development and transfer of green technologies. For instance, the U.S.-China Clean Energy Research Center focuses on clean coal and electric vehicles.

- **Development Assistance:** Increasing financial and technical assistance to developing nations for sustainable development projects, including the expansion of renewable energy and sustainable agriculture.

Corporate Collaboration

- **Corporate Social Responsibility (CSR):** Companies should incorporate sustainability into their business models, shifting from profit maximization to triple-bottom-line accounting (people, planet, profit). For example, Unilever's Sustainable Living Plan integrates environmental and social considerations into its supply chain.

- **Public-Private Partnerships:** Collaborations between governments and corporations can yield innovative solutions. The Global Alliance for Clean Cookstoves aims to reduce indoor air pollution in developing countries by promoting cleaner stoves

- **Industry Standards:** Voluntary industry standards, such as the Forest Stewardship Council (FSC) for sustainable forestry and the Roundtable on Sustainable Palm Oil (RSPO), promote responsible sourcing practices.

Civil Society Collaboration

- **Non-Governmental Organizations (NGOs):** NGOs like Greenpeace, the World Wildlife Fund (WWF), and Friends of the Earth play a crucial role in advocacy, research, and capacity building. Their grassroots initiatives and international campaigns have raised awareness and pushed for stronger environmental policies.

- **Indigenous Communities:** Indigenous communities possess invaluable knowledge of sustainable land management. Their inclusion in policy-making and conservation projects is essential for equitable resource management.

- **Youth Movements:** Youth-led movements, such as Fridays for Future and Extinction Rebellion, have revitalized environmental activism and put pressure on governments and corporations to take immediate action.

Global Commons Governance:

THE GOVERNANCE OF GLOBAL commons, such as the high seas, atmosphere, and Antarctica, requires collective action. The United Nations Convention on the Law of the Sea (UNCLOS) should be strengthened to protect marine biodiversity beyond national jurisdictions.

- **Universal Declaration of Environmental Rights:** Developing a Universal Declaration of Environmental Rights could set ethical standards for environmental protection, similar to the Universal Declaration of Human Rights.

- **Sustainable Development Goals (SDGs):** The SDGs provide a comprehensive framework for sustainable development. Governments and corporations should align their policies and business strategies with the SDGs, focusing on targets such as clean energy (Goal 7) and responsible consumption (Goal 12).

Ethical Governance:

- **Transparent Policy-Making:** Transparency in environmental policy-making fosters public trust and ensures accountability. Participatory governance, where civil society and marginalized communities have a say in decision-making, is crucial.

- **Accountability Mechanisms:** Independent monitoring bodies and whistleblower protection can help hold corporations and governments accountable for environmental violations.

- **Adaptive Governance:** Policies should be flexible and adaptive to changing environmental conditions. This requires continuous monitoring, feedback loops, and the ability to quickly respond to emerging challenges.

ADDRESSING ENVIRONMENTAL challenges in a globalized world demands a philosophical shift towards ecological justice and equitable resource distribution. Practical solutions must integrate technological innovations, policy reforms, and collaborative approaches among states, corporations, and civil society. Philosophically, the emphasis should be on collective action and ethical governance, advocating for a multilateral approach to sustainable development that ensures a fair and just future for all. By grounding global policies in environmental ethics, we can work towards a sustainable world that values both human well-being and the intrinsic worth of nature.

Synthesis

Throughout this chapter, we have explored environmental sustainability and globalization across multiple dimensions. By examining the philosophical underpinnings of environmental ethics, sustainable development, and global responsibility, it becomes evident that addressing environmental challenges requires a multifaceted and ethically grounded approach.

The philosophical frameworks of land ethic (Aldo Leopold), deep ecology (Arne Naess), and ecological citizenship (Andrew Dobson) underpin our understanding of ecological justice, emphasizing that human activities must respect the intrinsic value of all species and ecosystems. The theories of ecological justice further extend John Rawls's concept of justice as fairness to include intergenerational and intragenerational equity, asserting that the benefits and burdens of environmental policies should be distributed fairly among all populations and future generations.

The concept of sustainable development, popularized by the Brundtland Commission's report Our Common Future, integrates ecological stewardship with economic and social progress. It challenges us to rethink our economic systems and prioritize triple-bottom-line accounting, balancing people, planet, and profit. Its key challenges include, Global

Inequality and Political Will, which pose that achieving sustainable development necessitates addressing the economic disparities between developed and developing nations, ensuring equitable resource distribution and access to clean technologies; and, despite the widespread recognition of sustainable development goals, translating them into concrete policies requires political will and overcoming resistance from vested interests

.:

Philosophically, the global environmental crisis calls for a shift from state-centric to cosmopolitan ethics, where nations recognize their shared responsibility towards the planet. This is embodied in the concept of ecological citizenship, which emphasizes individual and collective actions that transcend borders. The key challenges here are that of nationalism vs. global responsibility, where rising nationalist sentiments often undermine global efforts, with countries prioritizing short-term economic gains over long-term ecological preservation; and the lack of enforceable mechanisms in the international environmental agreements, leading to inconsistent implementation and accountability. Here's a simplified roadmap for sustainable practices in a globalized world.

1. Collective Action for Climate Change Mitigation:

- **Strengthening International Agreements:** Enhance the Paris Agreement by setting stricter emission targets and implementing transparent monitoring systems. Expand the role of the United Nations Framework Convention on Climate Change (UNFCCC) to enforce binding commitments and facilitate technology transfer.

- **Regional Cooperation:** Develop regional frameworks for climate adaptation and mitigation, similar to the European Union's Green Deal. Facilitate knowledge-sharing between nations on climate-resilient agriculture and renewable energy technologies.

2. Equitable Resource Distribution and Ecological Justice:

- **Global Environmental Fund (GEF):** Increase funding for projects that promote equitable resource distribution and prioritize vulnerable communities. Support community-based renewable energy initiatives and sustainable agriculture practices.

- **International Environmental Court:** Establish an International Environmental Court to hold states and corporations accountable for environmental crimes.

3. Promoting Innovation in Sustainable Technologies:

- **Research and Development (R&D):** Increase investment in R&D for precision farming, renewable energy storage, and circular economy solutions. Encourage public-private partnerships to accelerate the commercialization of sustainable technologies.

- **Global Technology Transfer:** Facilitate technology transfer to developing nations, enabling them to leapfrog to cleaner and more efficient technologies.

4. Cultural Transformation and Environmental Awareness:

- **Education and Awareness Campaigns:** Implement environmental education in school curricula to foster ecological citizenship. Launch global awareness campaigns to promote sustainable consumption and production.

- **Inclusion of Indigenous Knowledge:** Integrate indigenous knowledge into environmental policies and practices, recognizing its value in promoting sustainable land management.

5. *Ethical Governance and Transparency:*

- **Inclusive Policy-Making:** Ensure that environmental policy-making includes marginalized communities and civil society organizations. Strengthen participatory governance structures to enhance transparency and accountability.

- **Adaptive Governance:** Design policies that are flexible and adaptive to changing environmental conditions. Incorporate continuous monitoring and feedback loops to refine and improve policy effectiveness.

THE PATH FORWARD FOR sustainable practices in a globalized world lies in embracing a holistic approach that integrates economic, cultural, and political dimensions. Philosophically, the emphasis should be on ecological justice and global responsibility, advocating for collective action and ethical governance that transcends borders. By synthesizing the insights and challenges discussed, we can outline a comprehensive roadmap that balances economic growth with ecological preservation. This roadmap must prioritize the following:

- **Global Frameworks for Climate Action:** Strengthening international agreements like the Paris Agreement and UNFCCC to enforce binding commitments and transparent monitoring systems.

- **Technological Innovation and Transfer:** Accelerating R&D in sustainable technologies and facilitating technology transfer to developing nations.

- **Equitable Resource Distribution:** Supporting vulnerable communities through global environmental funds and implementing international environmental justice.

- **Cultural Awareness and Indigenous Knowledge:** Promoting environmental education and integrating indigenous knowledge into sustainable practices.

- **Ethical Governance and Collective Action:** Enhancing transparency, accountability, and inclusivity in environmental policy-making and fostering collaboration among states, corporations, and civil society.

By following this roadmap, we can achieve a sustainable world that values human well-being and the intrinsic worth of nature. Ethical governance and a collective commitment to sustainable development are essential to ensuring a just and livable future for all.

Concluding Part 2: Ethical Conundrums of Globalization

Throughout Part 2, we have journeyed through the web of ethical conundrums arising from the multifaceted processes of globalization. By examining the challenges of nationalism versus global integration, migration and human rights, and environmental sustainability and global policies, we have sought to understand the complexities of these global issues and the moral imperatives they demand.

In Chapter 4, we explored the resurgence of nationalism amidst an increasingly interconnected world. The rise of nationalist movements and protectionist policies has posed significant challenges to global integration, highlighting deep-seated tensions between national interests and cosmopolitan ideals. Nationalist sentiments have fueled protectionism, disrupting global trade and investment flows. Trade liberalization and global economic integration, once heralded as pathways to prosperity, have instead led to job losses, economic inequality, and the erosion of local industries, sparking nationalist backlashes. Identity politics and cultural homogenization have intensified the cultural undercurrents of nationalism. The perceived loss of cultural identity to global cultural trends has prompted efforts to preserve national identities, often through exclusionary rhetoric. The sovereignty of nation-states has come under strain as supranational entities wield increasing influence. Nationalist movements challenge the legitimacy and authority of international organizations and treaties, demanding the restoration of political autonomy.

In Chapter 5, we examined the ethical dilemmas surrounding migration and human rights. Global migration trends, influenced by conflict, economic disparities, and environmental changes, have sparked intense debates over the rights and responsibilities of host nations and international bodies. Migrants contribute to labor markets and send remittances back home, boosting economic growth. However, their integration often faces resistance due to concerns over job competition, wage suppression, and social welfare strains. Migration challenges societies to balance integration with multiculturalism. Host countries grapple with the complexities of assimilation versus cultural preservation, leading to tensions around identity, belonging, and social cohesion. Immigration policies and international law face scrutiny over their ability to protect migrant rights. The rise of populist politics has led to stricter immigration controls, undermining global commitments to human rights.

In Chapter 6, we addressed the escalating environmental challenges in the age of globalization. Climate change, deforestation, and unsustainable consumption threaten global ecosystems and demand collective action. The transition to green economies and sustainable development remains uneven, with developing nations struggling to balance economic growth and environmental preservation. Global trade contributes to deforestation, pollution, and resource depletion, while the lack of equitable resource distribution exacerbates environmental injustice. Environmentalism has emerged as a global cultural movement, yet indigenous knowledge and practices often remain marginalized. The cultural implications of environmental degradation impact local communities and their way of life, calling for inclusive policies that respect indigenous rights. International environmental agreements and policies, such as the Paris Agreement, have made strides in addressing climate change but lack enforceable mechanisms. National interests and geopolitical dynamics complicate global cooperation on environmental protection.

The ethical conundrums explored in here illustrate the interconnectedness of global challenges across multiple dimensions. The resurgence of nationalism, the ethical dilemmas of migration, and the urgency of environmental sustainability are deeply intertwined, each influencing and amplifying the others. Addressing these challenges requires a nuanced understanding of the global landscape, where economic, cultural, and political factors are tightly bound together. Solutions must recognize and navigate this complexity.

Moral and political philosophy plays a crucial role in guiding global policies. The principles of justice, equity, and universal human dignity must underpin efforts to balance national interests with global cooperation. Moreover, the interconnected nature of these challenges calls for collective action. States, corporations, international organizations, and civil society must collaborate to create ethical and sustainable solutions that transcend borders.

Balancing nationalism and global integration requires reconciling national identities with cosmopolitan ethics, promoting international cooperation while respecting cultural diversity. Similarly, Upholding migrant rights demands global frameworks that recognize migration as a human right and facilitate ethical immigration policies. Simultaneously, achieving environmental sustainability necessitates a global commitment to equitable resource distribution, ecological justice, and innovative technologies.

This part of the book has highlighted the urgency of addressing the ethical conundrums of globalization. Nationalism, migration, and environmental sustainability are not isolated challenges but deeply interconnected phenomena that require a holistic, ethically grounded approach. By understanding and embracing moral and political philosophy, we can forge a path toward a just and sustainable future that balances the complexities of global integration with the ethical imperatives of justice, equity, and human dignity.

A Call to Action

TO ADDRESS THE ETHICAL challenges posed by globalization, it is imperative that policymakers, scholars, and global citizens come together to engage proactively and collaboratively. The complexities of globalization touch every facet of our interconnected world, and only through informed, ethical approaches can we hope to navigate these challenges effectively. We need to issue a call to action, emphasizing the critical need for continuous dialogue and cooperation.

Policymakers are at the forefront of managing the impacts of globalization. Their decisions shape international trade, environmental policies, and human rights frameworks. We urge them to:

- **Adopt a Long-Term Ethical Vision:** Move beyond short-term political and economic gains to formulate policies that prioritize justice, sustainability, and global cooperation.

- **Strengthen Multilateral Institutions:** Empower international organizations like the UN, WHO, and WTO to address global challenges through inclusive governance structures.

- **Engage with Ethical Experts:** Integrate philosophical insights into policy development by consulting with ethicists and scholars, ensuring that decisions reflect global justice principles.

- **Support Vulnerable Populations:** Craft migration, trade, and labor policies that protect marginalized groups, refugees, and workers, upholding their dignity and rights.

Scholars possess the intellectual rigor and analytical skills necessary to dissect globalization's ethical challenges. To maximize their impact, they should:

- **Bridge Theory and Practice:** Produce research that translates ethical theories into actionable policy recommendations, making academic work accessible to broader audiences.

- **Foster Interdisciplinary Collaboration:** Work with economists, environmental scientists, and political analysts to craft holistic solutions that address the multifaceted impacts of globalization.

- **Engage Publicly:** Write for popular media, give public lectures, and participate in advisory roles to influence public opinion and policymaking.

- **Mentor Future Leaders:** Integrate global ethics into educational curricula, inspiring the next generation of policymakers, activists, and thinkers to approach global challenges with moral clarity.

Global Citizens have a role in shaping the ethical landscape of globalization. Every individual must:

- **Stay Informed:** Educate ourselves on global issues, from climate change to economic inequality, by consuming diverse and credible sources of information.

- **Advocate for Ethical Policies:** Support initiatives and organizations that advocate for justice, sustainability, and human rights in global governance.

- **Practice Ethical Consumption:** Make conscientious consumer choices that support fair trade, environmentally friendly practices, and ethical labor standards.

- **Engage in Civil Society:** Participate in community organizations, advocacy groups, and public forums to foster grassroots movements that drive ethical change.

Addressing the pervasive challenges of globalization requires an unprecedented level of collaboration and ethical commitment. Policymakers, scholars, and global citizens must work in unison to craft informed approaches that reflect our shared moral obligations to one another and the planet. Continuous dialogue, proactive engagement, and unwavering dedication to justice and sustainability are crucial as we strive to shape a future where globalization uplifts all of humanity.

Let us seize this moment to build a more just, inclusive, and sustainable world by proactively confronting the ethical conundrums of globalization together!

———

Epilogue: A Philosophical Framework

Throughout this book, we have ventured into the multifaceted world of globalization, examining its economic, cultural, and political dimensions through the lens of moral and political philosophy. By dissecting the phenomena of global trade, cultural hybridization, and supranational governance, we have encountered both the promises and perils of a deeply interconnected world. As we close this exploration, it becomes crucial to synthesize these insights, reflecting on how they collectively contribute to our understanding of globalization and its ethical implications.

In Chapter 1, we explored how economic globalization has generated unprecedented wealth but also exacerbated inequalities within and among nations. The theories of classical economists like Smith and Ricardo, while foundational, struggle to fully capture the nuances of modern global trade. We delved into the philosophical implications of sweatshop labor, MNC practices, and global supply chains, using utilitarian, deontological, and Marxist frameworks to evaluate these practices critically.

Fair trade initiatives emerged as a pragmatic response, demonstrating the potential of alternative economic models that prioritize equity and dignity over profit maximization. Yet, despite these positive strides, challenges like tax avoidance, labor rights violations, and environmental degradation persist. Philosophers such as Rawls, Nussbaum, and Sen advocate for distributive justice, a capabilities approach, and global solidarity to address these systemic issues.

In Chapter 2, the cultural dimension revealed how globalization fosters both homogenization and diversity. The spread of global media, brands, and digital platforms challenges traditional cultural identities, raising concerns about cultural imperialism and loss of diversity. Yet, it also offers unprecedented opportunities for intercultural exchange and understanding.

Theoretical frameworks like postmodernism, existentialism, and cultural studies provided valuable lenses to analyze these trends. The rise of Netflix and other global media exemplifies both the potential for cross-cultural engagement and the risks of cultural homogenization. Philosophical perspectives such as Appiah's cosmopolitanism and Bhabha's hybridity underscore the importance of promoting global cultural dialogue while safeguarding marginalized voices.

In Chapter 3, we examined the political dimension, focusing on the challenges of nationalism, sovereignty, and democratic deficit in a globalized world. The resurgence of nationalism challenges the cosmopolitan ideals of global integration, while international organizations like the UN and EU face criticism for their lack of democratic accountability.

By contrasting cosmopolitanism with realism and analyzing the doctrine of Responsibility to Protect (R2P), we highlighted the complexities of balancing state sovereignty with global cooperation. The Syrian conflict served as a case study, demonstrating the intricate interplay of international interests, humanitarian concerns, and state legitimacy.

In Chapter 4, we explored how the resurgence of nationalism challenges global cooperation, often driven by economic, cultural, and political anxieties. The interplay between protectionism, identity politics, and sovereignty necessitates a nuanced philosophical response that balances national interests with global ethical obligations. Philosophical frameworks like primordialism and modernism provided insights into the roots of nationalism, while cosmopolitanism offered a counter-narrative advocating for shared global responsibilities.

Chapter 5 addressed the ethical dilemmas surrounding migration and human rights, as global migration trends expose the fragility of international law and human dignity. The Syrian refugee crisis and U.S. immigration policy highlighted the disparities in global responses to migrants and asylum seekers. Ethical theories like care ethics and justice as fairness, combined with human rights philosophy, underscored the moral imperative to protect migrant rights and develop inclusive policies for integration.

Chapter 6 brought environmental ethics to the forefront, emphasizing the global responsibility to protect the environment amidst economic and political interests. The Paris Agreement and Amazon deforestation exemplify the challenges of international environmental governance. Theories of ecological justice, sustainable development, and stewardship guided our analysis of green economies, environmentalism as a cultural movement, and the effectiveness of global treaties.

A recurring theme across chapters is the need for global economic justice, advocating for a restructuring of global economic systems to address disparities. To realize this vision, a forward-looking approach is imperative. Policymakers need to consider global economic justice as foundational to global policy-making. Progressive taxation and global financial regulations should be implemented to curb tax evasion and ensure equitable distribution of resources. Fair trade initiatives must be expanded, emphasizing ethical labor practices and environmental sustainability. Policymakers should also advocate for a universal basic income or minimum wage to address the disparities arising from automation and technological advancements.

Governance structures, both national and international, must evolve to reflect the ethical imperatives of transparency, accountability, and inclusivity. Global solidarity, guided by cosmopolitan principles, requires collaborative efforts to address shared challenges like climate change, migration, and wealth inequality. Similarly, Corporations should adopt corporate social responsibility (CSR) frameworks that align with global ethical standards. This includes committing to environmental sustainability, fair labor practices, and transparency in their global supply chains. By fostering partnerships with NGOs and local communities, corporations can enhance their social impact and contribute to a more equitable global economy.

In the cultural realm, a renewed emphasis on intercultural competence and ethical media practices is crucial. Educational programs that promote global citizenship and empathy can help combat cultural homogenization and xenophobia. Media platforms must commit to accurate representation and inclusion, promoting diverse narratives that respect cultural identities.

Political structures need comprehensive reforms to address democratic deficits and ensure accountability. International organizations like the UN, World Bank, and IMF should be reformed to reflect diverse global voices and facilitate equitable decision-making. Regional organizations like the EU can serve as models for balancing national sovereignty with supranational governance, but they too require reforms to mitigate nationalist reactions and strengthen democratic participation.

At the same time, addressing environmental challenges requires a multilateral approach that transcends national borders. The Paris Agreement should serve as a minimum standard, with nations committing to ambitious targets for carbon reduction and renewable energy adoption. Technological innovation in sustainable agriculture, renewable energy, and circular economy practices must be prioritized and incentivized through global policies and investments.

Philosophers play an important role in shaping global ethics, offering clarity, critique, and normative frameworks to guide policy and public opinion. Their engagement in academic discourse, public forums, and advisory roles is crucial in addressing the ethical challenges of globalization. Policymakers must proactively integrate philosophical insights into decision-making, ensuring that economic, cultural, and political strategies align with ethical considerations. This requires continuous dialogue with scholars, NGOs, and global citizens. Most importantly, global citizens have a shared responsibility to engage with ethical challenges, advocating for informed and just approaches to globalization's complexities. Collective action, ethical consumption, and intercultural dialogue are vital in building a more compassionate and sustainable world.

Globalization presents a web of challenges and opportunities that require a cohesive philosophical response. The insights from this book integrating moral and political philosophy into our understanding of globalization, help us gain critical insights into its ethical dilemmas and pathways toward a more just and sustainable global order. The synthesis of economic, cultural, and political dimensions provides a comprehensive framework for navigating globalization's complexities, guiding policymakers, scholars, and global citizens toward a future that upholds justice, dignity, and global solidarity. offer a roadmap for navigating globalization's ethical conundrums. The challenges are significant, but with informed dialogue, collaborative action, and unwavering commitment to ethical principles, a more just and sustainable global order is within reach.

Key Texts and Further Reading List

Philosophy and Ethics

1. RAWLS, JOHN. A THEORY of Justice. Harvard University Press, 1971.

A seminal work that introduces the concept of "justice as fairness," laying the foundation for contemporary political philosophy. Rawls discusses the principles of distributive justice that underpin egalitarian societies, emphasizing the importance of equity and human dignity.

2. Pogge, Thomas. World Poverty and Human Rights: Cosmopolitan Responsibilities and Reforms. Polity Press, 2002.

Pogge challenges the global order's structural inequalities and argues for a cosmopolitan approach to human rights and global justice. This book is instrumental in understanding ethical obligations in a globalized world.

3. Nussbaum, Martha. Creating Capabilities: The Human Development Approach. Harvard University Press, 2011.

Nussbaum expands on the "capabilities approach," advocating for development policies that prioritize human well-being over economic growth. Her framework provides ethical guidance for addressing global inequalities.

4. Singer, Peter. One World Now: The Ethics of Globalization. Yale University Press, 2016.

A revised edition of Singer's classic work that examines the ethical challenges posed by globalization, including climate change, trade, and human rights. Singer makes a compelling case for a cosmopolitan ethical perspective.

5. Appiah, Kwame Anthony. Cosmopolitanism: Ethics in a World of Strangers. W.W. Norton & Company, 2007.

Appiah explores the idea of cosmopolitanism and its implications for global ethics. His work offers insights into how diverse cultural identities can coexist within a global framework of shared values.

6. Walzer, Michael. Spheres of Justice: A Defense of Pluralism and Equality. Basic Books, 1983.

Walzer provides a pluralistic approach to justice, arguing for differentiated distributions in various spheres of life. His analysis is crucial for understanding cultural diversity and global justice.

Globalization Studies

1. STIGLITZ, JOSEPH E. Globalization and Its Discontents. W.W. Norton & Company, 2002.

Nobel laureate Stiglitz critiques the negative impacts of globalization, particularly through the lens of international financial institutions like the IMF and World Bank. He offers practical policy recommendations for reform.

2. Rodrik, Dani. The Globalization Paradox: Democracy and the Future of the World Economy. W.W. Norton & Company, 2011.

Rodrik argues that globalization, democracy, and national sovereignty are mutually incompatible. His analysis provides a nuanced view of the trade-offs involved in global economic integration.

3. Sassen, Saskia. Territory, Authority, Rights: From Medieval to Global Assemblages. Princeton University Press, 2008.

Sassen explores the transformation of state sovereignty and global governance structures in the context of globalization. Her interdisciplinary approach is valuable for understanding the political dimensions of globalization.

4. Sen, Amartya. Development as Freedom. Anchor Books, 1999.

Sen argues that development should be understood as the expansion of human freedoms rather than economic growth. His work has significant implications for global policy-making and the ethical considerations of development.

5. Harvey, David. The New Imperialism. Oxford University Press, 2005.

Harvey critiques the geopolitical and economic dynamics of contemporary globalization, linking it to neoliberalism and the accumulation of capital. His Marxist analysis provides a critical perspective on global power relations.

6. Scholte, Jan Aart. Globalization: A Critical Introduction. Palgrave Macmillan, 2005.

Scholte offers a comprehensive introduction to globalization studies, covering economic, political, and cultural dimensions. He critically examines the varying definitions and debates surrounding globalization.

Economic Globalization and Inequality

1. MILANOVIC, BRANKO. Global Inequality: A New Approach for the Age of Globalization. Harvard University Press, 2016.

Milanovic provides an in-depth analysis of global inequality, offering historical context and data-driven insights into the distribution of wealth and income in the age of globalization.

2. Piketty, Thomas. Capital in the Twenty-First Century. Harvard University Press, 2014.

Piketty's groundbreaking work on wealth inequality uses historical data to highlight the concentration of wealth and its implications for democratic societies. His analysis of "r > g" has sparked global debates on inequality.

3. Rodrik, Dani. Straight Talk on Trade: Ideas for a Sane World Economy. Princeton University Press, 2017.

Rodrik challenges conventional economic wisdom on trade and globalization, advocating for policies that prioritize national interests and democratic accountability in the global economy.

Cultural Globalization and Identity

1. HALL, STUART. CULTURAL Identity and Diaspora. Routledge, 1990.

Hall's essay explores the concept of cultural identity in the context of diaspora and globalization. His work is foundational in understanding the complexities of cultural identity and representation.

2. Bhabha, Homi K. The Location of Culture. Routledge, 1994.

Bhabha introduces the concept of "hybridity," challenging fixed notions of cultural identity. His postcolonial critique provides insights into how globalization influences cultural representation and power dynamics.

3. Tomlinson, John. Globalization and Culture. University of Chicago Press, 1999.

Tomlinson examines the relationship between globalization and cultural homogenization, arguing that globalization also enhances cultural diversity through hybridization.

4. Appadurai, Arjun. Modernity at Large: Cultural Dimensions of Globalization. University of Minnesota Press, 1996.

Appadurai introduces key concepts like "ethnoscapes" and "mediascapes" to explore the global flows of culture. His work offers a framework for understanding cultural globalization.

Political Globalization and Governance

1. HELD, DAVID. DEMOCRACY and the Global Order: From the Modern State to Cosmopolitan Governance. Stanford University Press, 1995.

Held advocates for cosmopolitan democracy, proposing reforms to international institutions and global governance structures. His work is essential for understanding the democratic challenges of globalization.

2. Keohane, Robert O., and Nye, Joseph S. Power and Interdependence: World Politics in Transition. Little, Brown and Company, 1977.

Keohane and Nye introduce the concept of "complex interdependence," exploring how economic and political ties shape global governance. Their work remains influential in international relations theory.

3. Falk, Richard. Power Shift: On the New Global Order. Zed Books, 2016.

Falk analyzes the changing dynamics of global power and governance, emphasizing the rise of non-state actors and global civil society. His work offers a critical perspective on the potential for global democracy.

4. Slaughter, Anne-Marie. A New World Order. Princeton University Press, 2004.

Slaughter argues that transgovernmental networks are reshaping global governance, highlighting the role of cross-border collaboration among government officials.

Environmental Sustainability and Global Ethics

1. GARDINER, STEPHEN M. A Perfect Moral Storm: The Ethical Tragedy of Climate Change. Oxford University Press, 2011.

Gardiner examines the ethical challenges of climate change, arguing that it constitutes a "perfect moral storm" due to the intergenerational, global, and theoretical complexities involved.

2. Jamieson, Dale. Reason in a Dark Time: Why the Struggle Against Climate Change Failed—and What It Means for Our Future. Oxford University Press, 2014.

Jamieson explores the philosophical and practical barriers to addressing climate change, offering ethical frameworks for future environmental action.

3. Singer, Peter. Practical Ethics. Cambridge University Press, 1993.

Singer's influential work addresses global ethical issues such as poverty, animal rights, and climate change. His utilitarian perspective provides practical guidance for ethical decision-making.

4. Klein, Naomi. This Changes Everything: Capitalism vs. The Climate. Simon & Schuster, 2014.

Klein critiques neoliberal capitalism and its role in exacerbating the climate crisis. Her work advocates for systemic economic and political changes to address environmental challenges.

5. Shiva, Vandana. Earth Democracy: Justice, Sustainability, and Peace. South End Press, 2005.

Shiva critiques corporate globalization and its impact on the environment and indigenous communities. Her concept of "earth democracy" emphasizes local sovereignty and ecological sustainability.

Appendices

Appendix 1: Glossary of Key Terms

A

1. **Artificial Intelligence (AI):** A branch of computer science focused on developing systems capable of performing tasks that typically require human intelligence, such as decision-making, language understanding, and visual perception,
2. **Asylum Seekers:** Individuals who have fled their country due to persecution or fear of persecution and seek refuge in another country but have not yet been granted legal refugee status.
3. **Autonomy:** The capacity of an individual or a state to make independent decisions without external influence or coercion.

B

1. **Bretton Woods System:** An international monetary system established in 1944 that included fixed exchange rates and the creation of the IMF and World Bank.
2. **Brexit:** The withdrawal of the United Kingdom from the European Union following a 2016 referendum.

C

1. **Care Ethics:** An ethical theory emphasizing interpersonal relationships and the moral significance of empathy and care in decision-making.
2. **Climate Change:** Long-term changes in global or regional climate patterns, often attributed to increased levels of atmospheric carbon dioxide due to human activities.

3. **Cosmopolitanism:** A philosophical perspective advocating for global citizenship, where individuals are part of a broader international community and moral obligations transcend national borders.
4. **Cultural Homogenization:** The reduction of cultural diversity through the spread and influence of dominant cultural norms, values, and practices.
5. **Cultural Hybridization:** The blending of elements from different cultures to create new, mixed cultural forms.

D

1. **Deforestation:** The large-scale removal of forests, often resulting in biodiversity loss, soil erosion, and disruptions to local and global climate systems.
2. **Digital Divide:** The gap between individuals who have access to modern information and communication technology and those who do not.

E

1. **Ecological Citizenship:** A concept emphasizing individuals' ethical responsibilities to the environment and advocating for active participation in sustainable practices.
2. **Electronic Waste (E-waste):** Discarded electronic devices and components, which often contain hazardous materials and pose environmental risks if not properly managed.
3. **Environmental Ethics:** A branch of philosophy focused on the moral relationship between humans and the environment, including the rights of non-human entities.
4. **Environmental Justice:** The fair treatment and meaningful involvement of all people in environmental laws, policies, and practices, regardless of race, nationality, or income.

F

1. **Fair Trade:** A movement promoting ethical trading practices that ensure fair wages, safe working conditions, and sustainable livelihoods for producers and workers in developing countries.
2. **Federalism:** A political system where power is divided between a central government and subnational entities, allowing for shared governance and autonomy.

G

1. **Global Governance:** The collective management of international affairs by states, international organizations, and non-state actors through cooperative norms, rules, and institutions.
2. **Global Solidarity:** The commitment to mutual support and cooperation among people and nations to address shared challenges and promote global well-being.
3. **Global South:** A term used to describe developing regions of the world, often referring to countries in Latin America, Africa, and Asia.
4. **Global Supply Chain:** The network of companies, suppliers, and logistical processes involved in producing and distributing goods on a global scale.

H

1. **Human Development Index (HDI):** An index developed by the United Nations to measure a country's social and economic development, including factors like life expectancy, education, and income.
2. **Human Rights:** Universal rights and freedoms to which all individuals are entitled, such as the right to life, freedom of speech, and equality before the law.

I

1. **Identity Politics:** Political movements or policies focused on the interests of specific social groups based on shared characteristics like ethnicity, gender, or religion.
2. **Indigenous Knowledge:** The traditional knowledge and cultural practices of indigenous communities, often tied to their historical relationship with the land and environment.
3. **International Law:** A set of rules and principles governing relations between states, international organizations, and individuals in international contexts.

J

1. **Justice as Fairness:** A concept developed by John Rawls proposing that a just society ensures fair distribution of resources and opportunities through principles derived under the "veil of ignorance."

K

1. **Kyoto Protocol:** An international treaty adopted in 1997 aimed at reducing greenhouse gas emissions globally, preceding the Paris Agreement.

L

1. **Land Ethic:** An environmental philosophy developed by Aldo Leopold advocating for a respectful and sustainable relationship between humans and the natural environment.
2. **Liberalism:** A political and philosophical ideology emphasizing individual rights, democracy, and free-market economies.

M

1. **Multiculturalism:** A policy or ideology advocating for the coexistence of diverse cultures within a society, promoting mutual respect and cultural diversity.
2. **Multinational Corporation (MNC):** A company that operates and has assets in multiple countries but maintains headquarters in one country.

N

1. **Nationalism:** A political ideology that emphasizes loyalty and devotion to one's nation, often advocating for national sovereignty and identity preservation.
2. **Neoliberalism:** An economic ideology advocating for free-market capitalism, deregulation, and reduction in government spending.

P

1. **Paris Agreement:** An international climate change agreement adopted in 2015, aimed at limiting global warming to well below 2°C above pre-industrial levels.
2. **Primordialism:** A theory of nationalism arguing that nations are ancient and natural entities based on shared kinship, language, and culture.
3. **Protectionism:** An economic policy that restricts imports through tariffs and regulations to protect domestic industries.

R

1. **Realism:** An international relations theory emphasizing the role of power, national interest, and competition among states in global politics.
2. **Refugees:** Individuals who flee their country due to persecution, conflict, or violence and seek protection in another country under

international law.

3. **Responsibility to Protect (R2P):** An international norm asserting that states have a responsibility to protect their populations from genocide, war crimes, and other atrocities.

S

1. **Sovereignty:** The supreme authority of a state to govern itself without external interference.
2. **Sustainable Development:** Development that meets present needs without compromising the ability of future generations to meet their own needs.

T

1. **Transnational Corporations (TNCs):** Corporations that operate and have investments in multiple countries but maintain control from a central headquarters.
2. **Treaty:** A formal, legally binding agreement between two or more states or international organizations.

U

1. **Universal Declaration of Human Rights (UDHR):** An international document adopted by the United Nations in 1948 that defines universal human rights standards.

V

1. **Veil of Ignorance:** A concept in John Rawls' theory of justice where individuals design societal principles without knowing their position in society to ensure fairness.

W

1. **Westphalian Sovereignty:** A principle derived from the Peace of Westphalia (1648) emphasizing the inviolability of state borders and non-interference in domestic affairs by other states.

Appendix 2: Overview of Major International Organizations

United Nations (UN)

Established: 1945

Purpose: Maintain international peace and security, promote human rights, foster social and economic development, and uphold international law.

Key Bodies: General Assembly, Security Council, International Court of Justice, UNESCO, UNICEF, UNHCR, WHO.

World Trade Organization (WTO)

ESTABLISHED: 1995

Purpose: Facilitate international trade, resolve trade disputes, and create a framework for trade negotiations.

Key Bodies: Ministerial Conference, General Council, Dispute Settlement Body.

International Monetary Fund (IMF)

ESTABLISHED: 1944

Purpose: Provide financial assistance to member countries facing economic instability, promote global monetary cooperation, and facilitate international trade.

Key Bodies: Board of Governors, Executive Board, Managing Director.

World Bank Group

ESTABLISHED: 1944

Purpose: Provide financial and technical assistance for development projects in low- and middle-income countries.

Key Bodies: International Bank for Reconstruction and Development (IBRD), International Development Association (IDA), International Finance Corporation (IFC).

European Union (EU)

ESTABLISHED: 1993 (Treaty of Maastricht)

Purpose: Promote economic and political integration among European states, uphold democratic values, and ensure stability in the region.

Key Bodies: European Parliament, European Council, European Commission, Court of Justice of the European Union.

Organization for Economic Co-operation and Development (OECD)

ESTABLISHED: 1961

Purpose: Promote policies that improve economic and social well-being worldwide, provide a forum for governments to share experiences and coordinate economic policies.

North Atlantic Treaty Organization (NATO)

ESTABLISHED: 1949

Purpose: Provide collective security against military threats and promote democratic values among member states.

African Union (AU)

ESTABLISHED: 2001

Purpose: Promote unity and solidarity among African nations, foster economic development, and ensure peace and security on the continent.

Association of Southeast Asian Nations (ASEAN)

ESTABLISHED: 1967

Purpose: Promote regional economic, political, and security cooperation among Southeast Asian countries.

Appendix 3: International Agreements and Conventions

Environmental Agreements

- Kyoto Protocol (1997):

- International treaty to reduce greenhouse gas emissions.

- Paris Agreement (2015):

- Global pact to limit global warming to well below 2°C above pre-industrial levels.

- Convention on Biological Diversity (1992):

- Agreement to conserve biodiversity, sustainably use biological resources, and ensure equitable sharing of genetic resource benefits.

Human Rights Conventions

- Universal Declaration of Human Rights (1948):

- Defines fundamental human rights to be universally protected.

- International Covenant on Civil and Political Rights (1966):

- Protects rights such as freedom of speech, religion, and fair trial.

- International Covenant on Economic, Social and Cultural Rights (1966):

- Guarantees rights related to work, education, and an adequate standard of living.

- Convention on the Elimination of All Forms of Discrimination Against Women (1979):

- Promotes gender equality and women's rights.

Trade and Economic Agreements

- General Agreement on Tariffs and Trade (GATT) (1947):

- Precursor to the WTO, reducing trade barriers globally.

- North American Free Trade Agreement (NAFTA) (1994):

- Promotes trade between the U.S., Canada, and Mexico (now replaced by USMCA).

- Comprehensive and Progressive Agreement for Trans-Pacific Partnership (CPTPP) (2018):

- Regional trade agreement among 11 Pacific Rim countries.

Security and Disarmament Treaties

- Non-Proliferation Treaty (NPT) (1968):

- Prevents the spread of nuclear weapons and promotes disarmament.

- Chemical Weapons Convention (1993):

- Prohibits the development, production, and use of chemical weapons.

- Arms Trade Treaty (2013):

- Regulates international trade in conventional arms and prevents illegal arms transfers.

Appendix 4: Key Case Studies from the Book

1. Economic Dimension Case Studies

- Sweatshop Labor: Examining the ethical implications of sweatshop labor and fair trade practices.

- Global Supply Chains: Highlighting the vulnerabilities and ethical challenges of global supply chains exposed during the COVID-19 pandemic.

- Digital Currencies: Analyzing the rise of cryptocurrencies and their potential impact on global finance and economic justice.

2. Cultural Dimension Case Studies

NETFLIX'S INFLUENCE on Culture: Exploring how global media platforms shape and are shaped by cultural dynamics.

Cultural Hybridization vs. Cultural Homogenization: Contrasting the positive and negative cultural impacts of globalization.

Virtual Reality and Augmented Reality in Cultural Experience: Assessing the ethical implications of virtual cultural experiences.

3. Political Dimension Case Studies

- The Syria Conflict: Analyzing the complexities of the Syrian conflict and its global implications.

- Brexit: Evaluating the economic, cultural, and political ramifications of the United Kingdom's departure from the European Union.

- Global Terrorism and Cyber Warfare: Understanding the evolving nature of security threats in a globalized world.

4. Ethical Conundrums Case Studies

- Nationalism vs. Global Integration: Examining the challenges posed by nationalism to global cooperation.

- Migration and Human Rights: Investigating the ethical dilemmas surrounding the rights and treatment of migrants.

- Environmental Sustainability: Highlighting global responsibility in protecting the environment amidst economic and political interests.

Don't miss out!

Visit the website below and you can sign up to receive emails whenever Waleed Mahmud publishes a new book. There's no charge and no obligation.

https://books2read.com/r/B-A-GAYSB-DTFQD

BOOKS 2 READ

Connecting independent readers to independent writers.

Did you love *Decrypting Globalization*? Then you should read *Power &
Ethics: A Brief History Of Western Moral and Political Philosophy*[1] by
WALEED MAHMUD!

2

Dive into the philosophical journey that shaped the Western world, from
the ancient Greeks to the digital age. "Power & Ethics: A Brief History of
Western Moral and Political Philosophy" is an exploration of the ideas that
have defined millennia of human thought and societal evolution.

This book offers more than just a historical recount; it invites to
understand the profound debates and the philosophical foundations that
have influenced modern ideologies and our understanding of a just society.
Through the pages, readers familiarize themselves with the likes of Socrates,
Plato, Aristotle, and move through the transformative periods of the
Renaissance, the Enlightenment, and into the throes of modern and
postmodern challenges.

---

1. https://books2read.com/u/mg80J6

2. https://books2read.com/u/mg80J6

As our world grapples with issues of democracy, ethics in technology, and global justice, this book connects past wisdom with present dilemmas, providing a critical perspective that is both enlightening and necessary. It's not just a book for philosophers or academics; it's crafted for anyone who seeks to understand the deep moral and political currents that continue to shape our world."Power & Ethics" is your guide through the ages, as it illuminates the ongoing discourse on rights, justice, and the ethical challenges of the 21st century. Engage with this narrative that not only recounts philosophical milestones but encourages you to question, critique, and perhaps redefine your understanding of the good life.

Prepare to be challenged and inspired on a journey that not only recounts the history of moral and philosophical thought but also examines how these enduring ideas can help us navigate the complexities of modern life. Join me in a dialogue that spans millennia and discover how ancient wisdom can inform contemporary solutions for a just and equitable world.